TEACHING TO READ

TEACHING TO READ

Historically Considered

MITFORD M. MATHEWS

THE UNIVERSITY OF CHICAGO PRESS

Chicago & London

Library of Congress Catalog Card Number: 66–20588

THE UNIVERSITY OF CHICAGO PRESS, CHICAGO & LONDON
The University of Toronto Press, Toronto 5, Canada

© 1966 by The University of Chicago

Published 1966

Second Impression 1967

Printed in the United States of America

If the invention of the ship was thought so noble . . . how much more are letters to be magnified, which as ships pass through the vast seas of time.

BACON, *The Advancement of Learning* (1605)

PREFACE

Wherever the English language is used, the problem of how a child can best be taught to read is widely discussed and unceasingly worked upon. What is perhaps not so widely known is that this confusion over reading is assuredly four hundred and fifty years old. It may be older, but records fail us.

Writing in 1908, Dr. Edmund Burke Huey, Professor of Psychology and Education in the Western University of Pennsylvania, said: "A survey of the views of some of our foremost and soundest educators reveals the fact that the men of our time who are most competent to judge are profoundly dissatisfied with reading as it is now carried on in the elementary school." The present situation could not be better described. In an effort to improve upon what was being done at that time, Dr. Huey wrote his book, *The Psychology and Pedagogy of Reading*. In the introduction he said: "We have surely come to the place where we need to know just what the child normally does when he reads, in order to plan a natural and economical method of learning to read. We have come to the place where we need to pass in review all the methods that have been tried in all the centuries of reading, and to learn any little that we can from each." Huey's book was remarkably interesting and valuable. What effect it had on the classroom procedure of teaching children to read I do not know.

My object in writing is somewhat akin to Huey's, but far

less ambitious in its scope. Attention here is altogether restricted to reading that which is expressed in letters of an
alphabet. By this limitation we avoid any need to consider
the thousands of years of reading before the advent of the
Greek alphabet.

By focusing attention on the most significant events in
the history of teaching children to read English as their
native language, it is hoped that at least a little help may be
afforded those engaged in the long quest to "plan a natural
and economical method" of teaching children to read. If
this should prove to be the case, I shall be amply rewarded
for my efforts.

The University of Chicago

ACKNOWLEDGMENTS

In writing this book I have incurred obligations to some who are now beyond the reach of my thanks. Foremost among those who aroused my interest in the subject were Miss Zonia Baber and Miss Flora Cooke, both members of Colonel Parker's faculty who resigned from the City Normal with him in 1899. They had studied under and taught with Colonel Parker for many years. Miss Cooke was one of the best teachers of elementary reading Parker ever trained. Miss Baber was a devoted teacher of geography and the founder of the Chicago Geographic Society in 1898. Long after their retirement from active teaching these old friends and admirers of Colonel Parker kept in touch with each other, and I was privileged to hear much of what they said about the "war" Parker waged with those who regarded his as a mere "play school," a pretentious "mud-pie factory." Into their accounts they brought the chief actors of these stirring times, by no means omitting "old Charlie Thornton," the villain of the piece.

Others have helped by providing inspiration and also highly competent hard work in my behalf. Prominent among these is Professor Robert L. McCaul of the Department of Education at the University of Chicago, who, knowing of my interest, has over the years directed me to material which but for him I would have missed. Dr. Frederick F. Lighthall of the same department has shown great interest in what I have tried to do. He and Professor McCaul went over my manuscript with great care. I have profited also from the thoughtfulness of Dr. Harold B. Dunkel of the Department of Education, who often called my attention to things pertinent to this study. In addition, he too read my entire manuscript and made suggestions which enabled me to improve it.

To others of the University of Chicago staff I am under obligation: to Dr. Benedict Einarson and Dr. Blanche Boyer of the Department of Classical Languages and Literatures, Dr. Helena Gamer of the Department of Germanic Languages and Literatures, and Dr. William T. Hutchinson of the Department of History, I am particularly indebted.

Most of all, I am under obligation to my wife, without whose help as secretary, typist, consultant, and adviser, this work would never have been undertaken, much less completed.

CONTENTS

THE ABC'S INVENTED
AND FIRST USED

About three thousand years ago people who spoke Greek happened to be neighbors of those using a Semitic language, and a peaceful relationship prevailed between them at different places at the eastern end of the Mediterranean Sea. The Semites were the supposed descendants of Shem, the oldest son of Noah. Among them was a people known as the Phoenicians who were noted traders and seafarers. It was with them that the Greeks had most to do, and in the friendly exchanges that took place, some of the Greeks and Semites learned to speak each other's language.

The Phoenicians could write by means of letters, and this art intrigued bilingual Greeks. They soon began to try to write their own language in the symbols or letters of their Semite neighbors. In different parts of Greece men worked away at devising an alphabet, using the Semitic one as the source of many of their letters, a difficult undertaking because the two languages involved, Greek and Phoenician, were not at all related. They belonged to two entirely different families of language, and the Greeks could not pronounce some of the letters in the Semitic alphabet. They could not, for example, pronounce the *sh* sound of the Semitic letter *shin*.[1] The first letter in the Semitic alphabet was also among those the Greeks could not pronounce. The initial sound of this character is a glottal stop, which is

[1] Many words, such as *Jesus, Jerusalem, Salome, Samson, Samuel, Saul, Solomon,* testify to the Greeks' inability to pronounce the *sh* sound these words had in Hebrew.

made by a momentary complete closure of the glottis. The
Greeks had no such sound in their language, so they did not
bother about it, but took what they regarded as the second
sound in the name of the Semitic letter and called it *alpha,*
making it the first letter in their alphabet.

The Phoenicians did not write vowels, nor did they list
them in their alphabet, although in speaking they of course
used vowel sounds freely. For those brought up speaking a
language, the writing of vowels is more a convenience than
a necessity. Systems of shorthand practically dispense with
vowels, but what is written in them is easily read by those
trained to do so. There was nothing about the Greek language which hindered its users from including vowels in
their alphabet, however, and this they accordingly did.
After long experimentation in various parts of their island
kingdom the Greeks had what they wanted: a complete set
of symbols or letters with which they could represent
every sound in their language. This alphabet in its finished
form had all the letters in a fixed order, an arrangement
suggested by the Semitic alphabet. And every letter had a
name, following the fashion of the earlier alphabet. The
Greeks must have realized from the outset that the letters
they were adopting or devising were going to be memorized
by those learning to read. It facilitates memorizing a list or
series of things to have them in a fixed order and to have a
name for each of them.

The more one knows about this magnificent achievement
of the Greeks the more one marvels at what they did. Dr.
I. J. Gelb describes theirs as "the alphabet that subsequently
conquered the world. Much as the hundreds of alphabets
used throughout the world may differ from each other in
appearance, they all have characteristics of outer form,
inner structure, or both, which first originated in the small
area surrounding the eastern Mediterranean." He goes on to
say that with minor exceptions "there is only one system
of writing in use today. And that is the alphabet of Semitic-
Greek origin."[2]

---

[2] I. J. Gelb, *A Study of Writing* (Chicago, 1952), p. 184. For a general
account of the role which the Semites played in the development of the

Probably the first use the Greeks made of their ability to write was in business and administration. They had no doubt observed that the Phoenicians used their ability to write in commercial activities. It may be significant that the Greek word for "letter," meaning missive, is *epistolē*, a word which originally meant "command." Probably at first such communications proceeded from administrative superiors. But the works of Homer were early reduced to writing and used in teaching boys to read.

Anybody who understood the alphabet could write. He neither had nor cared for a dictionary to guide him in spelling. He sounded each word he wished to write and then set down in order the letters representing the sounds. When the Greeks first began to write they were faced with certain practical problems. One of the first of these was to decide on the direction the line of writing should take. The Semites began at the right and went toward the left, but the reverse procedure finally won out with the Greeks, and by about the fifth century B.C. the left to right direction in writing was well established.[3]

For a long time Greek writing was not separated into words but was set down in solid lines. Some of the oldest surviving manuscripts of the New Testament were written in this uninterrupted fashion. Connected discourse impressed the Greeks as flowing on like a stream without any breaks. In a work by Plato (*ca.* 429–347 B.C.) a speaker mentioned the teeth, tongue, and lips as producing the "river of speech," which he described as "the fairest and noblest of all streams."[4] Working out such problems as confronted them, the Greeks took "the last important step in the history of writing. From the Greek period up to the present, nothing new has happened in the inner structural development of writing. Generally speaking, we write con-

---

alphabet, see Holger Pedersen, *Linguistic Science in the Nineteenth Century* (Cambridge, Mass., 1931), pp. 176–88. For a fuller treatment, see Martin Sprengling, *The Alphabet* (Chicago, 1931).

[3] Gelb, *op. cit.*, pp. 21–22, 68, 155, 178, 187, 230, 246. Also see "Boustrophedon" in the *Oxford English Dictionary* (Oxford, 1933) and in the *Encyclopaedia Britannica* (London, 1946).

[4] Cited in Sir John Edwin Sandys, *A History of Classical Scholarship* (New York, 1958), I, 89.

sonants and vowels in the same way as the ancient Greeks did."[5]

As soon as there existed among the Greeks a body of written material, reading became both possible and desirable. Boys could now be set to learn to read and write. Their first task was to master the names and forms of letters with great thoroughness. It was not easy to do this, for printing lay far in the future, and the letters—all made by hand—differed considerably in form. The reader was helped, however, by the fact that in early times all the letters were capitals, the small letters developing later out of the practice of writing rapidly.

The boy who had mastered a letter, or thought he had, was told to pick out every occurrence of it in a specific piece of writing. There is a vivid suggestion of the thoroughness with which Greek boys were expected to master the letters in a passage in Plato's *Republic,* written at least 350 B.C. Socrates and Glaucon are conversing, and Socrates says:

Now in learning to read . . . we were proficient when we could recognize the few letters there are wherever they occur in all the multitude of different words, never thinking them beneath our notice in the most insignificant word, but bent upon distinguishing them everywhere, because we should not be scholars until we had got thus far. . . .
Also we must know the letters themselves before we can recognize images of them, reflected (say) in water or in a mirror. The same skill and practice are needed in either case.[6]

Emphasis was placed upon the boy's learning the letters in their proper alphabetical order. To assist him in this, the teacher might give him a list of common names, the initial letters of which were in order down the alphabet—just as if we were to prepare a list such as: *Abe, Bill, Clara, Dan, Ed,* and so forth. Another exercise for the same purpose

[5] Gelb, *op. cit.,* p. 184. There are many accounts of the alphabet. The best of them are listed by Gelb, pp. 254–55. Those especially interested in the origin of the Greek alphabet should see Martin P. Nilsson, "Die Übernahme und Entwickelung des Alphabets Durch die Griechen," *Historisk-filologiske Meddelelser,* I (1917), 6. Excellent treatments of the English letters are found in the *OED* and in the *Century Dictionary* (New York, 1889–91).
[6] Plato, *The Republic,* ed. F. M. Cornford (Oxford, 1941), p. 88.

was to give the pupil a list of words denoting professions, the names of which began with the different letters in their proper order, such as *Actor, Baker, Cook, Doctor,* and so forth.[7] To make sure that their pupils had mastered the letters perfectly, Greek teachers appear to have required their charges to recite them backwards and forwards, up and down the alphabet column.[8] Centuries later English children were required to recite the alphabet in this manner, and the likelihood is that the practice was ancient.

It is quite probable that the Greeks set the letters, in proper order, to a simple air and had the pupils sing it in a way still popular among parents and their children. A metrical alphabet, though in a mutilated form, has been found and ascribed to a time before 429 B.C. It formed the prologue to what Kenneth Freeman called a "spelling drama, in which the whole process of learning to spell was expressed either in iambic lines or in choral songs."[9]

The second demand made upon pupils in Greek reading classes was that they learn syllables perfectly. The first ones taken up were simple combinations of vowels and consonants, such as *ba, be, bē, bi, bo, bu, bō; an en, ēn, in, on, un, ōn.* As the pupils advanced in their ability to pronounce such combinations, three-letter groups were taught them—*ban, ben, bēn, bin, bon, bun, bōn.*[10]

The emphasis which the Greeks placed on syllable learning developed naturally out of the phonetic structure of their language. One of the first things a schoolboy learns about Greek is that in it a word has as many syllables as it has vowels and diphthongs. Greek may be called a syllable-oriented language. In it syllables were basic, to a degree we have difficulty in appreciating because English is word oriented. We are not able to look at a word and tell how

[7] J. Grafton Milne, "Relics of Graeco-Egyptian Schools," *Journal of Hellenic Studies,* XXVIII (1908), 121–32.

[8] *Ibid.,* p. 121.

[9] Kenneth J. Freeman, *Schools of Hellas* (London, 1932), p. 88; Milne, *op. cit.,* p. 123. W. Rhys Roberts in his *Dionysius of Halicarnassus* (London, 1910), p. 269, refers to a passage in Athenaeus telling of how children recited these combinations in a kind of chant.

[10] Erich Ziebarth, *Aus der Antiken Schule* (Bonn, 1913), pp. 3 ff. See also Sandys, *op. cit.,* I, 88.

many syllables it has; we have to pronounce it to find out. With the Greeks it was different. Syllables were speech units that had to be learned extremely well. Under the circumstances, the custom of writing in solid lines with no separation into words was by no means the handicap to the Greek pupil that it would be to us. He had in any event to be able to recognize syllables and to pronounce them readily. Thorough drill on them was essential.

The syllable learning begun by the Greeks continued in use for more than two thousand years. In English the practice of drilling children on syllables continued because it was the best way the teacher had of acquainting the child with the sounds that letters have in actual use. It was a device exploited fully in Webster's *Elementary Spelling Book*, often referred to as the "Ole Blue-back." Here consonant-vowel combinations came first—*ba, be, bi, bo, bu, by*—followed by vowel-consonant combinations—*ab, eb, ib, ob, ub*. Then came three-letter combinations in great abundance. We shall see later under what conditions this teaching technique passed out of use.

Greek teachers at this second stage drilled the pupil further in the sounds of the letters by having him engage in word- and syllable-building. Starting with an expression such as *ar*, the teacher showed the pupil how he could get other expressions by prefixing different letters to form *bar, gar, dar*, and so forth. Similarly, from *er* he could form *ber, ger, der*.[11]

Words were the last things the Greek boy had to take up. Dionysius of Halicarnassus, writing about 20 B.C., gave a concise summary of the whole process of learning to read:

When we are taught to read, first we learn off the names of the letters, then their forms and their values, then in due course syllables and their modifications, and finally words and their properties, viz. lengthenings and shortenings, accents, and the like. After acquiring the knowledge of these things, we begin to write and read, syllable by syllable and slowly at first. And when the lapse of a considerable time has implanted the forms of words firmly in our minds, then we deal with them without the least difficulty, and whenever any book is placed in our hands

11 Freeman, *op. cit.*, p. 89 n.

we go through it without stumbling and with incredible facility and speed.[12]

As Dionysius suggests, reading went right along with practice in writing. Exercises written by pupils under the master's guidance or at his dictation have survived. A teacher might write for his pupil a list of initial letters and ask him to expand these into words with particular endings, as if we should write C D E R I P and direct the pupil to expand them into words of two syllables in -pel. If the pupil succeeded, he might come up with such a list as Compel, Dispel, Expel, Repel, Impel, Propel.[13]

We need not describe any further the way Greek boys were taught to read, but one point is of special interest. As the pupil advanced in writing, he was given moral instruction by way of what he was asked to write. In the copies set for him, some virtue was made clear: industry, discretion, respect for the gods, were set forth in an approving light.[14] This association of learning with morality and religion has a very long history, extending back to the very beginnings of literacy.

Although various peoples had been writing for thousands of years before the Greeks, the latter outstripped all those who had preceded them in this field. The secret of their phenomenal advance was in the vividness of their conception of the nature of a word. They reasoned that words were sounds, or combinations of ascertainable sounds, and they held inexorably to the basic proposition that writing, properly executed, was a guide to sound. Their firm adherence to this view caused them to be dissatisfied with the failure of the Egyptians and the Semites to take full account of all the speech sounds, the vocalic ones in writing being slighted.

Other peoples, such as the Babylonians and the Egyptians, had caught glimpses of the desirability of having signs represent *sounds,* not *things,* but they were never able

12 Roberts, *op. cit.,* p. 269.

13 Milne, *op. cit.,* p. 124.

14 *Ibid.,* pp. 125–28; Edgar J. Goodspeed, "Greek Documents in the Museum of the New York Historical Society," *Mélanges Nicole* (Geneva, 1905), pp. 181–82.

to break with convention to the extent of setting aside picture writing in favor of letter writing. The fundamental defect of picture writing was that it was not based upon sounds at all. The Greeks saw this basic weakness and by avoiding it achieved everlasting distinction.

Scholars speak of "alphabetic writing" as that in which every letter represents one, and only one, speech sound, and in which every sound is represented by one, and only one, letter or symbol. The Greeks certainly aimed at, and must in large measure have achieved, "alphabetic writing" more than two and a half thousand years ago, at a time when their nearest neighbors did not realize the tremendous significance of such a thing. Once a system of alphabetic writing is adjusted for any language, reading what is written becomes simple. A native user of such a language, already well practiced in its sounds, can learn to read it in a very short time. And he can write as soon as he has learned to make the letters or symbols in a legible manner.

This point needs no belaboring. There must be many people who have heard of the great American missionary and teacher, Frank Charles Laubach, who is world famous for having made it possible for many backward people to pass from illiteracy to literacy in a few days. He and his helpers have prepared more than two hundred primers in about one hundred and sixty-five languages. The number of those who have learned to read by the use of these books runs into the millions.[15]

Every schoolboy should know the story of Sequoya, the celebrated Cherokee Indian born about 1760 somewhere in Tennessee. When he was a grown man he was injured in a hunting accident. No longer able to take part in the labors and pleasures of the chase, he turned his attention to preparing an alphabet which would enable his people to read and write. Although he was severely handicapped by not knowing how to read or write, or even to speak, English, he devised a system of symbols by means of which a Cherokee could in a few days learn to read and write. Sequoya was

---

[15] There is an excellent account of Laubach and his work in the *World Book Encyclopedia* (Chicago, 1966).

perhaps the greatest man his nation ever produced, and his memory is appropriately perpetuated by the big evergreen trees in California which are often referred to as sequoias.[16]

Possibly learning to read as the Greeks and Romans did was not particularly difficult. Those who taught children to read and write were regarded with great disdain and contempt. Whenever possible, slaves were assigned to this monotonous, unimaginative task.[17] In old Athens there was a saying of one who was missing that he was either dead or had become a schoolmaster and was accordingly ashamed to appear in polite society. It was thought that kings and others of high rank who had lived evil lives would, in the next world, be forced to maintain themselves by teaching reading and writing. Epicurus complained of Nausiphanes, "He abused me and called me a schoolmaster." Demosthenes in attacking Aeschines made much of the fact that his father was a schoolmaster, and only an assistant at that, in an institution of the lowest order, a reading and writing school.[18]

There must have been a reason for this universal attitude toward elementary teachers among people as intelligent as the Greeks and Romans. The most probable explanation of it is that teaching to read was widely recognized as something anybody could do. There was nothing difficult about it. Its acceptable execution called for neither learning nor talents; no distinction could be attained in such a mediocre occupation.

[16] Frederick Webb Hodge, *Handbook of American Indians* (Washington, 1907, 1910), II, 510 ff.

[17] Freeman, *op. cit.*, p. 83. Paul Monroe's *Source Book of the History of Education for the Greek and Roman Period* (New York, 1902) contains excerpts from Greek and Roman authors covering the whole range of formal education among the Greeks and Romans. The proverb, "He is either dead or teaching the A B C's," dates from 415 B.C., when it was used as a reply to questions about the fate of those Athenians who did not return from the disastrous expedition against Syracuse. The answer meant that they had either died or been captured and sold as slaves. See Andreas Schollus, *Adagia sive proverbia Graecorum* (Antwerp, 1612), p. 83.

[18] Lewis F. Anderson, *History of Common School Education* (New York, 1909), p. 11; Freeman, *op. cit.*, p. 81.

READING ENGLISH—AT FIRST

While the Greeks were still at work on their alphabet, a group of them—chiefly traders—went to Italy, about 750 B.C., and settled the ancient city of Cumae, about ten miles west of Naples. In this new location they had as neighbors the Etruscans, the most important of the many peoples who in early times occupied much of Italy. For a long time relations between the Greeks and the Etruscans were quite friendly. Under such circumstances, the letters which the colonists brought with them were taken over by their neighbors and used by them chiefly in inscriptions, some of which have endured to the present time. These show that it was a form of the Greek alphabet employed at Delphi about the seventh century B.C. that passed into the use of the Etruscans.

These borrowers, in taking over Greek letters, did not take the names the Greeks had given them. The Greeks themselves were extremely careful about this matter of letter names. As a rule they took the Semitic names, *aleph, beth, gimel, daleth,* and vocalized them into *alpha, beta, gamma, delta.* So zealous were they in this matter that they devised names for such letters as they could not secure from the Phoenicians but had to provide otherwise.

The result of this neglect by the Etruscans was that when the Romans in their turn secured Greek letters from the Etruscans they did not get the names along with the letters. The Romans allowed the sounds of the vowels to serve as their names. As names for the consonants they used the letter itself accompanied by a distinctly pronounced vowel sound. *Consonant* is a word of Latin origin and signifies "sounding with." By calling these letters *consonants* the Romans showed that they knew the nature of the characters and also appreciated the difference between this and the other class of letters, which they called by a name signifying "sound," and from which our word *vowel* comes.[1]

By their short-cut method of naming the letters the Romans paved the way for the delusion which later prevailed, to the effect that the *names* of the letters are their *sounds*. If the fullfledged Greek names had been carefully kept, no such mistake could ever have come up to bedevil teachers and pupils alike. It certainly never bothered Greek teachers or schoolboys.

Just as the Greeks did, the Romans soon had schools in which their sons learned to read. The instructional method was the same as that which prevailed in Greek schools, so there is nothing new to learn from an extended consideration of them. And just as the Greek schoolboys did, the little Romans learned their letters first. Quintilian, a celebrated Roman grammarian of the first century of the Christian Era, deplored the tendency in his day to allow the child to

learn the names and order of the letters before they learn their shapes. This method hinders their recognition of them, as, while they follow their memory that takes the lead, they do not fix their attention on the forms of the letters. This is the reason why teachers, when they appear to have fixed them sufficiently in the minds of children, in the straight order in which they are usually first written, make them go over them again the contrary way, and confuse them by variously changing the arrangement, until their pupils know them by their shape, not by their place. It will be best for children, therefore, to be taught the appearances and names of the letters at once, as they are taught those of men.[2]

Following the learning of the letters came the mastering of syllables. In this way the child learned how the

[1] Rhys Carpenter, "The Alphabet in Italy," *American Journal of Archaeology*, XLIX (1945), 455–56, 460.

[2] John Selby Watson (ed.), *Quintilian's Institutes of Oratory* (London, 1875–76), I, 16.

letters sounded in actual use. Quintillian said: "They [syllables] must be learned throughout; nor are the most difficult of them, as is the general practice, to be postponed, that children may be at a loss, forsooth, in writing words." This great Roman teacher was not in favor of hurrying the child: "It is incredible how much retardation is caused by reading in haste; for hence arise hesitation, interruption, and repetition, as children attempt more than they can manage; and then, after making mistakes, they become distrustful even of what they know."[3]

Like the Greeks, the Romans thought of reading as an oral process. The ancients felt very strongly the relationship between what was spoken and what was written, and they assigned primacy to the spoken word; the written word was clearly secondary and was provided only to enable those who came later or were at a distance to recapture the actual speech, the sounds, the author's actual words. Socrates did not write anything; he had found that conversation was the avenue to truth. Written words were by comparison poor substitutes: "like the creations of the painter they have the attitude of life; and yet if you ask them a question, they preserve a solemn silence."

Alphabetic writing won its victory over picture writing just because it preserved sounds and enabled the reader to repeat the author's very words. To get the full benefit of what he read it was necessary for him to read aloud. It was this practice of reading aloud, even though alone, which enabled Philip to know that the Ethiopian official was reading from the prophet Isaiah as he rode along in his chariot going from Jerusalem down to Gaza (Acts 8:30). When St. Augustine went to Milan to confer with St. Ambrose, he was surprised and perplexed to find that Ambrose, for some reason which Augustine and his friends could not quite make out, often read silently. On his return home St. Augustine mentioned this peculiar habit of St. Ambrose in explaining why the two of them had not conversed more.[4]

[3] *Ibid.*, I, 16.
[4] See Josef Balogh, "Voces Paginarum," *Philologus*, LXXXII (1927), 84–109, 204–40. See also Augustine's *Confessiones*, ed. Andreas Labhardt (Frauenfeld, 1949), p. 55.

During the Renaissance, reading undoubtedly connoted oral reading. Monks in the Middle Ages created a devil named Titivillus, whose function was to collect fragments of words mumbled, or skipped, or read silently in the recitation of the divine office. These he carried by bagfuls down to hell where they were duly registered against the offenders. This piece of medieval humor helped to keep the brothers conscious of doing their best in reading orally.[5]

Hendrickson in his excellent article on "Ancient Reading" tells of a friend of his whose father, deeply versed in Hebrew lore, instructed him as a boy "that one must never read any of the sacred literature with the eye alone, but must always, even if only soundless, form the words with the lips." The reason for this injunction was that "only thus the command could be observed, that not one tittle of the holy word should ever be lost."[6]

The Romans ruled in England for three hundred and fifty years. By the time they withdrew at the beginning of the fifth century many in England were acquainted with the Latin language and literature. Christian missionaries had set up schools quite early; and it is thought that perhaps sometime in the seventh century, in these schools or because of their inspiration, English was written for the first time. The procedure was simple; knowing both English and Latin, the missionaries, or their best pupils, selected Latin letters to represent English sounds. The result was that English at this early time was written as "alphabetically" as those doing the writing were able to make it.

Of course these early writers did not do as well as trained phoneticians could have done, but that they did at least reasonably well is indicated by a comment made about 1150 by an anonymous Icelandic author: "Yet Englishmen write English with Latin letters, as many as can be rightly pronounced in English, but when these no longer suffice, they add other letters, as many and of such a nature as they

[5] See the entry "Titivil" in the Oxford English Dictionary (Oxford, 1933).
[6] G. L. Hendrickson, "Ancient Reading," Classical Journal, XXV (1929–30), 183–86, 193. See the entire article by Ralph W. Williams, "Reading and Evolution," Journal of Developmental Reading, IV (Autumn, 1960), 3–11.

need, rejecting those that cannot be rightly pronounced in their language."[7]

As this intelligent Icelander suggested, the alphabet in which the first English was written was quite different from that in use today. *J* was not then an independent letter, but merely a variant of *I*. In the Greek alphabet it did not have the now familiar dot over it; the Greeks crossed their *t*'s but did not dot their *i*'s. Eventually to give the letter more visual importance scribes fell into the habit of placing a dot over it; and for the same purpose of making the letter more distinct it was often extended a little below the line of writing and its tail given a slight turn to the left. But until the end of the eighteenth century the realization that *I* and *J* were merely forms of the same letter was so strong that in dictionaries all the words beginning with either letter were alphabetized in one group. This is the way such words were entered in Johnson's dictionary in 1755. The *I* and *J* words were separated, possibly for the first time in a dictionary, by Noah Webster in 1806.

The accounts of the origins of other more recent letters such as *U, V, Y,* and *W* are full of interest, but a consideration of them would lead us too far afield.[8]

As soon as English began to be written, people began to learn to read it. It is unfortunate that virtually nothing is known about how reading was taught for seven or eight hundred years after the first English was set down in written form. It is not likely that there was during these centuries anything like a popular enthusiasm for learning this particular skill. There were no such things as printed books, only manuscripts, and these were chiefly in the hands of rich people (of whom there were not many) and churchmen.

More than any other class in the population, priests and monks were interested in reading. Their interest was chiefly in Latin, however, as the Scriptures were in that language. But the ecclesiastics were interested in translating parts of the Bible into English and in teaching English-

[7] Einar Haugen, "First Grammatical Treatise," *Language,* XXVI (October–December, 1950), 12.

[8] In the *Century Dictionary* (New York, 1889–91) the antecedent forms of each of the letters are shown.

men, both young and old, to read such translations. Their most distinguished pupil was King Alfred (849–99): he could read English and encouraged others to master the skill; he could also read Latin and made translations from that language into his own. He did all he could to support schools in which pupils, including his own son, learned both languages.

But the times were so filled with trouble that not much progress could be made with schools for learning. During the ninth and tenth centuries the Danes harassed the country and directed their efforts particularly at churches and monasteries because of the wealth of such institutions. Not long after the Danes had established themselves in authority over a large portion of England, Norman invaders from what is now France appeared, winning a notable victory at Hastings in 1066, and initiating a conquest that swept over the whole land.

The Normans brought their own language, a form of French, and soon their speech was well established in Britain, especially among people of power and influence. English for centuries occupied a place of inferiority. Anyone of consequence used the speech of the new masters; yokels and swineherds and their like used English. In these times so filled with hardship for the common people, there was not much enthusiasm for reading English. And during these centuries the attitude of churchmen toward English translations of the Bible altered; those who undertook such translations were denounced.

Yet under these most unfavorable circumstances there were those who wrote English and instructed others in how to read it. No doubt parents, when they could, taught their children to read, but there were also "petty schools," certainly as early as thé thirteenth and fourteenth centuries and probably earlier. Such schools as existed were under the guidance of poorly prepared teachers: a tailor, a shoemaker, a weaver, a crippled old man, or a destitute old woman might turn pedagogue on at least a part-time basis, though they were only able to stumble haltingly through the simplest sentence. From the little that is known of these early pitiful mixtures of kindergarten, nursery, and baby-sitting elementary schools, it is easy to see that the motivation was strongly religious. In a poem written about 1400 the following lines, here given in modern spelling, introduced the child to his first book:

> When a child to school shall set be
> A book him is brought
> Nailed on a board of tree,
> That men call abc.[9]

Note that the beginner did not bring his book from home; it was supplied by his teacher. It was sometimes called an *ABC,* but more often a *battledore-book* or *hornbook.* A handy device which kept its place in the elementary schools for centuries, it resembled a tiny ping-pong paddle, suitable for a baby's hand. On one side of it was pasted a leaf of paper or parchment on which were the ABC's, some simple syllables, and the Lord's Prayer. The contents varied slightly, but the essential part was the ABC's, often arranged in the form of a Latin cross. This single leaf of instructional material was protected from wet, dirty fingers by a thin transparent sheet of horn, hence the name *hornbook.* The cross motif was conspicuous in the arrangement of its contents. Often there was a Greek cross at the very beginning of the ABC's, so that the child had constantly before him a reminder of Christ who died on the cross for such sinners as he. And just before giving his attention to the letters themselves, the child, under the teacher's guidance, offered up a prayer suited to his years and attainments:

> Christ's cross be my speed
> In all virtue to proceed.[10]

By way of still further making sure that the learner did not escape the symbolism of the Christian cross, his teacher often called the alphabet the *Christ-cross-row,* alluding to the arrangement of the letters in the form of a Latin cross on many of the hornbooks. Another early name for the

[9] Thomas Wright and James Orchard Halliwell, *Reliquiae antiquae* (London, 1841–43), p. 63.
[10] Thomas Morley, *Plaine and Easie Introduction to Practicall Musicke* (London, 1937), p. 38.

alphabet was the *cross-row*, with reference to the Greek cross often placed before the ABC's.

No matter what form the cross had, or where it was placed on the hornbook sheet, the child encountered it at the very threshhold of his formal education, and one of his first assignments was to draw a picture of it. If he mastered the making of it, but failed ever to advance far enough to learn to write his name, then his "Christ-cross" could be accepted as his signature. To this day one unable to sign his name to a document is allowed to make his "mark," and this is often in the form of a cross. So constantly was the cross associated with and represented by the letters arranged in the form of a cross that *Christ-cross* came to be a shortening of *Christ-cross-row* and served as a name for the alphabet. Through phonetic reduction and shifts in meaning it became *crisscross* as used at the present time.[11]

If a child possessed sufficient toughness of physical and mental fiber to survive a thorough drill on the alphabet and syllables, he advanced to a real book, the name and nature of which again give a hint of the religious motivation behind learning in those early days. He got a *primer*. At first this was a prayer book or devotional manual, pure and simple. The earliest of them go back to the fourteenth and fifteenth centuries. The name "primer" is clearly from the Latin word meaning "first," but, as the *Oxford English Dictionary* expresses it, "the actual reason for the name does not appear." There are those who would connect it with *Prime* in its ecclesiastical use as the first canonical hour of the day in the divine office.

Another indication of the close relationship between religion and the ability to read is seen in the old custom of allowing one in the toils of the law to plead the *benefit of clergy*. If upon being handed a book, a man could read it, even poorly, this performance was accepted as a proof of his scholarship and secured for him exemption from trial in a secular court.

There is no way to estimate the rate of progress of pupils in these early schools. Both teachers and pupils undoubt-

[11] See the entry "Criss-cross" in the *OED*.

edly varied greatly in industry and ability. Nor is there any way of knowing whether acquiring the ability to read English was relatively easy or distressingly difficult. From the fact that no lamentations about the difficulty of the undertaking can be found until about 1500, one might incline to the view that in the early centuries pupils learned more readily from such instruction than they did later, but real evidence in support of this view is lacking.

LEARNING TO READ
BECOMES DIFFICULT

On the last day of October, 1517, Martin Luther, by posting his famous ninety-five propositions on the door of the castle church in Wittenberg, inadvertently touched off the Protestant Reformation. Compayré, writing particularly of the situation in France, said that the primary school was the child of Protestantism, and that the Reformation was the cradle in which it was rocked.[1] He could hardly have described better the situation in England.

In the new era it was imperative for a man to learn to read the Bible; the salvation of his soul depended upon his doing so. Jesus himself directed man to search the Scriptures, and suggested that eternal life might be the reward. The desire to acquire the skill of reading and to see that one's entire household did the same was very great. We may be sure that schools multiplied and that the poor old ineffectual women and men who had been serving as teachers were joined by those somewhat better prepared for their task.

In general, the method used by those who taught beginners to read in the sixteenth century was virtually that employed by the Greeks and Romans: first one learned the names of the letters; then one learned letter sounds through work on vowel-consonant, consonant-vowel combinations and syllables. When enough drill of this type had been engaged in, one began to read. Initially, each word was spelled

[1] Gabriel Compayré, *History of Pedagogy* (Boston, 1907), p. 113.

and pronounced before one could move on to the next.

Difficulties were encountered by both teachers and pupils at every step in this process. Although the teachers used every means they knew of to make the letters easy,[2] pupils often learned them only with the greatest difficulty. Even when they had mastered them to the teacher's satisfaction, experience proved that they were not far advanced on the way to reading. Nor was their progress assisted by generous applications of the rod.

Teachers of the better sort thought they knew where the trouble was. Children that were mere babies, three years old in many cases, were bundled off to such miserably poor schools as were available. Therein lay one of the difficulties of the situation, and one about which the teachers could do little. The second major obstacle came in the fact that the letters of the alphabet no longer served as reliable indicators of sounds.

The tendency of letters is to remain fixed in form. The tendency of speech sounds, which letters represent, is to change. Inevitably, then, letters and the speech sounds for which they stand tend to lose rapport, the one to remain fixed and the other to undergo change. Those who wrote English during the first centuries of its existence as a written language had at their disposal a ready way of adjusting what they wrote to the changes taking place in the speech sounds. They spelled as they pronounced. This they could do then without the slightest embarrassment because spelling had not become fixed; the writer was free to spell as he pronounced. The results of this practice show up on any printed page of English. For example, in the Old English period (*ca.* 450–1125) there were in the language a number of words beginning with h followed by the consonants *l, n, r.* Those who spoke English got into the habit of not pronouncing the *h* in such words. Accordingly, people

---

2 John Brinsley, *Ludus Literarius* (London, 1612), pp. 15 ff. The author here tells of the various devices; Charles Hoole, *A New Discovery* (Syracuse, 1912), pp. 33 ff., discusses their uses more fully. On pp. 33–40, Hoole tells "How a Child May Be Taught with Delight to Know All his Letters in a Very Little Time."

ceased to write the full combination, with the result that in English today there are many words, such as *ladder, lady, lank, leap, lid, loaf, lord, lot,* that in the earliest period were spelled with an initial *hl-*. Similarly in words beginning with *hr-* the initial sound dropped away and only that of *r-* remained. Spelling, following the sound as it should always do, reflected this change and such words as *raven, reed, ridge, ring, roof,* and *rung* resulted.

But after the art of printing reached England about 1475, spellings in use at that time tended to become fixed and no longer able to denote changes in sound. Consider some Old English words beginning with *cn-* having the value of *kn-*, and later so spelled. The pronunciation of this *kn-* combination continued until about the middle of the seventeenth century, but was then reduced to the *n* sound. The spelling, now being held through the influence of printing, remained, and today we have to write *knave, knead, knee, kneel, knife, knight, knoll, know,* though nobody pronounces the initial *k*.[3]

All the long vowels of the Old English period began slowly shifting in sound as the centuries passed. A brief consideration of the first one will be sufficient for illustrative purposes. In Old English long *a* represented a sound that was approximately that of the vowel now heard in *ah, palm, father*. By Middle English times (about 1125 to 1475) this vowel sound had become that heard in *talk, raw, fought*. By this time, however, England was under French control. One result of this foreign domination was that from about 1230 to 1350 the writing of English was in the hands of Anglo-French scribes. This was disturbing for English spelling, but not seriously so, for these scribes also tried to write phonetically. They did not, however, have any symbol for the sound into which long *a* had shifted. They did the best they could to represent it by writing *oo, o,* or, rarely, *ao*.[4]

The sound continued to change little by little until in

[3] See the *Oxford English Dictionary* (Oxford, 1933), under "H," "Hr-," "Kn-."

[4] W. W. Skeat, *Primer of English Etymology* (Oxford, 1924), pp. 18, 31, 34 ff.

Tudor-English times (1500-1600) it had become that of the long *o* in *no*. Scribes then used *oa* to represent this sound, but if it came at the end of a word they wrote the sound as *-oe*. Here were two ways of writing the same sound shown in such spellings as *oak, oath; toe, doe*. A third arose in the following way. In Old English there were many nouns, such as *stān, hām, rāp, abād,* in which the long *a* sound occurred. In that early period English nouns were declined, but as centuries passed the case-endings were more and more neglected in pronunciation until they disappeared altogether or survived as a faintly pronounced vowel.

Of these vowel endings, *-e* was quite common and has persisted until the present time. Today in words which the Anglo-Saxon scribes wrote and pronounced *stān, hām,* and so forth, we write *stone, home, rope, abode,* and give the vowel the sound of long *o*. The final *-e* has not been pronounced in centuries, but it is retained because it has come to be felt as an indicator of the long sound of the vowel in the body of the word. This brief explanation of how the same sound in modern English has come to be expressed in three different ways is sufficient for illustrative purposes. But as a result of other circumstances in the history of the language, the same long *o* sound is also spelled as shown in such words as *hautboy, beau, yeoman, sew, oh, brooch, soul, flow*.

From the earliest times there has been a strong tendency in English to borrow words from other languages. For centuries these borrowings did not disturb the original pattern of written English, for the borrowed words were spelled as they sounded in English. *Debt* was borrowed early, but spelled *det;* similarly with many other words such as *isle,* spelled *ile; subtle,* spelled *suttle,* even by John Milton, who also wrote *suttlety, suttly*.

At the time of the revival of learning in the sixteenth century, a policy was adopted by some scholars of spelling borrowed words in such a way as to indicate the source of such terms. They said they did this as a kind of confession of obligation, as a memorial of appreciation. Over the vigorous protests of many scholars of much sounder views, "etymological" spellings, so called, became established.[5]

By the time of Queen Elizabeth (1558–1603), two conflict-ing principles of spelling were at work—the older phonetic or alphabetical one, and what Skeat called the "pedantic or retrospective." Neither principle was carried out fully, with the result that greater spelling confusion than ever pre-vailed. Moreover, in the seventeenth and eighteenth cen-turies great changes took place in vowel sounds, but by that time printing had so nearly fixed the spellings that changes were difficult. Today we spell about as they did in the time of James I (1603–25) and pronounce as well as we can. In addition to spelling *debt, island, subtle, balm, indict, pneu-monia, psalm, ptomaine*, we write the same vowel sound as it shows up in such words as *ruby, rule, do, move, fruit, bruise, group, through, moon, rheumatism, flue, grew, two.* No wonder Professor Pei described English spelling as "the world's most awesome mess."[6]

In addition to the confusions, greatly multiplied,[7] stem-ming from the sources just suggested, at least one other should be taken into account. Abercrombie has shown con-clusively that by 1633, if not earlier, the word "letter" was often used in the sense of *speech sound.*[8] Into the ancestry of this usage we need not go; Abercrombie has done this most interestingly and has given ample illustrative passages showing that the use cited was by no means rare.

In the sixteenth and seventeenth centuries many teachers must have thought of letters in this sense of "speech sounds." They drilled their charges unmercifully on the *names* of the ABC's, thinking that the names of the letters were their sounds. Such teachers thought that when a child had mastered the letters by their names he had mastered

[5] *Ibid.*, pp. 29–41. Also see Albert C. Baugh, *History of the English Language* (New York, 1935), pp. 255 ff., 275.

[6] Mario Pei, *Story of English* (New York, 1952), p. 310.

[7] For the variant spellings which even such apparently easy words as *able, ache, acre, hat, heron* have had, see these words in the OED.

[8] David Abercrombie, "What Is a 'Letter'?" *Lingua*, II (1949–50), 54–63. The author makes it clear that this meaning of "letter" arose naturally from earlier confusion in the work of the Latin grammarians (beginning certainly by the time of Priscian, about A.D. 500) involving the Latin *litera*. It is strange that in the OED there is no trace of this sense of "letter," which Abercrombie shows was in wide use for a long time.

their sounds and should therefore be able to read. When it was amply demonstrated that a child so taught could by no means read, the teachers were bewildered and often angered. Clearly, they thought, the rod was called for; but that was ineffectual too.

This confusion of letter names with letter sounds lasted for a long time and even now sometimes occurs. As we shall see later, Horace Mann was a victim of this misconception. Today it is not difficult to find those who think that when they consciously pronounce words they are pronouncing *letters*. It is conventional to speak of letters that are *sounded* and those that are *silent*. This convenient way of speaking helps to perpetuate an ancient delusion and obscures for many people the proper idea that letters, theoretically at least, merely stand for or represent speech sounds. They have no other function.

As letters became progressively less and less dependable indicators of sounds, as spellings became less and less alphabetical, and as confusion between the names and the sounds of letters came more and more to prevail, difficulties increased for those trying to learn to read and for teachers undertaking to guide them. These difficulties in connection with reading aroused exceptional interest in a century and a half extending roughly from 1511 to 1658. Commenting upon this period, Harold B. Dunkel says: ". . . never before or since have language teaching and language learning been so important as they then were, and never have so many first-rate minds given major attention to them."[9] Several superior English scholars had their attention called to the distressing plight of those who tried to teach children to read their own language.

This close scrutiny of what had come to exist in the English language was the result of an altercation that broke out among scholars over the correct pronunciation of classical Greek. Erasmus was the first, or among the first, to maintain that Greek written before the birth of Christ should be given the pronunciation it probably had at the

[9] Harold B. Dunkel, "Language Teaching in an Old Key," *Modern Language Journal*, May, 1963, pp. 203–4.

time, and not that of the Greek currently in use. Scholars took sides on this proposition, and arguments were vigorous.[10]

Those on the side of Erasmus looked into the history of English for examples with which to convince their opponents that in their own language great changes had come about both in pronunciation and spelling within a relatively few centuries. They reasoned that similar changes must have taken place in the pronunciation of Greek. We need not go further into this learned quarrel except to mention that Erasmus' group won the controversy. What is of more significance in our investigation is that when these highly trained linguists realized what had happened to English pronunciation and spelling, they saw at once a possible remedy for the reading problem.

English should be written alphabetically—that is, the number of letters in the alphabet should be increased until every sound in the language was represented by one letter. No letter should represent more than one sound. Furthermore, spelling should by all means follow sound. With these two basic propositions in mind, the best-qualified scholars in England set to work to persuade those who used English (as opposed to Latin) to make the two changes suggested. Sir Thomas Smith and John Hart were prominent among those who battled valiantly in the latter part of the sixteenth century to improve the writing and spelling of English.

One of the first things Smith did in his part of the campaign was to speak disparagingly of some of the English letters. He censured C for having two sounds—that of S in such words as *city* and *certain,* and that of K in *can* and *camp.* In a treatise he wrote in Latin in 1568 on "the right and emended writing of the English language," he said: "If S is a letter and K is a letter, as the Latin alphabet, which you wish me to follow, clearly shows, then I do not know what power [i.e., office or function] is left to this vagabond C, unless it is some kind of monster or hobgoblin, some-

---

[10] E. J. Dobson, *English Pronunciation* (Oxford, 1957), I, 38 ff. See also John Strype, *Life of Sir John Cheke* (London, 1705), pp. 15 ff.

times masculine and sometimes feminine, sometimes a snake, and sometimes a crow."[11] In showing the inadequacy of the existing twenty-four letter alphabet, Smith was preparing for the presentation of a better one of his own given at the close of his treatise. His alphabet had thirty-four letters, by which he thought to provide a letter for each sound in the language.

Sir Thomas may justly be called the first English phonetician, but he was soon surpassed by John Hart who, in the opinion of a highly competent student of English pronunciation, "deserves to rank with the greatest English phoneticians and authorities on pronunciation."[12] Hart also produced an alphabet, which he gave in his *Methode* of 1570. He called attention to the misnaming of the conventional letters and gave implicit directions for the proper naming of those he provided. Misnaming of the letters, he said, was so serious that if a sensible man, ignorant of letters, should be asked what *t, h, r,* spelled (giving these letters by their names), he would say "teacher," "for so are your letters taught, as might be thus, te, ache, er, which sounds iustly, as you teach those letters to be named."[13] Many people in Hart's time believed that it was wicked to add to or take from the number of letters in the alphabet.[14] At least some of them knew that English letters were of Latin origin, and all good men agreed that Latin was a holy language. It had been one of the three used in the inscription placed above the head of Christ upon the cross, and the sanctity of the Saviour had made all three of them—Greek, Latin, and Hebrew—holy.[15] Those who espoused this pious belief were not averse, however, to modifying the letters by markings placed above, under, or beside them. Among these broad-minded people there were probably some who knew that Hebrew, the most sacred language of the trio,

11 Sir Thomas Smith, *De recta & emendata . . . Scriptione . . .* (Halle, 1913), p. 22. In Latin, which Smith used, *serpens* (a snake) is feminine, and *corvus* (a crow) is masculine.

12 Dobson, *op. cit.,* I, 62, 88.

13 Bror Danielsson (ed.), *John Hart's Works* (Stockholm, 1955), pp. 234–35.

14 Dobson, *op. cit.,* I, 120.

15 Lewis F. Anderson, *History of Common School Education* (New York, 1909), p. 189.

had tolerated the placing of signs on some of its letters to serve as vowel indications.

Richard Hodges, "a School-master dwelling in South-wark, at the midle-gate within Mountague-close," was one of those willing to use diacritical marks on the existing letters. In 1644, he brought out a book showing what he considered to be the easiest and quickest way for the learner to master spelling and reading and writing. The excerpt on the following page from the preliminary matter shows Hodges' system of marking the letters and his evaluation of the difficulties for both teachers and pupils in the usual way of learning to read.[16]

The proposals of those who sought to smooth the way for those learning to read by providing them with a new or greatly modified alphabet failed. The efforts made showed that those who used English were devoted to the conventional alphabet, no matter what its imperfections might be. The names of the would-be reformers, such as Sir Thomas Smith, John Hart, William Bullokar, and Richard Hodges, are now known only to students.

In sixteenth- and seventeenth-century England efforts to teach children to read increased markedly. Although every device or practice inherited from the past or newly arrived at by clever teachers was employed to make the letters easier for children, teachers did not swerve from the ancient classical method of having the child start with a mastery of the letters, then of syllables, and finally of words and sentences. Children were given tidbits for each letter they learned. The alphabet was set to a simple air and the children taught to sing it. Thomas Morley, the celebrated musician, neighbor for a time of William Shakespeare, made use of such a musical arrangement of the letters.[17] Pupils were even taught to recite the alphabet backward. In Shakespeare's time "Holophernes" was a name for a pedantic and pompous schoolmaster. In *Love's Labor's Lost* Shakespeare invited his audience to laugh with him at

[16] Richard Hodges, *The English Primrose*, ed. Heinrich Kauter (Heidelberg, 1930), p. 2.
[17] Thomas Morley, *Plaine and Easie Introduction to Practicall Musicke* (London, 1937), p. 38.

Tô the Reader.

especially for the gaining of Sacred knowledge, without which the minde cannot bee good: but so many are the difficulties, in the common way of Teaching tô read English, that few wil undertake tô bee Masters in that kinde, unlesse necessitie and want cast them upon it; nor wil they long continue the Profession, if by any other imployment they can subsist. And if Masters finde the work sô tedious & grievous, it is impossible it should bee pleasing tô the Scholars. 'Tis most true, that they poor boys bee often chiden, rebuk't, knockt and whipt, when the fault is not in them, that they apprehend not what is taught, but in the uncertain, and perplext, and intricate expressing of our Tongue, by letters wrong named; and by their various sounds and forces attributed tô them. This is not any singular opinion of mine, but hath been, and is averred by diverse Learned and industrious men, both in the former, and this present age. And shal bee fully manifested in the following Tables of the Letters, and in the Practice thereupon: for therein I purpose, with as-much perspicuity as possible I can, and indeavour with as-much brevity as may bee, tô shew the inconveniencie and uncertaintie, in our expressing

this old traditional character of Italian comedy. In the first book of *Gargantua,* when Rabelais tells of the education of his hero, he says that Holophernes taught the young giant the alphabet backward in five years and three months. There was more than an element of truth in this satire. John Brinsley, in 1612, referred to the "common manner practiced in Schooles" of learning the alphabet "which is by oft reading over all the letters forwards and backwards untill they can say them."[18] Charles Hoole mentioned that the usual manner of teaching a child letters was to have him go over all of them in the alphabet or Christ-cross row "both forwards and backwards, until he can tell any one of them, which is pointed at." This way, he observed, was very effective with some "ripe witted" children, but others under the same treatment "have been thus learning a whole year together (and though they have been much chid, and beaten too for want of heed) could scarce tell six of their letters at twelve monts' end."[19]

It is possible, of course, that here and there teachers may have experimented with some methods other than the traditional one, but the lack of details no doubt indicates accurately that such experiments were sporadic and came to nothing in the long run. Hoole was entirely committed to the ABC method, but he cited Brinsley as directing teachers to have pupils pronounce and even spell a little before they knew a letter in the book. This they did by having the child sound the five vowels on his fingers "like so many bells" until he was able "to say which finger was such and such a vowel." Next the teacher put single consonants before the vowels, and then the vowels before the consonants. "But this is rather to be done in a private house, than in a publick Schoole," Hoole commented.[20] Later he said: "Amongst those that have a readier way to reading, I shall onely mention Mr. Roe, and Mr. Robinson, the latter of whom I have known to have taught little children not much above four years old to read distinctly in the Bible, in six weekes time, or under; their books are to be had in print, but every one

[18] Brinsley, *op. cit.,* p. 15.
[19] Charles Hoole, *op. cit.,* p. 33.
[20] *Ibid.,* p. 34–35.

hath not the art to use them."[21] It is most unfortunate that this remarkable method was not set forth in more detail and thus preserved. These comments by Hoole are no more than faint hints that sometimes a teacher might have tried to overcome the ever present difficulties of teaching a child to read by departing from the traditional ABC approach. At any rate, whatever these efforts may have been, nothing came of them.

[21] *Ibid.*, p. 42–43.

READING PROBLEMS AND SOLUTIONS IN GERMANY

FROM ICKELSAMER TO GEDIKE

In Germany the problems which elementary teachers and their pupils faced in beginning reading were the same as those which prevailed in England: the letters were difficult to learn, and a mastery of them contributed little to the child's ability to read. Instead of seeking the solution to their difficulty as the English did in an effort to adjust the alphabet to the sounds in the language, the Germans early devoted their best efforts to devising a new method of instruction in reading.

The most prominent of those Germans who began to cast about for a better method early in the sixteenth century was Valentin Ickelsamer (?1501–?1542). When he had finished his course at the university, he resolved to devote his life to improving his native language and to teaching children to read it.[1] Experience soon convinced him that the ABC method was faulty, and he began to study the possibilities of improving upon it. He turned to the Latin grammarians, especially Quintilian, and as he read ancient authorities, he pondered the nature of the letters and the nature of reading. Ickelsamer reasoned that speech sounds must have been in existence long before they were identified and represented by letters. A consideration of this

---

[1] The account given here is from Theodor Moritz Vogel, *Leben und Verdienste Valentin Ickelsamers* (Leipzig, 1894).

obvious fact led him inevitably to the conclusion that speech sounds were original and primary, and that the letters which represented them were secondary. Since letters were secondary, it was an error to make them primary in any system of teaching beginners to read. He would place first things first and at the very beginning direct the attention of his pupils to sounds, and then to the letters which stood for them. Only when a pupil had mastered a speech sound and was able to identify it everywhere it occurred should he learn the letter that stood for it. The teacher should be extremely careful to make sure that the name given to the letter was the proper one, that is, its sound.

Persuaded of the correctness of his new conception, Ickelsamer set to work with his beginners. To teach them speech sounds he used at first simple, well-known words. *Ot*, short for *Otto*, a boy's name, was a good one with which to begin. He showed the child this word, wrote it on the board, and on pieces of paper so each pupil might have it. As they looked at the word, he pronounced it carefully for them and had them imitate him. When he was satisfied with their pronunciation, he analyzed the word into its sounds. He taught the pupils just how he made the sounds and how they should do precisely the same in their pronouncings. He was careful not to say a thing about letter names. When he had done enough with *Ot*, he took up other simple words—*Hans, Wolf, Hund, Katz, Fuchs*.

It was natural for Ickelsamer to overdo work on sounds. He advanced from simple words to longer and more difficult ones. The analysis of words into their sounds intrigued him, and no doubt he was able to induce at least some of his pupils to enjoy these exercises. He urged parents to help their children by encouraging them to display their analytical abilities on words at home and to learn further refinements of the skill.

As soon as the pupils had learned to distinguish clearly the individual sounds in their speech, and to know which sound each letter represented, they were ready to read; for reading, according to Ickelsamer, was nothing more than naming the letters quickly and properly, that is, by their sounds, not by their conventional names. This new method of acquainting children with speech sounds, and teaching them to appreciate the letters—not in terms of their mis-leading names but in terms of their sounds—saved the be-ginners from confusing the two things. Thus taught, they were in an admirable position to proceed, just as school-boys had in ancient times, to begin to read, slowly at first but with a satisfactory gain in speed as facility in associ-ating sounds and letters increased.

Ickelsamer had such excellent success with his system that in 1527 he prepared a primer, *The Shortest Way to Reading*, to share with teachers and parents the advantages of what he had learned. Basing his statements on some ex-tremely favorable experiences with certain pupils he said that anyone taught by this system could learn to read in a few days; he himself had taught an adult to read in eight days and really saw no reason for anyone's taking more than one day for the task.

He was not able, however, to induce others to endorse his method. They pronounced it excellent for anyone who had unlimited time to devote to individual pupils, but they thought the analysis of words into sounds was beyond the abilities of most teachers. Ickelsamer had virtually agreed with this criticism when he wrote: "How one should name the letters correctly is not in use by many, and not many even know about it, but those who do know it, so like to be the only learned ones, and esteemed and respected therefor, that they will not teach it properly to anybody, and keep it in their schools and heads."[2]

Ickelsamer has the distinction of having been the first, or among the first, to depart from the traditional ABC method of teaching a child to read. By overemphasizing the work on sounds he failed to become widely influential, but his work helped later innovators to succeed.[3]

Many approaches—they can hardly be called "methods"

[2] Cited in Artur Kern, *Lesen und Lesenlernen* (Freiburg, 1937), p. 112.

[3] Vogel, *op. cit.*, pp. 36–37, and Karl Kehr, "Geschichte des Leseunter-richts," *Geschichte der Methodik des deutschen Volksschulunterrichts* (Gotha, 1889), pp. 43 ff., deal with Ickelsamer and lay some stress on efforts by successors to simplify what he had done by allowing pupils to begin to read before they had mastered all the sounds and letters.

—to the problem of teaching reading followed that of Ickelsamer, but the ABC method prevailed over all of them. The practitioners of this conventional way, through their struggles to preserve it, and in exploiting what they regarded as its excellencies, went beyond the bounds of reason. Since learning the letters was difficult for the children, the proposed remedy was to increase the insistence on thorough mastery of them—to have the pupils recite them backward as well as in the usual fashion down the alphabet row, jumble the letters in every possible manner, and race the children through them.

Syllable learning being desperately dull work, then by all means one must have more of it. The learning of syllables became a fetish. Teachers apparently worked hard to devise new and more appalling combinations with which to test the pronouncing powers of their charges.[4] Some cunning teacher thought of having dice with letters on their faces. Children rolled the dice and struggled to pronounce the combinations made of the letters exposed on their faces. "Reading machines" of different kinds were invented for the mass production of letter combinations.[5]

Spelling was hard and cheerless. Again, the remedy was to have more of it. The following is a sample of what industrious Germanic genius was capable of when it really devoted itself to this matter of putting together tough groups of letters and words: *schmurx, speimolch, sprulschax, thraimust, tschitschatschots, pseutscherpsen, kozkozkuzkiz*. The Bible and other ancient writings were ransacked for such terms as: *Tryphena, Ptolomäus, Kiriathaim*,

[4] There was, of course, nothing new about these techniques; it was simply that increasing insistence upon them became intolerable.

[5] Kehr, *op. cit.*, pp. 30 ff., gives a brief account of some of the more common mechanical devices used along with primers to get beginners started. On p. 33 he discusses the dice used in some detail, and on pp. 35–36 he gives pictures of two common types of reading machines. The invention of such gadgets will probably continue forever. The latest of which I have heard is the Edison Responsive Environment Instrument, tried out in 1964 in at least one kindergarten in Freeport, New York, to teach children the letters. It is an electronic computer, which in addition to typing, talks in six languages, reads, and shows pictures. It is the size of a desk and costs $30,000. The *Chicago Daily News,* January 8, 1964, p. 1, carried an AP notice of it. Linguistic blocks to be rolled as dice by beginners are marketed by Scott, Foresman and Company.

Jekuthiel, topped off by such prizes from contemporary usage as *Almosenamtsverpflegungsgelder, Viceoberappellazionsgerichtspräsident, Dudelsackpfeifenmachergesell.* If the teachers are to be believed, some pupils actually enjoyed grappling with such monsters as these and vied with each other to see who could spell and pronounce them best.[6] But such excesses led to the downfall of the ABC method with which they were identified.

One of the most bitterly eloquent voices raised in indignant protest against them was that of Samuel Heinicke (1727–90), the founder at Leipzig in 1778 of the first institution in Germany for the training of the deaf and dumb. He regarded such practices as insane—"a droll way of teaching," a "senseless playing with sounds," a "mere fiddlesticks," a "babble-factory," a "pim-pel-pam-pel," indeed "the most shameful, most injurious among all the follies which have gone up and down God's earth." In one of his diatribes he said: "The spelling method is a greater prejudice than burning witches and heretics; indeed it is a greater crime than the rack and all the inhumanities lumped together. For it is in defiance of all natural and revealed laws; it begets stupidity, illness, and death itself. It is child-torture—a slower and surer child-murder. A country which numbers twenty million inhabitants loses every year at least ten million dollars through this fiddling about with spelling and senseless trafficking with words."[7]

Such sulphurous fulminations elicited responses in a similar spirit from those well satisfied with things as they were. One of the spelling-school masters of the time declared Heinicke's outbursts were nothing but mere cricket-catchings, a shopful of subtleties, good for nothing but to while away the time for loafers, and he expressed his surprise that Heinicke had made such a spectacle over a mere rat's-tail.[8]

But as educators bickered, the "Age of Enlightenment" was coming. The Intellectual Revolution of the seventeenth

[6] Heinrich Fechner, *Grundriss der Geschichte der wichtigsten Leselehrarten* (Berlin, 1884), p. 11.
[7] Quoted in Kehr, *op. cit.,* p. 63.
[8] *Ibid.,* p. 64 n.

and eighteenth centuries was reaching a climax as epochal as the Renaissance or the Reformation. This new movement, with its roots extending far back into the sixteenth century, affected high and low—farmers, lawyers, scientists, philosophers, courtiers, kings. Representatives of all classes thought of themselves as "enlightened," and so they were—at least far more so than those who had preceded them. During the Enlightenment great progress was made in learning about the physical world. Alexander Pope, early in the eighteenth century, struck the keynote of this new attitude toward Nature: "Nature and Nature's laws lay hid in night: God said, Let Newton be! and all was light." The study of natural science became immensely popular. Observatories and museums multiplied. Progress was made in biological sciences; metaphysical speculation made a great appeal; mathematics, zoology, chemistry, minerology, anthropology—all felt the new impulse of this broad, European intellectual movement.

At this time, when the natural was substituted for the supernatural, and science tended to take the place of theology, those who were "enlightened" regarded the entire universe of matter and mind as guided and controlled by inescapable natural law. Human reason was glorified and almost deified, and it was confidently believed that man would henceforth use this faculty and obey Nature.[9]

In the light of these new concepts, all existing institutions, no matter how much popular veneration they enjoyed, were in danger of being most critically examined to see if their teachings and practices conformed to this better appreciation of Nature and Nature's laws. Rousseau held that a man should study Nature if he would develop his faculties. The educator especially should make his first study the order of Nature. Thus conventional methods of teaching reading came under close critical scrutiny. A remarkable philosophical explanation was found for the diffi-

[9] See Isaiah Berlin, *The Age of Enlightenment* (Boston, 1956). See also Carlton J. H. Hayes, *A Political and Cultural History of Modern Europe* (New York, 1938), I, 496. The lines from Pope are from his "Epitaph Intended for Sir Isaac Newton." For a brief but clear account of the application of the "Wholeness" philosophy to the teaching of beginning reading, see Kehr, *op. cit.*, pp. 122 ff.

culty of teaching the subject and for the poor results achieved. Teachers, instead of working in Nature's way, were proceeding in an exactly opposite manner. They were starting the child with what should be the end of the learning process and ending with that which should be the beginning.

FROM GEDIKE TO JACOTOT

The first German to make use of this great philosophical concept of naturalness in the interest of beginning reading was Friedrich Gedike (1754–1803), one of the most influential Prussian educators of his day. In 1779 he pointed out that children only three years old were set to learning the alphabet, often spending as much as two years at it. The child then entered upon an even worse drudgery—syllable learning. When at last he was able to read a little, he did so in a shockingly slow, inflectionless, uncomprehending manner. He pronounced the words but had no interest in them, for they were beyond his ability to understand.

Gedike thoroughly disapproved of this procedure. He saw that the child's difficulty was not that he was stupid but that he was ignorant; there was nothing in the letters and the syllables to increase his knowledge. What he needed was oral instruction in practically everything. The child in his development paralleled the development of the human race. Through skilful guidance he should live through his cultural inheritance. He should learn about numbers and listen to stories and songs suited to his age and be encouraged to express himself and to draw pictures and to exercise his imagination. His attention should be directed to the world about him—to grass, flowers, birds, stones, trees, brooks, hills, fields, animals.

By the time the child was ten or twelve, if he had been properly guided, he would be ready to learn to read, but not in the conventional manner for that was contrary to Nature. God worked in a synthetic fashion, His activity in Creation exemplified this. He began with the simplest of elements and proceeded to most complex "Wholes." In creating Man, He began with the simplest of all substances, the "dust of the ground," and ended with a noble, highly complicated Whole, a finished man, complete in all his parts. In precisely the same manner God had created the Cosmos, the Universe. He took the earth He had made, the sun, the moon, the stars, the constellations, and adjusted them to each other on a scale utterly beyond the comprehension of mere Man, and at the end He had the last and final stupendous Whole, the Cosmos.

This synthetic method was reserved for God alone; Man had to be content with the opposite method. Nature presented him with Wholes—a flower, a tree, an animal, a mountain. In his effort to learn about and to appreciate each of these, Man had to start with a particular Whole. If he wished to know all about a flower, he must dissect it, slowly, carefully, going constantly from a larger to a smaller unit of its composition, until he had advanced to its microscopically small cell structure and root system. If a man would learn about a beast, he must follow the same process; he must proceed from the Whole to its smallest parts.

In learning to read in the conventional way, the child was set to work in a manner quite contrary to Nature. He was confronted with elements, that is, letters, at the outset. What should have been the end of his quest was made the beginning. Under the tutelage of poorly prepared adults, the child continued his way—slowly and painfully because he was going in the wrong direction—until he at long last arrived at a book, exactly the place from which he should have started had he been properly taught.[10]

Thus Friedrich Gedike reasoned in 1779. He felt sure that a book was the logical whole with which the child should begin, but he must have realized that such a beginning was hardly practicable. When at last he had worked out a procedure he regarded as philosophically justified and practical, he used it in teaching his five-year-old daughter, and under his guidance she learned to read in two months. In 1791 he brought out a primer: *Kinderbuch zur ersten*

---

[10] Friedrich Gedike, *Aristoteles und Basedow* (Berlin and Leipzig, 1779), pp. 93 ff., and by the same author, *Einige Gedanken* (Berlin, 1791), pp. 2–10.

Übung im Lesen ohne A B C und Buchstabieren ("Children's Book for the First Practice in Reading without the ABC's and Spelling"). In the foreword Gedike explained his conception of the natural method of procedure for the human mind in going from the whole to its parts, from results to their origins. He would have the child learn letters through seeing them in use in words. Thus his procedure would be in accordance with Nature, that is from the whole to its parts. In this way the child would appreciate at once the real value of letters. Kehr described this primer as follows:

In [it] every letter has its page in which it, as it were, plays the chief role. It stands individually spaced out four times, printed twice in red and twice in black. In the first line are the words, each of them containing the letter which is to be learned, printed all in red; then come lines in which the letter alone is red in every word, and then come other lines in which the letter alone is black. In the first place, the character is the first letter of the word; after that it stands also in the middle. The last line on every page has the same words that stood in the first line, but not in the same order, and here they are all printed in black.[11]

Gedike defended this presentation of letters along with words in his preface. He had been criticized for having the child learn German as though it were Chinese. He argued that his book acquainted the child at the outset with the important fact that German words are made up of constantly recurring elements—that is, letters—as Chinese writing is not.[12]

Gedike regarded the following as the most important part of the preface to his *Kinderbuch:*

It is neither necessary nor useful to *begin* learning to read with a knowledge of the individual letters, but it is not only far more pleasant but also far more useful for the child if it learns to read *entire words* at once, because in this way it will be occupied immediately with whole ideas, but on the contrary the ABC's and spelling supply the child only fragments of ideas.

According to the customary method, the child first learns, with great difficulty, the individual letters, the capitals as well as the small ones.* The shape of an individual letter costs the child

11 Kehr, *op. cit.,* p. 100.
12 Gedike, *Einige Gedanken,* p. 8.

several days, indeed several weeks and months, and still, at every glance, the letters become confused with each other, because the picture of the bare letters makes too weak an impression on the eyes and imagination of a child, and is associated with no idea. People for a long time have been aware of the unnaturalness and torture of the ABC method, and tried various games proposed to make learning the individual letters easier for the child. They have invented all kinds of reading machines; they have pasted up individual letters, and tried to "play" them into the mind of the child; they have even had the letters baked by pastry cooks and given them to the children to eat.

All this proves how keenly people have felt what a torture the study of the ABC's is for children, but the "unthinking-ness" of this study has still not been relieved by all this playing, merely disguised somewhat. Even to this day, most children are tortured for years with the ABC's in order then to advance to the equally thought-lacking Ab, Eb, Ib, or Ba, Be, Bi. One would think that people really intentionally proposed to destroy the childish understanding in the bud, since they train the child like a starling to pronounce individual sounds about which it does not think in the least, and to recognize the symbols of them. Is it difficult to see that Nature's way does not proceed from letters, or indeed from marks—to names and from names to ideas, but, just the reverse, from ideas and things to names and words, and from these to letters, or, in short, not from symbols to meanings but from meanings to symbols?

According to the prevailing method, the child first learns to recognize the parts, the letters, and then the Whole, the word, for otherwise it will get its ideas in the wrong manner, and first proceed from the comprehension of the Whole—provided this Whole is not too great for the understanding of the child—to a more accurate observation of the parts themselves. As a rule, the synthetic method, which leads from parts to wholes, from causes to results, is more the way of dexterity and system than the way of Nature, made more for the purpose of putting in order what is already known and examined, than for finding out and examining. The analytical method which proceeds, on the contrary, from the Whole to the parts, from the results to the causes, is incontestably the natural way of the human mind, and especially of the mind as it is first stirred into action. Would it be unnatural then to carry this method over into learning to read? Would it be only in this instance repugnant to common sense to proceed from the perception of the Whole to a knowledge of the parts? People have tormented children long enough in conformity with the synthetic method to teach them to recognize words through letters. How would it be if we tried analytically, and exercised children in the contrary manner, to learn to know letters through words and along with words?

* Usually the child first learns the capital letters and then the lower case ones, although these latter ones give the child much more difficulty than the former, and although the small letters occur far more often than the capitals. Thus has custom, even in such small matters, made the unnatural the rule.[13]

This selection by Gedike of the most important part of his preface omits a paragraph of considerable interest:

One should not think that the child by this method knows only the words which it has actually learned, and that the recognition of these is merely an affair of the memory. No! Through the mysterious sense of analogy he will increasingly find out words on his own, or, if one prefers to say so, learn to guess, but also at the same time, he will sense even more mysteriously, why it must be this word and no other.[14]

Gedike's system did not make a favorable impression on the schoolmen of his day. John Frederick Zöllner expressed the almost unanimous judgment of the method in explaining it "more as a beautiful psychological-pedagogical experiment than as a gain for pedagogics." He further pointed out:

There will have to be many new exercises, if children who have learned to read by this method are going to be sure about unknown, much-compounded words, and able to help themselves. Indeed, many so accustom themselves to grasp quickly the impression which an entire word makes on the eye that they for years confuse words that are similar in appearance, and with the utmost difficulty learn to read with positive assurance. In addition to this, it happens that they still, when it is too late, have to be practiced in spelling in order to be able to write, with the result that neither time nor effort is saved.[15]

Gedike's primer went through three editions, but Heinrich Fechner explained that this was an indication, not of the popularity of the method, but of the author. Two of those who more or less closely followed in Gedike's footsteps were Ernst Christian Trapp and Philip Wackernagel. Trapp helped the child learn quickly and easily words de-

[13] Ibid., pp. 6–7.
[14] Quoted in Fechner, op. cit., pp. 43–44. See also Kern, op. cit., pp. 123–25, and Kehr, op. cit., pp. 100–101.
[15] Quoted in Fechner, op. cit., p. 44.

noting various common things by placing appropriate labels
on well-known objects, such as a book, a table, or a feather.
Then he provided the child with similar labels, and the
learner's task was to match the labels he had with those on
the objects. Trapp said, "In this way the picture of the
whole word impresses the children without their suspect-
ing anything about their parts, or letters." After the child
had learned a sufficient number of words in this fashion,
Trapp gave him a primer in which the words he knew were
used freely, and other badly needed ones, such as *the, and,
are, is, does,* and *what,* that could not be taught by objects,
were provided. Fechner said of this plan: "That such a
method is not very educative, that it can produce results
only slowly, and that it makes much greater demands on
the memory of the pupils than the much reviled spelling, is
self-evident."[16] Apparently this technique was never in
wide use.

The primer of Wackernagel was designed particularly for
mothers to use with their children at home. The mother
would read the selections over and over to the child, who
looked on, until he memorized them and could then recite
them by heart. This exercise continued until no matter
where his mother opened the book the child could begin
reciting. And conversely, the mother could tell the child the
general content of a selection and he could turn to it in his
primer. The idea was that the child, having learned a word
by its appearance, would go searching through the book to
find where it occurred again, or to find longer words of
which it formed a part. He would also learn letters and
their sounds in this process of familiarizing himself with
words; the letters and sounds which came at the beginning
of words would be the first to arouse his interest.

Fechner said of this approach: "That the method is applicable with very capable children privately instructed,
cannot be denied; proofs of its successful use are available.
That the way is very time-consuming and is extremely difficult is also well established. Of its use in crowded school
classes there can be no discussion—not even if the school-

16 *Ibid,* p. 44.

book to be used were cheaper than the Wackernagel one, which costs three marks."[17]

The work of these men and of others who agreed with them shows that by the end of the eighteenth century a word method of teaching reading, based upon philosophical principles, was being tried out in Germany. It failed to meet the approval of educational leaders of the time; they found its demands on the pupil's memory excessive, its results slow in coming, and its applicability to crowded classroom conditions quite impossible. Karl Kehr summed up the situation thus:

Gedike was the forerunner of a new developmental-phase in the history of elementary method. It also fell to his lot to be the forerunner of the phonics method and the writing-reading method. His works secured recognition, but his proposals did not find their way into the schools. There had first to come another man who with more powerful strength blew the alarm-trumpet of the time and roused the sleeping spirits from their sluggish security. This man was J. Jacotot.[18]

FROM JACOTOT TO THE NORMAL-WORDS METHOD

Jean Joseph Jacotot (1790–1840) was a brilliant French scholar and educator. In 1818 he became Professor of French Literature in the university at Louvain in Belgium. He faced a difficulty from the start; he did not know Dutch and three-fourths of his students did not know French. As he pondered this problem, he chanced upon a Dutch translation of Fénelon's *Les aventures de Télémaque*. This book gave Jacotot an inspiration. With the help of a student who could interpret he called the attention of his students to this translation and directed them to learn French by memorizing the French original, getting the meaning of what was said from the Dutch version.

Under his inspiration the students went to work with a will. As they memorized page after page of the French, they recited it to Jacotot who corrected any mistakes and urged

17 *Ibid.*, pp. 44–45.
18 Kehr, *op. cit.*, p. 101.

them to repeat, repeat, repeat until there was no likelihood of their forgetting it. From time to time he asked them to write their understanding of the text in French. To his great surprise, the students showed remarkable ability in reading and writing French. Their spelling and their grasp of French grammar, both learned from this intensive memory work, was amazing.

What his students had done set Jacotot to thinking about instruction in general. He apparently knew of Gedike's experiments in having children begin to read with whole words. What Gedike had said about Nature may have impressed him. He seems to have pondered the German's plan and philosophy in connection with what he had experienced at Louvain. In 1823 he began to bring out a series of pedagogical works under the title *L'Enseignement universel* ("Universal instruction"). He became famous at once. Hardly a day went by without visitors who came to see him from all over Europe, Russia, and the United States, and went home inspired by the Jacotot method and great admirers of its discoverer.

Only one of the books in Jacotot's pedagogical series is pertinent to our investigation; it is the *Langue maternelle* ("The Mother Tongue"). In it he explained in detail how he thought a child should be taught to read.

He was convinced that one learns a thing first in its total form. A child does not learn first a note, then a tune, and last a song; he learns the song first of all. Do you show a child first the stamen of a flower and last the total flower? Do you teach a child to recognize an animal by showing him one of its bones? Do you show him all the pieces that enter into the making of a house and last the house itself, or do you point out the entire completed house first of all? Did Jesus give the disciples first definitions and rules, or did he give them the facts, the reality, to start with? In teaching to read, why proceed from sounds, utterly unknown to the child, or from letters which are quite dead?[19]

[19] *Ibid.*, p. 104. This summary of Jacotot and the part he played in laying the foundation for the Normal-Words Method is from Kehr, *op. cit.*, pp. 101 ff. Kehr said he followed the presentation given by J. P. Krieger in his translation of the *Langue maternelle* in 1830. My description of Jacotot's

Give the child first that which is complete—a "Whole." Jacotot, remembering his students at Louvain, thought instruction in learning to read might well begin with Fénelon's *Les aventures de Télémaque,* a book which appeared in 1669 and went through at least one hundred and fifty editions, having been translated into all the languages of Europe. It dealt with the adventures of Telemachus in quest of his father Ulysses, long overdue from the Trojan War.

It requires no genius to see why Jacotot selected this as a suitable book with which to begin reading instruction. On the score of "Wholeness" it easily qualifies, for it is nearly four hundred pages long, divided after the pattern of the *Iliad* and the *Odyssey* into twenty-four parts or "books." It must have been intensely interesting to youthful readers— the adventures of Telemachus involved such episodes as his visit to the abode of the dead and a meeting with his grandfather—although it is true that the work is in reality a profound treatise on personal morals and sound principles of good government,[20] and called for much explanation by the teacher.

According to Jacotot the teacher's first task was to read the book to the pupils; they were expected to listen closely and at the end of the reading were in possession of a "Whole," that is, a total body of material. Considering the serious purpose of the book, it may be that some pupils had to listen to it read again, and even a third time before grasping fully the "Wholeness" of it. But with this "Whole"

---

method of teaching his students French is taken from Dr. Hugo Göring's "Leben und Lehre Joseph Jacotot's," in his *Joseph Jacotot's Universal-Unterricht* (Vienna, 1883), pp. viii–ix, xiii. Jacotot's method has been discussed in many books; the literature on the subject is referred to by Krieger and by Göring. See Göring, pp. clxxvii–clxxix, for a list of the writings about *Universal Instruction.*

On pp. 1–3 of his book, Göring translated Jacotot's Foreword to *Universal Instruction.* So far as teaching to read was concerned, Jacotot insisted that the pupil be given one book and taught to understand it thoroughly, and then shown how to derive from it anything and everything else he desires to know. See his *Enseignement universel . . . Langue maternelle* (Louvain, 1827).

[20] Fénelon wrote this remarkable book to instruct his royal pupil, the Duke of Burgundy, son of Louis XIV, in morals, and to provide him with a system of political ethics. Any adequate presentation of the book to pupils must have gone into its more serious aspects, though they do not lie on the surface.

well in mind, where he could contemplate it in its entirety, the pupil now prepared to participate under his teacher's guidance in dismantling it into its parts, advancing little by little to successively smaller units of the total whole. The teacher, having completed the reading of the whole book a sufficient number of times, then took up the first sentence in it: "Calypso was unable to console herself for the departure of Ulysses." He had the children memorize this sentence so that they could give it forward or backward or in any other fashion. They had to memorize every one of its words, first as they stood in the sentence, then backward, then in any order.

The teacher next took the first word, "Calypso," separated it into its sounds, and taught these to the pupils. Each letter in the word was then taken up, and its relationship to the sound for which it stood brought out. The children, sufficiently drilled, could give all the sounds and could assemble them into the entire word. They could do the same for the letters, relating each to its appropriate sound, and arranging all of them into the complete word. Through this entire book, sentence by sentence, word by word, letter by letter, sound by sound, the pupils were to be guided. By the time they reached the end, the meaning, etymology, history, pronunciation, and spelling, of every word had been carefully explained and learned. Pupils thus instructed came at last to understand what Jacotot meant by his instructional axiom: Everything is in everything.

German teachers who desired to follow the leadership of the renowned Jacotot balked at infringing on the limits of eternity by reading to their pupils an entire book, possibly more than once, and then picking it to pieces, sentence by sentence, word by word, sound by sound, and finally letter by letter. Why could not a sentence serve as a "Whole"? They believed it could, and it was certainly a more manageable unit.

By 1830 there had appeared in Germany a primer based upon the Jacotot method.[21] The sentence given as a desir-

---

[21] Kehr, *op. cit.*, pp. 106 ff. Kehr says the author of this primer was Friedrich Weingart, a locally prominent minister and teacher who worked not far from Gotha.

able "Whole" was this: "Socrates, the wise son of Sophron-iscus, spoke one day in the circle of his students of the all-powerful foresight of divine providence,—how it sees everything and hears everything, and is present everwhere and takes care of everything, and of how a man the more he feels and recognizes it the more he honors it."[22] This sentence was long and the subject-matter well beyond the comprehension of a four-year-old, so reduction continued to be made in the direction of shorter, more suitable "Wholes." The theorists at last got down to about the simplest possible sentences, such as "Alma paints." But this was not entirely satisfactory either. Perhaps the pupil did not know a girl named Alma, or perhaps the Alma he knew did not paint. Could not a single word be accepted as a "Whole"? Obviously it could. It has a beginning and an end; it is a total; it is a unit. Out came the inkpots and goose-quills, and an avalanche of primers resulted. Kehr in his "Geschichte" lists about forty such primers. They apparently differed chiefly in the number of words they supplied as the best ones to use with the beginner. No doubt they were words denoting objects which the teacher could show or draw for him on the blackboard. Above all, they were words spelled in the normal manner, the letters having the values usually given them.

In the manner thus briefly sketched, by constantly reducing the amount of material first offered the child, Jacotot's "Whole" consisting of a long book of about two hundred thousand words was brought down to a single word. Many designations were used for the words employed in this new way. Kehr referred to them as: ordinary words, instruction words, representative words, sample words, clue words, basic words, normal words. There were various names given the new system: Analytic-Synthetic Method and Normal-Words Method were used more often than the others. In discussing the desirability of this new method, Kehr pointed out how thoroughly it was in accord with Nature, for one first perceives a whole, just as on an elevation

---

[22] Kehr, *op. cit.*, p. 106, points out that in this primer Weingart employed a parable by Adolf Krummacher, and this sentence was the first one in it.

one first receives a total impression of the countryside on which he looks, later advances to an appreciation of the groups of houses he sees, and may finally fix his attention on one particular house.

In giving an account of the practical application of the Normal-Words Method, Kehr listed the seven essential steps to be taken by the teacher. First, the object denoted by the normal word chosen for the lesson should be presented, or at least a picture or drawing of it. Then the word itself should be shown in its entirety and analyzed into its sounds and syllables. In Kehr's estimation this analysis was "decidedly the most important part of the method." It involved the clear exposition of the sounds, and of the letters which represented them, though no mention at all was made of the names of the letters. They were presented one by one for the children's consideration, but only in terms of the sounds for which they stood. When the word had been thoroughly analyzed, the sounds and letters were put together again into the complete word. Hand in hand with this analysis and synthesis of the word went the writing of it. The teacher traced the word slowly for the children, stressing the chief features of its form, having them watch closely the tip of the pointer with which he went over the letters. Then he retraced the word, this time having each child follow the movements of the pointer with the index finger of his right hand. Then all the children wrote the word on their slates, and having written it, they all read it. In this way the children learned the value of the letters in terms of the sounds for which they stood. Nothing was said about their memorizing the words; the forms of the letters, the sounds they represented, the syllables, were the things aimed at. The names of the letters were not mentioned at this initial stage; their sounds alone were given.[23]

When Horace Mann and his second wife visited Germany in the summer of 1843, they saw a class of beginners being taught by a skilful Prussian teacher using this method. Although Mann could not understand German,[24] his wife

[23] *Ibid.*, pp. 114 ff.
[24] Mary Peabody Mann, *Life of Horace Mann* (Washington, 1937), p. 175.

could, and from what she told him and from what he saw he wrote quite vividly. There were sixty children in the class. The teacher, after a few opening remarks to put the children at their ease, drew on the board the picture of a house. Beside it he wrote the word *Haus* in German script and printed it also "in the German letter." With a long pointed rod having a white tip so that its motions might be more easily followed, the teacher ran over the forms of the letters, the children following the movements of the pointer with their fingers in the air. Then the children copied the word on their slates. Drill in the sounds of the letters followed; the names of the letters were not given, merely their sounds. After teaching the *h* sound and that of *au*, the teacher brought out the letter blocks for *h* and *au* and placed them together, instructing the children to combine the sounds. Finally *s* was sounded, first by itself and then with the others, and the entire word was spoken.

The word being thus disposed of, the teacher showed the children how to draw the picture of a house, the ability to draw being "a power universally possessed by Prussian teachers." The hour-long lesson concluded with a discussion of houses, the teacher supplying most of the information but inquiring of the children things within their knowledge. He ended with some general information about houses, "intermingling the whole with lively remarks and pleasant anecdotes."[25]

The advantage of this process of selecting and using normal words was that it taught the child his letters more quickly, more thoroughly, and far more pleasantly than had ever been done by the usual manner. Simple words were used merely as vehicles to bring the letters more vividly and interestingly to the child's attention. They were not memorized. Their instructional value and use ceased as soon as the child had mastered the speech sounds and the letters representing them. From this point on, reading instruction proceeded in the usual manner. The avoidance of the wearisome, discouraging, unimaginative manner of teaching a child the letters by having him first meet them

[25] *Common School Journal,* VI (1844), 117–18.

in simple words he already knew and in connection with well-known objects seems to have originated in Germany, but if so, it quickly spread. A revulsion at the tortures and beatings attendant upon the traditional method as many teachers applied it was certainly not confined to Germany.

As Horace Mann sat in the class of the Prussian teacher, he thought he was seeing something that urgently needed to be called to the attention of his people back home. In fact, he was seeing in operation a relatively new way of teaching children their letters which was, as we shall find in the following chapter, essentially the same method as one in use in New York State as early as 1834. The same approach reached Boston before Mann became Secretary of the Board of Education, and even as he sat in the class of German children, teachers in New Orleans were deriving great satisfaction from using words to teach children their letters and the sounds for which they stood.

This method spread quickly in Germany. Kehr tells of how it was found far more satisfactory than the somewhat earlier phonics method which had at first been hailed joyously by many teachers as the philosopher's stone found at last. The phonics method lost favor because teachers who used it allowed their enthusiasm for giving scientific instruction in sounds to get entirely out of hand.[26] For the infants before them they classified speech sounds on the basis of the organs most dominant in producing them and pontificated learnedly about explosives, pure sounds, breath sounds, aspirated sounds, soft sounds, sharp sounds, and so on.[27]

The chief reason for the popularity of the Normal-Words Method was that teachers found it a far better way of teaching the ABC's than anything that had gone before it. Kehr, in a book written for teachers, gave a full account of what was done with reading in the school he knew best. The teachers used this method and used object-teaching in connection with it. In the first grade, four hundred and

26 Kehr, *op. cit.*, pp. 68 ff.
27 *Ibid.*, pp. 37–77.

eighty hours of the child's time were devoted to reading. Professor Kehr said:

The objective of reading instruction in this first grade is that the children in the course of a year have practiced and learned the reading of written and printed German to the extent that they are able to read accurately, and to some degree, fluently, little easy selections. Mechanically-fluent reading is of prime importance and must be striven for with all permissible means. The school has attained a good part of its over-all objective if it has fulfilled this requirement. The teacher has to place special emphasis on *all* the children's attaining the objective, and that those children of perhaps less ability do not remain behind in one group. Not more than ten percent, at the most, of the first year's class should remain behind as stragglers.[28]

The entire section on reading at the elementary level is an excellent setting forth of opinions then widely held about beginning reading. Kehr mentioned that the basic meaning of "to read" (*lesen*) was "to gather" and thought that one who reads "gathers" letters into sounds, sounds into syllables, syllables into words, and words into sentences, "into thoughts, into connected discourse." So he distinguished *syllable-reading, word-reading, sentence-reading,* and *reading in connected discourse.* Depending upon fluency, comprehension, and emphasis, reading was viewed as *mechanical reading, mechanically-fluent, logically-correct,* and *euphonically-beautiful reading.* Kehr said: "Mechanical reading in itself has nothing to do with the understanding of what is read, for it consists merely and only in the correct pronunciation of symbols written or printed as syllables and words." The child in learning to read advanced through these grades of proficiency. If *mechanical reading* took place without stopping and hesitation, then it became *mechanically-fluent reading.* "For attaining mechanically-fluent reading there is only one means—industrious practice." Syllable-reading should not be neglected, for it was the foundation of all the later stages. He solemnly warned against reading too fast, calling it "the mother of bad reading. One does not learn to read well through reading fast; but through reading well, he learns to read fast."

[28] Karl Kehr, *Die Praxis der Volksschule* (Gotha, 1895), pp. 204–5.

Nothing is more disgusting than to have the children in a school in the second and third grade still unable to read with much fluency. What does all the alphabetic correctness, the understanding, even the beauty of pronunciation, help if the necessary fluency is lacking and if the flow of the words is interrupted through unseemly, disturbing pauses![29]

[29] *Ibid.*

EARLY READING EXPERIMENTS
IN THE UNITED STATES

The influence of what was being done abroad, particularly in Germany, to improve the methods of teaching reading was felt across the ocean. Early nineteenth-century American journals of education were heavily laden with articles describing European experiments in the entire field of elementary education, and particularly in reading.[1] Gedike and Jacotot were both influential in American experiments of the first half of the last century.

Some of those interested in elementary education were particularly anxious to improve ways of teaching children their ABC's. Ordinarily, it was a tortuous, time-consuming, discouraging operation for both teacher and pupil. Those whose goal was a better method of teaching the letters felt that if this initial barrier could be removed a great step forward in teaching and learning to read would have been taken. Others had a much more comprehensive goal: they

[1] For a discussion of the great wave of German immigration to this country in the nineteenth century, see Henry A. Pochmann, *German Culture in America* (Madison, Wis., 1957), pp. 40 ff. For an account of American students in Germany in the early part of the century, see Pochmann, pp. 66 ff. Beginning early in the nineteenth century many American educators went abroad, especially to Germany. See Edgar W. Knight, *Reports on European Education* (New York, 1930). These reports Knight (p. 2) called "One of the most influential forces of all those at work in behalf of public education in the United States during the second quarter of the last century." Alexander Dallas Bache was certainly one of the most competent of those who went abroad. See his *Report on Education in Europe* (Philadelphia, 1839), pp. 291 n., 657. For what he said about European methods of teaching to read, see especially pp. 183, 256, 291 n., 657.

aimed at an entirely different method of teaching the child
to read. They would solve the ABC problem by postponing
it until the child had learned to read simple material and
was therefore eager to acquire greater reading skill. The
influence of Jacotot's teaching, as it had been reduced to
practice in the Normal-Words Method in Germany, is apparent in the concern of the first group. The influence of
Gedike's ideas (which Jacotot had also heartily endorsed)
is obvious in the second group.

In this chapter we shall devote attention to the efforts of
those in the first group who aimed at the quicker, pleasanter
way of teaching a child the letters. In 1826 a contributor to
the *American Journal of Education,* pointing out the difficulties in "the present mode of the attainment of that art,"
that is, reading, suggested that the sounds of the letters be
taught along with their names.[2] In this same volume of the
Journal appeared an announcement of a forthcoming
"Reading Book for Infants." Of it the editor says:

> It is with uncommon pleasure that we inform our readers of
> the above publication. It is now in preparation by Mr. Samuel
> Worcester of Gloucester, Mass. a gentleman eminently qualified
> for the undertaking.
> This proposed book is to contain a series of reading and
> spelling lessons combined. It will embrace all or most of the
> valuable improvements suggested by the recent English publica-
> tions on the instruction of infants. It is copiously illustrated by
> neat cuts, and is in every way rendered amusing as well as
> instructive.
> From what we have seen of the manuscript, and the designs,
> we have no hesitation in recommending it as the most ingenious
> and practical volume which has yet appeared, for the purposes
> of domestic education or of primary schools.[3]

We shall notice this work of Worcester's again later, but
the editor's statement about its making use of what had
appeared in the best English publications on the subject
makes pertinent the following excerpt which appeared in
the first volume of the *American Annals of Education*
(1830–31). It comes from an account of the method of

2 *American Journal of Education,* I (1826), 196.
3 *Ibid.,* I, 379.

teaching to read used in the Sessional School in Edinburgh, as given by Professor Pillans, "a distinguished friend of Education, and professor in the University of Edinburgh."

English reading, according to the prevailing notion, consists of nothing more than the power of giving utterance to certain sounds, on the perception of certain figures, and the measure of progress and excellence, is the facility and continuous fluency with which those sounds succeed each other from the mouth of the learner. If the child gather any knowledge from the book before him, beyond that of color, form, and position of the letters, it is to his own sagacity he is indebted for it, and not to his teacher.

The rule, expressed or implied, which is generally followed in schools, is, that the duty incumbent on the master consists in giving the pupil, as speedily as possible, mechanical dexterity in reading, without wasting time, or distracting his attention with the sense of what he reads. He may allow it to be desirable that the child should comprehend what he reads; but still he thinks it right to sacrifice this object to the more pressing and immediate demand upon him, to return the child to his parents a fluent reader, in a given time.[4]

It is interesting to notice that those teaching reading in the Sessional School in Edinburgh did not bother themselves in the least, at the beginning stage of reading, with whether the child understood what he read. The task of the beginner was to pronounce as accurately and as fluently as he could; understanding would come later, they felt. The same view was expressed by Professor Kehr fifty years later.

Professor Pillans appeared not to have been enthusiastic about this conception; he thought it both possible and desirable to teach the child the habit of "carrying the sense along with the sound." He said that as an aid to this end, Mr. Wood, Superintendent of the Edinburgh Sessional School, had the child master the alphabet, and then started him at once on easy words, with no attention to the syllabic combinations. The alphabet was taught in portions, and only a few letters at a time. We shall become better acquainted with Mr. Wood and his method in the next chapter.

On August 6, 1830, the Reverend T. H. Gallaudet, writing

[4] *American Annals of Education,* I (February, 1831), 69 ff.

from Hartford, Connecticut, addressed a letter to an editor
friend of his. In this communication he explained how for
seven years he had been teaching his children:

The words *horse, dog, cat,* are written, in a very plain and
legible hand, on three separate cards. One of them is shown to
the child, and the name of the object pronounced; and then the
second and the third in the same manner, *without any reference
to the individual letters which compose the word.* After repeating this a few times, the child is asked, 'what is that?' holding up
one of the cards, and so of the rest. Let the cards then be placed
together, and the child required to select those denoting the
several objects, one after the other. Vary the order of doing this
until the child becomes perfectly familiar with the words; which
will be in a very short time.

The next day, another card, containing the name of some other
familiar object, may be added, and the child practised in the
same manner upon the four cards. The number of cards may
soon be increased to six, to ten, to twenty, to fifty.

Here I have been accustomed to stop, and begin to teach the
child the letters of which the words are composed in the following manner. Take the word *horse,* and covering all the rest, show
the letter *h,* giving its name. Do this with the other letters in
succession, repeating the process, until the child is perfectly
familiar with the four [sic] letters. Then lay down the fifty cards
in order, and ask the child to find the letter *h* among them, then
o, r, s, and *e.* This will readily be done. He has thus learned four
[sic] letters of the alphabet. Vary the order in which the cards
are laid, and require the child to point out again the letters *h,
o, r, s, e.* Let this be done till he is familiar with them. Pursue the
same course with the card containing the word *dog,* and so on,
until the child is perfectly acquainted with all the letters on the
cards. They may then be written down in the order of the alphabet, and the child taught to repeat them in that order.

A few lessons will enable him to know the same letters, and
the same words, in their printed form.[5]

In the last paragraph of this letter, Gallaudet said that if
leisure permitted he planned to prepare a *"Primer* for children on the plan above described." He did prepare this
primer, which will be discussed later.

Gallaudet was a man of unusual training and intelligence.
He had traveled abroad to learn all he could about the
methods used in Europe in teaching the deaf and dumb. He

[5] *Ibid.* (August, 1830), pp. (49) 373 ff. The paging in this volume is somewhat irregular.

had excellent opportunities there to find out about educational practices with regard to reading.[6] It is clear from his letter that as early as 1823 he was having his children learn their letters by means of words, and that they mastered the words used in the process so that they could read "both by inspection and from memory."

J. Orville Taylor wrote of how words were being used at least as early as 1834 in the district schools of New York State in teaching children their ABC's:

The way of teaching children their letters, which has always been found pleasant and successful, is, holding up in the sight of all the children two or three letters of considerable size, and whose union spells the name of some familiar object. For example, let the letters O X, standing under the picture of an ox, be shown to the children. The names of the letters are pronounced by the teacher, and by the children in concert after him. When the names of these two signs are known to the children, the teacher may tell them a story about the ox. By being interested with the *idea* which the letters represent, it will be almost certain that the children remember their names. The two letters may then be given to each of the children, who return to their seats, pleased with the signs which have been connected with such a pleasing *idea* or story. After a suitable interval the teacher may examine them, and if the names of the letters are remembered, they may be taken away, with a promise of showing them others, in connection with a picture and a story, in a short time.

The teacher again asks the attention of the children, and shows them the three letters, b, o, y; one of them the same they had in the first lesson, that he may try the memory. The picture of the boy is seen over the letters; and after the children have learned the names of the two signs, b, y, the teacher relates a story of a little boy he once knew or heard of. The children return to their seats with the two letters of which they have just learned the names. How much time, and labour, and impatience, and compulsion on the part of the teacher, and dislike, and fretting, and hatred on the part of the pupil might be saved, if instructers would permit children to get knowledge *in* school in the same manner that Nature teaches *out* of it!

This method of teaching the alphabet demands but a few moments of time from the teacher, and makes it a delightful employment for himself, for he sees the young minds before him taking their first steps in knowledge, and at the same time

---

[6] See the account of his life by his son: Edward Miner Gallaudet, *Life of Thomas Hopkins Gallaudet* (New York, 1888).

their little features lighted up with joy in their new enterprise. In one week's time he may make every child familiar with all its letters.[7]

Taylor explained that after the child had learned his letters in this pleasant and easy fashion, the teacher's next task was to acquaint him with the sounds which they represent. He apparently did not know much about phonetics for he spoke of some of the letters as having more than a hundred "different, distinct sounds or powers." The child needed guidance in distinguishing between the names and the sounds of the letters "for to the child the name of the letter is its sound."

In the plan Taylor sketched, both letters and simple words were used, but attention to the letters slightly preceded that devoted to the words which they formed. His indication that the method he described was widely used in New York State may have been accurate, but it is helpful at this point to consider a report submitted at the New York State Convention of County Superintendents held at Syracuse in April, 1845:

> In a course of *school* education the alphabet first claims attention, and upon the manner in which this and the earlier reading lessons are taught, depends, in a great degree, the future *love* of the child for books and his subsequent mental action as connected with them. The first lessons should be so given as to excite thought and delight the mind; but a directly counter effect has been more commonly produced—that of stifling thought and disgusting the mind; and this mental inactivity and indifference have often been kept up so long, upon the alphabet and spelling columns, as to become a fixed habit, following the pupil through his subsequent school course.
>
> It is suggested, therefore, that the alphabet be taught in all cases by familiar words, of not more than three letters; that the words thus selected be present, if possible, in some form, to the eyes of the whole class at once. The teacher then converses with his class about the object which the word represents, and, if he can, draws a plain outline of it on the blackboard; the letters are then named by the teacher and the pupils and the word pronounced. Sometimes the *powers* of the letters are given at the same time, and this is deemed the most rational and practical way of teaching this department of Orthography. As soon as a

[7] J. Orville Tayor, *The District School* (New York, 1834), pp. 142 ff.

few words are learned in this way, a short sentence is introduced, which is read and copied as before, not only in Roman,
but, as the pupils advance, in script also. . . . The interest excited
in a class by an exercise so conducted, is truly gratifying. No
difficulty whatever is found in teaching ordinary pupils, of
proper age, three letters a day, and your committee have known
frequent instances in which the alphabet has been taught in a
week, and in some cases in four days, by the method named.[8]

The method which Taylor outlined and the one the superintendents approved were almost identical. In the Taylor
presentation, the letters preceded the words by a mere matter of seconds or minutes; in the other procedure, the words
were first presented, and immediately thereafter the letters
of which they were composed. The difference between the
two approaches may well have been more theoretical than
real. A teacher might have used one or the other indiffer-
ently. At any rate, the object of both was to assist the child
to a mastery of the letters as quickly and pleasantly as
possible. And, on the evidence just shown, they both
achieved this end admirably. Notice too that the procedure
which the superintendents recommended did not differ
essentially from the German Normal-Words Method already discussed. They were both ABC methods slightly
disguised.

The "letter-to-word" or "word-to-letter" method was
known and used in England by 1838. In the Borough Road
School in Southwark, London, established about 1800, a
similar method of teaching the alphabet was employed—
not "in the usual way—a single letter at a time, but in connection with words having a definite meaning; a plan which
experience has found to be the best."[9]

Not long after Taylor's book appeared, some elementary
teachers in Boston became interested in trying to teach the
alphabet in a different manner from the prevailing one. On
August 2, 1836, the Primary School Committee of Boston
"Voted—That such teachers as may be disposed to use
Gallaudet's Primer, for teaching the alphabet, may do so in
the way of experiment, and report to the district committee

[8] *Common School Journal*, VII (1845), 227.
[9] *Ibid.*, I (1838–39), 100.

their opinion of its value." The primer referred to was *The Mother's Primer,* the one Gallaudet had hoped he might have time to prepare.

The teachers, having asked for and received permission to teach the letters in a new manner, went ahead with their experiment, and on November 7, 1837, made a report of which the following is the most pertinent part:

> They have carefully examined the Mother's Primer, and caused the experiment to be made in several of the schools, and from the favorable reports which have been received from the teachers of the success they have met with in advancing the children from the fourth to the third class, your committee are induced to recommend its adoption in our Primary Schools; believing as they do that it is easier as well as more expeditious and interesting to the pupil, than the old, unintelligible, and irksome mode of teaching them to call certain arbitrary marks, or letters, by certain arbitrary sounds.
>
> Your committee have been informed by one of the teachers, who has for the last year adopted this proposed mode of teaching, that pupils taught in this way, are enabled, in four months to read very well in plain reading, and spell words of one syllable, even with silent letters; whereas it generally takes a longer period of time, by the old method, to teach them the alphabet of large and small letters.[10]

I have not been able to secure a copy of *The Mother's Primer,* but there is available an account written in 1840 of how it had "been tried in various families and schools, and with great success." Children were taught words at the outset following the method Gallaudet said he had used with his children. When they had mastered a number of words and had done some reading by means of them, they learned letters from these words, not in regular order in the alphabet. "The subsequent steps, after the alphabet is learned, both with regard to spelling and reading can be varied at the discretion of the teacher. The mode of doing this pursued in *The Mother's Primer,* which is intended to harmonize with the above-mentioned plan, can be seen in that work."[11]

In each of the different aspects of the new procedure

---

10 Horace Mann, *Reply to Remarks* (Boston, 1844), pp. 111 ff.
11 *Connecticut Common School Journal,* III (1840–41), 42.

which we have considered—the one mentioned by Taylor, the one described by the superintendents, and the one outlined by those who used *The Mother's Primer*—the words employed served the purpose of assisting the child to a mastery of the letters.

The success of the Boston teachers in advancing pupils from the fourth to the third class—that is, from the first to the second grade[12]—and in teaching them to read "very well in plain reading" in four months and to spell words of one syllable "even with silent letters," was in keeping with another Massachusetts teacher's success in New Orleans a few years later. Professor John A. Shaw of Bridgewater, having taught for several years in Massachusetts, accepted a position in New Orleans, where he soon became a principal and a superintendent. Writing in 1845 about how reading was being taught under his direction in this southern city, he said:

Children of five years of age are admitted to the schools, most of whom are ignorant of the alphabet. The first lesson for those who do not know their letters, is, to read, after the dictation of the teacher, such an exercise as the first reading lesson in Goodrich's primer—*ox, fox*; or the first in Worcester's—*a man, a cat.* The little learners are in classes of six or eight. After repeating the words, sometimes simultaneously, sometimes separately, the names of the letters composing the words are told to them, and their attention is called to each of the two or more letters, in any manner which may be most likely to enable them to retain their names in remembrance. They are likewise required to spell each word, while looking at its respective letters, and then again with the book closed. All this, of course, can be done at first, and for some time after, only by following the dictation of the teacher. But the names of the letters, and their powers in combination with each other, soon become known to the pupil, and the teacher's aid is less and less needed.

This mode of instruction I much prefer to that usually pursued in former times, and by most teachers now—of calling upon children, one by one, to repeat the alphabet, day after day and

[12] This way of numbering the grades or classes, beginning with the fourth and advancing to the first, shows German influence. Germans reasoned, logically, that "first" connotes *best*, and should be worked up to from the *lowest*, that is, the fourth in this instance. This method of designating the grades continued sporadically until about the close of the nineteenth century.

month after month, till they can name all the letters, and then, of spending some months upon spelling-lessons, in columns of syllables and words as arranged in our spelling-books. I prefer it for the following reasons, to name no others. First, the alphabet is learnt in less than half the time required by the other process; for the children take much more interest in learning it when they are led to see its connection with words, with reading, with ideas; which they do immediately see, when taught in this manner—which they see as soon as the names and sounds of any of the letters are known; whereas, when taught in the more usual way, they have not the slightest idea of the use of a single letter, till they have learnt the names of twenty-six unmeaning characters. Furthermore, when the teacher, after having spent months in impressing upon their memories the names of these twenty-six marks, proceeds to teach them their powers as combined in syllables and words, in columns of the spelling-book, this stage of their progress is divested, like the former, of most that ought to interest the learner, by presenting them with mere unmeaning sounds, such as *ab, eb, bla, bly,* etc., and next with words not arranged in sentences, and consequently affording no exercise for the understanding. . . .

Those who will consult Worcester's Primer, and other books for young learners, some of which have been several years in use from Maine to Louisiana, will find our mode of teaching the alphabet to be no novelty.[13]

This plan of teaching children their letters by means of words was a great improvement on the one that had been conventionally followed. It spread widely, and wherever it was employed it was effective and delighted both teachers and pupils. Horace Mann was one of its most enthusiastic and eloquent endorsers. He praised without restraint the views expressed by the superintendents at Syracuse, saying that they were "incorruptible and imperishable. Should they be overwhelmed in another Pompeii, to be exhumed eighteen hundreds years hence, they would even then be full, not merely of historical interest, but of immediate and available utility." He concluded this tribute with the ringing statement, "New York has the best common school system in the world."[14]

This popular departure from the traditional way of teaching the letters never had a distinctive name. At first it was

13 *Common School Journal,* VII (1845), 268 ff.
14 *Ibid.,* VII (1845), 209.

referred to loosely as the "new method," a term which for a time was used also of what later became known as the "word method." Since in each of these approaches to reading the child started with words, it was natural for "word method" to be applied to both techniques. Those careful to distinguish between the two often referred to the new way of teaching the letters as "the word method together with the phonic method," "the word method and phonic method," or "the word method followed immediately by the phonic method."

This imprecise terminology caused those on the scene, and later investigators as well, to ascribe to the "word method" successes and popularity really belonging to the alphabet method, in which the letters were learned through the medium of words. We shall discuss this confusion in more detail in chapters 9 and 16. And we shall distinguish the alphabet method of teaching a child to read by having him learn his letters through words as the *words-to-letters* approach, in contrast with the *words-to-reading* system often referred to now as the *look-and-say method,* or simply the word method.

"AS IF THE WORDS WERE CHINESE SYMBOLS"

Those whose primary goal was to teach children their letters in a much quicker, more pleasant manner than the conventional one, apparently succeeded admirably by the use of simple words. The pupil who had mastered the letters had also made the acquaintance of a few words. From this point on, he was taught to read in the usual way.

Among those who were not primarily interested in having the child learn the letters first but who sought a better method of teaching him to read was John Miller Keagy (1792–1837). He was not a teacher, but a physician. Soon after he obtained his medical degree he became so interested in the Lancastrian and Pestalozzian enthusiasms of the time that he made a study of elementary education. His views on the best method of teaching a child to read developed rather slowly. In 1827 he brought out *The Pestalozzian Primer* in which he took no exception to the usual way of having the child first learn the letters, then combinations, and finally words.[1]

As Keagy continued his interest in and study of primary education, he became impressed with the words-to-reading method. In 1832 he was invited to speak before the American Lyceum. In this lecture, entitled "An Address on Early Education," he deplored the use of the spelling book to put into the minds of children "endless catalogues of words or signs without a knowledge of the things signified." Under

[1] The best account of Keagy is in the *Dictionary of American Biography*.

such misguided tutelage, children "will pronounce the most familiar words without having the corresponding ideas awakened in their minds. It is in the spelling book that the almost universal habit of reading without thinking is acquired, the tendency of which says Dugald Stewart, is to abolish the intellectual faculties. To some, it may seem extravagant to assert that spelling books produce and rivet habits of *not thinking.*"

To remedy this evil situation, Keagy would begin the pupil in a "miniature" museum. This would contain all the "most useful articles, natural and artificial to be met with; first in our woods, our fields, our hills, then in our groceries, dry goods stores, druggists' shops, &c. With these preparations, a *thinking school* might be commenced with the most cheering prospect of success. In such an establishment, teaching to think and to understand, would be found to be a much more delightful and easy occupation, than the usual one of teaching not to think."

The doctor then went on to outline the duties of the teacher in such a museum, and passed to the beginning of reading:

The business of the teacher would be, first, to make himself well acquainted with the subjects of his lessons, and then to give oral instructions on them to his pupils; requiring them when he has done, to give an account of what he has told them. The latter point must not be dispensed with, or cases of inattention may not be detected.

In this way an immense mass of useful knowledge could be collected, before any attempt is made at the difficult business of learning to read and spell. After about 18 months, or two years, have been spent in this oral and thinking course, the child may be taught reading. And here he should by no means be taught his letters, or spelling at first, but *whole words* should be presented to him, to be pronounced at sight. This is the surest method of learning to read understandingly and speedily. The most familiar words and phrases must be given him, such as *hat, head, eye, mouth, pen, candle, book,* &c., with easy phrases on them. It is better not to give him words of more than two syllables, and to exclude entirely, for some weeks, the capital letters; but let him rather see the same words and phrases, in the common written character. This would early familiarize him with the reading of manuscript. He should read his lessons as

if the words were Chinese symbols, without paying any attention
to the individual letters, but with special regard to the meaning.
When the little pupil can read a series of such lessons with
facility, then, and not till then, let him be taught to analyze his
words or name his letters, and learn to spell. This method needs
neither recommendation, nor defence, with those who have tried
it: and were it adopted, we should soon get rid of the stupid and
uninteresting mode now prevalent. Both teacher and scholar
would experience a pleasure that is in vain to be looked for, in
the practice of the other plan.[2]

From what Keagy said in this address it seems quite possible that he had become acquainted with what Gedike had
proposed, and had mixed in with it much of what Pestalozzi
had taught. His reference to the success that had been
achieved with the word method is puzzling. It would have
been most helpful if he had mentioned when, where, by
whom, and to what extent it had been employed. That it
may have been used by some teachers is entirely possible,
for in 1828 Samuel Worcester brought out a primer in which
the following occurs: "It is not, perhaps, very important
that a child should know the letters before he begins to
read. It may learn first to read words by seeing them, hearing them pronounced, and having their meaning illustrated,
and afterwards it may learn to analyze them or name the
letters of which they are composed."[3] The use by teachers
of this primer can not, however, be taken as an assurance
that it was used in the way Worcester suggested here, for
John Shaw referred to Worcester's primer in justifying
what his teachers were doing.

Those who wrote and those who published primers were,
of course, interested in sales. They tried to produce texts
that would be valuable no matter what system of teaching
was used. In 1840 Josiah Bumstead, a Boston merchant and
writer of textbooks, brought out *My Little Primer*, which
Nila Smith has said was the first reader to be based upon
the word method. She quotes Bumstead as follows:

In teaching reading, the general practice has been to begin with
the alphabet, and drill the child upon the letters, month after

[2] *American Annals of Education*, II (1832), 462–82.
[3] Cited in Nila B. Smith, *American Reading Instruction* (New York,
1934), p. 86.

month, until he is supposed to have acquired them. This method, so irksome and vexatious to both teacher and scholar, is now giving place to another, which experience has proved to be more philosophical, intelligent, pleasant, and rapid. It is that of beginning with familiar and easy words, instead of letters.[4]

It seems likely that Bumstead was endorsing his primer no matter how the teacher began to teach the child. What he said about "beginning with familiar and easy words" might have referred to the words-to-letters approach discussed in the previous chapter or to the method put forward by Keagy.

About 1841, Horace Mann's second wife, Mary Peabody, brought out a little book entitled *Primer*. Mann described it as a "beautiful book . . . published in Boston. It is prepared on the same general principles with those of Worcester, Gallaudet, and Bumstead; and it contains two or three reading lessons and a few cuts for drawing, in addition to a most attractive selection of words. It is the result of many years' successful efforts in interesting young children in reading and spelling."[5]

We have seen that the primer by Worcester and the one by Gallaudet were used in teaching children their letters by the words-to-letters approach. A primer is not in itself a reliable indicator of the way teachers used it in their work. Of much more influence, probably, were the lectures on reading delivered by locally prominent people before groups of teachers and school administrators. One of these, worthy of much more space than we can afford it here, was the so-called Prize Essay delivered by Thomas H. Palmer before the American Institute of Instruction in August, 1837. The title of this lecture was "On the Evils of the Present System of Primary Education."

Palmer was apparently not a teacher, but he had served on a committee that examined teachers in his home town of Pittsford, Vermont. In the discharge of his duties he had visited many district schools and had been impressed by the inferior quality of the reading.

---

[4] *Ibid.*, p. 87.
[5] Horace Mann, *Spelling Books* (Boston, 1841), p. 36 n.

In the course of these visits, I was much struck with the heavy, dull, vacant countenances of the pupils, the cause of which quickly appeared. For, when the reading classes took their places, it was easy to perceive, that the mind was no farther engaged in the exercise than attention to the pronunciation of the words required. As to comprehension of the *meaning*, the language might almost as well have been Greek, Arabic, or Chinese, as English. An inveterate habit of mechanical reading is formed, (if reading, indeed, that can be called, which is nothing but a mere utterance of sounds) which not one in fifty can ever overcome. Here lies the grand impediment to the attainment of knowledge, the impassable barrier to self-education. . . .

The pupils commenced with the spelling-book, from which they learned the alphabet. Next came their a, b, ab, e, b, eb, &c. followed by spelling lessons of words of one syllable, in columns, without any connexion. Spelling words of two syllables came next in order. All this, you will perceive, is a mere affair of memory, in which the reason and judgment of the child are never called into action. For months, nay, in many instances, for years, he is occupied by barren sounds alone. He is taught to connect them, it is true, with certain characters; but of their use, viz. to convey the *ideas* of others to his mind, he as yet knows nothing. Now, surely, it must be sufficiently evident, that the active mind of a child cannot be exclusively occupied with such tiresome drudgery. While engaged with these *names,* his body alone will be present. His mind will be far distant, at play with his schoolmates, or at the family fireside. . . .

What was called *reading* was now introduced, which in no respect differed from what preceded, save that there *was* some attempt at meaning in the arrangement of the words, but as the chief object of the compiler seemed to be the collection of words easy to be pronounced, without reference to the capacity of the pupil, his efforts were as mechanical as ever. Indeed, the manner of reciting these lessons would have rendered nugatory all attempts of the compiler to carry sense as well as sound to the mind of the child. . . . Truly, a dependence on the spelling-book or dictionary, "is trusting to a broken reed, on which if a man lean, it will go into his hand and pierce him." (2 Kings 18:21).

The chief distinctions between the old mode of teaching reading, and the one I recommend, consist, 1st. in *commencing* with words and phrases, instead of the *names* of syllables. . . . The reason for commencing in this manner must be, I think, sufficiently obvious from what has already been said. . . . The dislike manifested to this innovation, arises principally from the idea that the *naming* of the letters leads naturally to the *sound* of the *word.* But this is evidently a mistake, arising from confounding the *names* with the *powers* of the letters, which in most cases are totally different. Striking examples of this occur in the words *hat* and *which;* any one may satisfy himself of the folly of this practice by slowly naming the letters, and then observing the sound of the word [viz. hat, aitch-a-tee, &c.] In fact, no reasonable person, who would calmly examine the subject, could for a moment doubt, that if a child, or an adult who could not read, were told that the three letters c,a,t, formed one of the following words, *hat, cat,* or *man,* from the sound of the letters, he could not tell for which word they stood. It is popularly, and perhaps truly said, that an ounce of practice is worth a pound of theory. Now this mode has been practised successfully in a number of schools. I have used it also with the best results in my own family. Some persons, perhaps, may think, that it would be well to bend to the popular prejudice on this score, as it could not be a matter of much moment whether a child commenced with letters or words. On the most mature reflection, however, I confess that I cannot see the subject in this light. Exceedingly desirous as I am of smoothing down opposition, and conciliating friends to reform, this would be among the last of the improvements that I would willingly resign. The *first* steps are of paramount importance. Interest the child in the commencement, let him clearly see the object and use of his studies, and you will be able to teach him from time to time the names of his letters, and then smaller combinations, while he is going on with his reading, and with but little risk of his acquiring the habit of mental wandering, that most powerful adversary of self-education, which I am so desirous of rendering universal. This method, which may be termed the analytical system, is truly the method of nature. In her communications to man, she always proceeds from generals to particulars. We know a tree, and can name it, long before we become acquainted with its constituents, the leaves, limbs, trunk, and root; a house, before we have even heard of the shingles, boards, timbers, brick, or stone; a man, before his parts, the head, neck, body, limbs, hands or feet. And, finally, we have formed a long vocabulary, before we know anything of syllables or letters.[6]

Another lecture that must have had considerable influence was that of the Reverend Cyrus Peirce given on April 15, 1843, before the same organization. He had been the Principal of the Normal School at Lexington and had taught advanced grades. He was asked to address the gathering without having had time to prepare a paper, so he spoke at considerable length.

Peirce had apparently never had any experience teaching first graders, for what he said has the tone of one who

[6] *American Institute of Instruction, Lectures,* VIII (1838), 216 ff.

"would do" thus and so. "I do verily believe that the carry-ing out of these two principles, would effect wonders of reform in the reading of our common schools."[7] He ex-plained that he would talk to the entering pupils and invite them to talk. In every way possible he would have them exercise their senses, especially those of hearing. He would question them on weight, size, color, taste, appearance, use, and so forth, of a variety of objects, as many as possible of which he would bring into the classroom and exhibit.

This preliminary stage of talking to the children he re-garded as most important, because it would give the chil-dren something to think about and discuss. While this conversational part of the instruction was going on, the children would "be entertained, and constantly occupied, while they are being subjected to RESTRAINT, wholesome in kind and degree." He commended highly a teacher he knew who on her way to school picked up a strip of leather, the rib of a dog, a fragment of a broken tumbler, and a pine cone which she showed the children and made the basis of half a dozen "interesting and instructive conversations" with her pupils.

In teaching the child to read, he advised that the begin-ning be made with words, not letters, printed on the black-board. These should be such as, combined, would form an easy sentence. He singled out for special praise the book prepared by Miss Peabody, in which "you will find full illustration of the whole method with words and sen-tences." He continued:

Write on the black-board several times and in various orders, the following words; large, has, two, cow, the, horns; cow, horns, large, has, two, the; has, cow, horns, large, the, two; horns, has, two, the, cow, large; and finally, combine them into the sentence, —'The cow has two large horns.' Again, take the following sentence, and resolve it into its component parts, writing the words in various orders. 'The dog has four legs.' Legs, four, dog, the, has; dog, the, four, has, legs; four, dog, has, the, four &c. Then combine them again so as to form the original sentence,— 'The dog has four legs.'

It may be necessary with very young scholars to make the

process still more simple. You take a child or a small class of children to you to give them their first lesson in reading. You show them on a card, sheet, blackboard, or in a book, a word, a simple, a *very* simple word. Let it be the name of some object which is perfectly familiar to them, as, cat, dog, horse, bird, cup. Show them the object itself, or the picture or representation of the object. Ask them whether they know what the object is, or what the picture is, or represents. Then show them the name, saying at the same time, This is its name; this is what it is called. . . . Show them the picture, and let them say cat, cat, cat.

After the word has been sufficiently studied in connection with the picture, the teacher removes the picture and has the child give the word.

Peirce justified this method in these terms:

Children begin to *talk* with words, and why should they not begin to *read* with words? It is nature's method. And moreover, it enables the teacher, from the beginning, to make reading an intellectual exercise; it furnishes something to talk about; and this alone is a sufficient recommendation of it. . . . Some think it better to begin with the *sounds* or *powers* of letters. A series of school books is now in the course of publication, based on this principle. This method is better than the old way of beginning with the *names* of the letters, though not so good, in my opinion, as beginning with *words.* It is not nature's method. To a child, the continual utterance of the sounds, or powers of the letters, must be a dry and uninteresting exercise. It gives no scope to the intellect. It furnishes nothing to talk about. It forgets that children have minds. . . .

Children learn to *talk* from *memory;* they may learn to read from memory. Let them make the experiment; let them try it fairly and faithfully. Even were it a work of mere memory, I believe they will succeed. But it is not a work of *mere* memory. Memory will be aided by analogy. An ingenious child, I will say a child of average curiosity and quickness of apprehension, will discern analogies in words, and take advantage of them. For instance, when he is familiar with the words 'fan,' 'pat,'—from these he can and would make out what to call the word 'pan,' the first part of which is like the first part of 'pat,' and the last part like the last part of 'fan.' So from 'man' and 'hat' he could make out what to call 'mat;' from 'depart,' 'impress,' by comparison, he could learn to name 'impart.' All this might be done with very little aid from the teacher, by calling the attention of the learner to the *general form or resemblance of the words,* without a knowledge of either the names or the powers of the letters. . . .

After the scholars are able to manage with ease simple sentences, such as are found in Gallaudet's and Worcester's Primers, Bumstead's First Book, or Swan's Primary Reader, let them be taught the names and sounds, or powers, of letters.

Peirce brought Maria Edgeworth into his essay: "This method of teaching reading by means of words instead of letters, was first recommended, I think, by Miss Edgeworth. It is practised by Mr. Wood, late principal of the sessional school, Edinburgh; by Jacotot, the celebrated teacher of the Borough school, and others." He said of this new method:

> It is founded in reason and philosophy; and it must become general. Nothing can be more irksome and unreasonable than the old method of learning the names of unmeaning sounds and characters, as it was formerly the practice to do. The child's attention was arrested and long detained in the very porch of learning, by being obliged to name, and even learn by heart, a series of characters, which have scarcely an associating tie to bind them in the memory. It seems like stringing beads on a thread of sand. What rendered the old method more absurd, is, that nothing but the name was taught; and the name gives no clue to the power, or sound of the letter, especially in combination with another letter.[8]

Harold Lamport called this lecture "epoch-making."[9] What Peirce said about the child's memory aiding him by analogy in acquiring additional words in the new system of instruction has been often repeated since Gedike expressed it in 1791. How, under the circumstances, analogy can possibly operate in behalf of a child who does not know one letter or its function from another is by no means apparent. Peirce's mention of the importance of the teacher's pointing out to the child the general form or resemblances and differences in the physical appearance of words is likewise an injunction that has been often repeated.

Peirce was in error in claiming Mr. Wood of the Sessional School in Edinburgh as a practitioner of the word method, although the work of John Wood was certainly well known among schoolmen at that time. Wood himself had in 1828

[8] See the entire lecture: *ibid*, XIV (1844), 143–84.
[9] Harold Boyne Lamport, "History of the Teaching of Beginning Reading" (Unpublished Ph.D. dissertation, University of Chicago, 1935), p. 274.

written a book on what he was doing there. This book was favorably reviewed in *Blackwood's Magazine* early in 1829,[10] and re-issued in Boston in 1830, where more favorable reviews of it appeared. It had been advertised among the books teachers should by all means have in *the Connecticut Common School Journal.*[11] Furthermore, Professor Pillans of the University of Edinburgh had in 1830 or 1831 lectured before the same organization that Peirce addressed, and had explained that Wood "had the child master the alphabet" and then start on easy words. In his book of 1828 Wood gave considerable attention to reading. At the beginning of the first chapter he devoted to the alphabet, he said:

> On the subject of Reading, the first matter which naturally comes under consideration, is the mode of teaching the ALPHA-BET. In this department the Sessional School cannot boast of any novelty or peculiarity. The child is first taught to name so many of the letters; then so many more, with which the former are afterwards mixed up; and so forth, till the whole alphabet is in this manner exhausted.[12]

Peirce appears to have made another curious blunder in describing Jacotot as "the celebrated teacher of the Borough School." The school alluded to was the then well-known Borough Road School in London,[13] with which Jacotot never had anything to do. In any case, he had been dead nearly three years when Peirce spoke.

Apparently John Russell Webb published a primer in 1846—*The New Word Method*—in the preface of which he gave an account of the origin of the word method. The story was no doubt propaganda for the primer, pure and simple, but it must be referred to here for it apparently deceived

10 *Blackwood's Magazine*, XXV (January–June, 1829), 106–34.

11 See *Connecticut Common School Journal*, II (1839–40), 251–53, for an excellent review. In the *Journal* (III, 48) there is an advertisement of the book.

12 John Wood, *Account of the Edinburgh Sessional School* (5th Edinburgh ed., 1840), p. 181.

13 For information about the Borough School, see Paul Monroe, *Cyclopedia of Education* (New York, 1911–13), I, 416. Alexander D. Bache visited the school; see his *Report.*, pp. 174–75. References to the school are in the *Connecticut Common School Journal*, I, 100 ff., 268 ff. It was the model school and training establishment of the British and Foreign School Society.

Dr. Nila Smith and Dr. Rudolph Flesch, both of whom seem to have accepted it at face value.[14]

The story tells of how on "an early summer morning of 1846, a young man, barely twenty-one years of age, was reading a newspaper in the sitting-room of his boarding place." This young man was the teacher of the village school, but he had been regarded as "odd" from boyhood. As he sat reading the paper while he waited for breakfast, a little four- or five-year-old girl of the household came and climbed into his lap while her mother was busy in the kitchen and her father was milking. Just as the child clambered into his lap, the young man noticed the word "cow" in the paper and pointed it out to her. He told her it stood for the creature her father was milking. She was greatly interested. She at once jumped down, caught up the paper, and ran to her mother to show her the word and to read it for her and explain what it meant. Her interest and excitement set the teacher to thinking about a new way of teaching children to read.

The plan which he developed aroused interest in the entire community. That fall when a teachers' institute was held at Watertown, New York, twelve miles away, those present sent for the young man to tell them about his wonderful new method. They were enthusiastic about what he said, and passed a resolution to have the method published. This was done, and the new way to teach reading spread widely.

This account, signed by Jay Russell, of how J. Russell Webb discovered the word method, ends with these words: "And this is how the Word Method originated, and how it was born into the world. Since then it has written its own history."[15]

[14] Smith, op. cit., pp. 88 ff.; Rudolph Flesch, Why Johnny Can't Read (New York, 1955), pp. 46 ff.

[15] Cf. this account with the following from Rudolph Rex Reeder, Historical Development of School Readers (New York, 1900), p. 79: "J. Russell Webb, author of the Normal Readers, has probably done more than any other educator to develop the word method in this country. He has frequently been mentioned as the author of the method, and has so advertised his own name in the title page of the Analytical Second Reader of 1866: 'By Richard Edwards, LL.D., and Russell Webb, author of the Normal Readers and the Word Method.' "

THE WORD METHOD ENDORSED
BY HORACE MANN

Horace Mann was by far the most eloquent advocate the orthodox look-and-say method of teaching children to read has ever had. Hunter Diack is in error in saying that Mann's "influence on the teaching of reading in America does not seem to have been very great."[1] What deceived Diack was that during his lifetime Mann's influence in this area was negligible, but when the word method came under fire more than fifty years ago, his pronouncements were found to be of great use.

Mann was born in 1796 in Franklin, Massachusetts, a little town named for the state's illustrious son, who, in appreciation, presented it with a library.[2] Mann came from an exceptionally poor family and early became accustomed to hard work and self-denial. Until he was fifteen he had only the meagerest schooling, being limited to the yearly sessions, eight or ten weeks long, available in the school nearest him. By rare good luck he met an itinerant schoolmaster whose proficiency in Latin and Greek inspired him. He set to work with a will, and in 1816 entered Brown University where he made a brilliant record in the classics and was retained as a tutor. He married the daughter of the president of Brown, became a lawyer, and was elected to the Massachusetts State Legislature. Here he played what was probably a decisive role in the creation of a State Board of

[1] Hunter Diack, *In Spite of the Alphabet* (London, 1965), p. 18.
[2] Merle Curti, *Social Ideas of American Educators* (Paterson, N. J., 1959), p. 102.

Education and was promptly selected as its first Secretary. He took up his duties on July 1, 1837.[3]

His services to the public schools came at a time when they were badly needed. Public education in his native state was at a low ebb, and in other states it was even worse. In 1826 hardly a third of the children of appropriate age in Massachusetts had the opportunity of attending any public school. The schools were miserably poor affairs with short sessions measured in weeks and presided over in many cases by teachers who were unable to do simple sums in multiplication and division. The year Mann took office three hundred teachers were driven from their schools by pupils who refused to submit any longer to senseless beatings and kindred cruelties.[4]

Such details as these give some indication of the conditions under which Mann began his labors for the good of the common schools. He did not spare himself. Until he resigned in May, 1848, he worked an average of fifteen hours a day, without allowing himself even one day off for recreation, often toiling for months without taking so much as an evening to call on a friend.[5] What he did in the field of reading was relatively insignificant in comparison with what he did in other areas.

In Mann's day, educational theories of all kinds were in the very air he breathed and in the literature he read. He took office about the time the illustrious Jacotot left Valenciennes in northern France for Paris, spending himself freely in teaching the poor and ignorant in that city until his death there. As Mann was toiling away at the classics at Brown, he may have learned something of what Jacotot was doing at the University of Louvain and how he was developing new theories of instruction. Naturally Mann cast about in his mind for more practical methods of language learning.

What he saw taking place in the schools he visited as

[3] There are many accounts of Mann's life: The account in the *DAB* is highly competent; the one by his second wife, Mary Tyler Peabody Mann, *Life of Horace Mann* (Washington, 1937), is devoted chiefly to Mann's correspondence.

[4] Curti, *op. cit.,* p. 107.

[5] *Ibid.,* p. 109.

Secretary of the Board of Education convinced him that something was badly wrong with the way children were taught to read. He saw children trying to learn the alphabet. He heard others who had finally learned the letters stumbling through syllables abundantly given in their spelling books to teach the sounds of the letters, only whose names they knew. Bigger boys were blundering through sentences, spelling each word and pronouncing it before passing to the next, which was likewise painfully spelled and pronounced and then annexed to the preceding one. Reading lessons became a horrible, discouraging performance.[6]

As the Secretary pondered what he saw and heard and discussed with his friends he came to the conclusion that the principle on which learning to read was based was utterly senseless and wrong. Mary Peabody, a Boston teacher who became Mann's second wife, supported his criticisms of the current reading method. Mann became convinced that spelling books were the source of the trouble.

One of his earliest and most noted lectures on education was "On the Best Mode of Preparing and Using Spelling-Books," which he gave in Boston, August 19, 1841. He condemned utterly the plan of starting the child with the letters, at which anywhere from three to six months were spent, while the mind of the child was all this time "undergoing a rapid process of stupefaction." Condemning the alphabetic column as presenting an utter blank, he said: "There stands in silence and death, the stiff, perpendicular row of characters, lank, stark, immovable, without form or comeliness, and, as to signification, wholly void." Then he passed on to the letters making up this most unattractive column. Of them he said, "They are skeleton-shaped, bloodless, ghostly apparitions, and hence it is no wonder that the children look and feel so deathlike, when compelled to face them. The letters are more minute too, than any objects which ever attract the attention of children. Children re-

---

[6] For Mann's early experiences as Secretary of the Board of Education, see the first volumes of the *Common School Journal*. They are well indexed, and by using the indexes s.v. "Reading," one can learn much about the reading situation.

quire some medium between the vast and the microscopic. They want some diversity, also, but the forms of the twenty-six letters have as little variety as twenty-six grains of sand." He spoke of the repulsion with which children viewed these skeleton-shaped ghosts. The brighter the children, the more they would be repelled by having to learn these microscopic specks of letters as alike in form as grains of sand. As the children were unattracted to letter-learning, "they must be driven to it by fear; and under the deadening influence of such fear is commenced, even in childhood, the soul's paralysis." He went on:

> Many of us, doubtless, can recollect some humane teacher, whose fortune it was to drag or whip us up through this Slough of Despond, who having caught some glimpse of the remorse-lessness of the alphabetic exercises, used to practise sundry devices to win his little prattlers to an acquaintanceship with the twenty-six idiot strangers. He used to tell us that *a* stands for apple, to call *o*, round *o*, *s*, crooked *s*, *t*, the gentleman with a hat on, &c.

Having disposed of the alphabetic column and the letters composing it, Mann took up "those cadaverous particles, ba, be, bi, bo, bu, &c." As has been shown in our opening chapter, these letter combinations trace their ancestry back to the Greeks. All the spelling books in Mann's time were loaded with them. They were given with no explanation of their use in teaching the sounds of letters in combination, and Mann's teachers apparently did not know their purpose.

At a time when children were more often than not regarded as imps of Satan and treated accordingly, Mann had great compassion for them. "Now it is upon this emptiness, blankness, silence and death, that we compel children to fasten their eyes. To say nothing of the odor and fungous-ness of spelling-book paper, who can wonder at the energy of repulsion exerted upon quick-minded children by this exercise? Upon others of less natural vivacity, a soporific effluvium seems to emanate from the page, steeping all their faculties in lethargy."

After having brought the child through the tables of *ba*,

be, bi, followed by *bla* "with its conjuncts," Mann described
the struggle with words:

After having repeated these letters and particles, thousands of
times, where the same sound is uniformly given to the same
letters or combination of letters, he is then taken into words,
where each of the principal letters, in the rapidity of its changes
from one sound to another, outdoes ventriloquism;—where the
first five vowels to which respectively he has been accustomed
to give the same alphabetic sound, assume twenty-nine different
sounds, so that according to the doctrine of chances, it will happen only once in five or six times that he will be correct, if he
sounds them as he was taught;—where the twenty-six letters,
and the same combinations of two or three of them assume
hundreds of different sounds, without any clue by which to follow them as they glide from one into another;—where letters
are often dropped out of notice altogether;—where g sometimes
becomes j, and x becomes gz;—where *th* changes every brea*th*
we brea*the*;— where tion and sion are shun; cial, sial, and tial,
are shal, (not shall, which is different still;) ceous, cious, tious,
are shus; geous and gious are jus, (not the Latin *jus* either;) sion
is zhun; qu is kw; wh is hw; ph is f, and c is uniformly concealed
in s, or sacrificed as a victim to k or z. . . .
In this way the child's previous knowledge of the alphabetic
sounds of the letters misleads; four times in five, if he recollects
them right, he will call them wrong, and be rebuffed; the more
thoroughly he has learned and the more correct are his applications of the previous knowledge, the more infallibly he goes
wrong. When a child is taught the three alphabetic sounds *l e g,*
and then is told that these three sounds, when combined, make
the sound *leg,* he is untaught in the latter casé what he was mis-
taught in the former. L e g does not spell *leg,* but if pronounced
quickly, it spells *elegy.*

Having led his hearers in his best satirical manner
through the horrors of the spelling book, Mann gave suggestions for a better way to teach reading. In doing this he
showed clearly that he, like Gallaudet, Keagy, Palmer, and
others already mentioned, was acquainted with what
Gedike in Germany and Jacotot in France had thought and
said about the subject. He introduced his whole-word approach as follows:

The advantages of teaching children, by beginning with whole
words, are many. Nothing has to be untaught which has been
once well taught. What is to be learned is affiliated to what is

already known. The course of the pupil is constantly progressive. The acquisition of the language, even from its elements, becomes an intelligible process. The knowledge of new things is introduced through the knowledge of familiar things. At the age of three or four years, every child has command of a considerable vocabulary consisting of the names of persons, of animals, articles of dress, food, furniture &c. The sounds of these names are familiar to the ear and the organs of speech, and the ideas they represent are familiar to the mind. All that is to be done, therefore, is to lead the eye to a like familiarity with their printed signs. But the alphabet, on the other hand, is wholly foreign to a child's existing knowledge. Having no relation to any thing known, it must be acquired entirely without collateral aids. In learning words, too, the child becomes accustomed to the form of the letters, and this acquaintance will assist him greatly in acquiring the alphabet, when the time for learning that shall arrive. I do not see, indeed, why a child should not learn to read as easily as he learns to talk, if taught in a similar manner. . . .

When we wish to give to a child the idea of a new animal, we do not present successively the different parts of it,—an eye, an ear, the nose, the mouth, the body, or a leg; but we present the whole animal, as one object. And this would be still more necessary, if the individual parts of the animal with which the child had labored long and hard to become acquainted, were liable to change their natures as soon as they were brought into juxtaposition, as almost all the letters do when combined in words. . . .

The first books or cards, from which reading should be taught to children, should contain whole words, with the meaning of which the learners are entirely familiar. I believe the earliest books, in this country, on this plan, were prepared by Worcester and Gallaudet. They contained pictures of persons and objects, each picture being accompanied by its printed name; and the names were afterwards repeated without the pictures.

As the picture presented to the child a more agreeable object than the word, it was thought, by some teachers, to be an impediment to progress; and the children were said to get the idea that the word was the peculiar name of that one picture, and to feel as though it were a kind of contradiction to apply it to any thing else. Within the last year or two, books have been prepared by Mr. J. F. Bumstead, of Boston,—on the same general plan in regard to words, but omitting the pictures altogether. Mr. Bumstead's books are now used in all the primary schools in Boston. The plan of teaching words first has succeeded, wherever it has been fairly tried; and I have no doubt that it will soon wholly supercede the old and doleful method of beginning with the alphabet. . . .

Provide books on this plan, and learning to read will cease to be a burden and a mockery. The teacher, in good faith, may invite a group of little children to come around her *to think of pleasant things;* instead of forcing them to gaze at idiot marks. Such lessons will be like an excursion to the fields of elysium, compared with the old method of plunging children, day by day, for months together, in the cold waters of oblivion, and compelling them to say falsely, that they love the chill and torpor of the immersion. After children have learned to read words, the twenty-six letters, as they stand marshalled in the alphabet, will be learned in a few hours.[7]

There is little that is new in Mann's eloquent discussion of spelling books. He was by no means the first to call attention to the difficulty children had in learning the letters and how little they were advanced thereby toward reading. The illogical nature of English spelling was known at least three centuries earlier. Even the subject of spelling books may have been suggested to him by Dr. Keagy's work.

In the spring of 1819, Keagy began to contribute papers on education to the *Morning Chronicle* of Baltimore. In 1824 he published a thirty-four page pamphlet, *An Essay on English Education Together With Some Observations on the Present Mode of Teaching the English Language.* In this he commented on the "absurdity of teaching by Spelling Books," believing that this prevented children from thinking of what they were reading. He said: "Our language is generally taught in such a way as to establish habits of reading without thinking." He thought when the "engine of reform" was set in motion "the present spelling book system, the unlucky invention of ignorant and barbarous times, will then no more paralyse the energies of the youthful mind." He had intended that the *Essay* "should be in some measure declamatory."[8] Mann was precisely the person capable of adding this "declamatory" element to the subject.

No matter what might have been the inspiration of the spelling-book lecture, it appears to have led to an interest-

[7] Mann delivered his lecture on spelling books before the American Institute of Instruction, and it was printed by this organization in its lecture series (XII [1842], 1–40).

[8] J. M. K[eagy], *An Essay on English Education* (Harrisburg, Pa.), pp. iv, 10, 27.

ing passage in *The Caxtons* (1849) by Bulwer-Lytton. While the author was at work on this novel he was well aware of theories about education then under discussion and may well have read Mann's essay. In *The Caxtons* he created a character named Dr. Herman, possibly as close as he cared to come to "Herr Mann" of Boston. He made this teacher, charged with the education of Pisistratus Caxton, the butt of ridicule. He said of him:

> Dr. Herman had written a great many learned works against every pre-existent method of instruction; that which had made the greatest noise was upon the infamous fiction of SPELLING BOOKS: "A more lying, roundabout, puzzle-headed delusion than that by which we CONFUSE the clear instincts of truth in our accursed systems of spelling, was never concocted by the father of falsehood." Such was the exordium of this famous treatise. "For instance, take the monosyllable CAT. What a brazen forehead you must have, when you say to an infant, C,A,T,—spell CAT; that is, three sounds forming a totally opposite compound—opposite in every detail, opposite in the whole—compose a poor little monosyllable, which, if you would but say the simple truth, the child will learn to spell merely by looking at it! How can three sounds, which run thus to the ear, *see-eh-tee,* compose the sound of cat? Don't they rather compose the sound *see-eh-té?*"

Immediately after this tirade of Dr. Herman's, Bulwer-Lytton, speaking in his own character, expressed his "mournful doubts" whether the new engines of instruction being devised would shoot "the youthful idea an inch farther" than did "the old mechanism of flint and steel."[9]

When Rudolph Rex Reeder came upon this Dr. Herman passage, he concluded that Lord Lytton was in sympathy with the word-method approach to reading.[10] His opinion has been accepted by others, apparently without examination.

There are two principal places in which Mann gave at some length his convictions on how a child should be

[9] Bulwer–Lytton's novel appeared serially in *Blackwood's Magazine* during 1848–49. The copy I used was Volume I of the edition of his works brought out in New York by Thomas Y. Crowell & Co. (13 vols. [18——]). The passage about Dr. Herman is on p. 26.

[10] Rudolph Rex Reeder, *Historical Development of School Readers* (New York, 1900), p. 78.

taught to read. His spelling-book lecture was the earlier of these. In his justly famous Seventh Report, submitted to the Massachusetts Board of Education on January 1, 1844, upon his return from Europe, there is a sixteen-page section on "Methods of Teaching Young Children on Their First Entering School." In this he gave the second of his detailed discussions on reading. A part of this report has been quoted above. The following continues that account:

Compare the above method with that of calling up a class of abecedarians,—or, what is more common, a single child, and, while the teacher holds a book or a card before him, and, with a pointer in his hand, says, *a,* he echoes *a;* then *b,* and he echoes *b;* and so on until the vertical row of lifeless and ill-favored characters is completed, and then of remanding him to his seat, to sit still and look at vacancy. If the child is bright, the time which passes during this lesson is the only part of the day when he does not think. Not a single faculty of the mind is occupied except that of imitating sounds; and even the number of these imitations amounts only to twenty-six. A parrot or an idiot could do the same thing. . . .

The advocate for teaching the letters asks, if the elements of an art or science should not be first taught. To this I would reply, that the 'Names of the Letters' are not elements in the sounds of words; or are so, only in a comparatively small number of cases. To the twenty-six letters of the alphabet, the child is taught to give twenty-six sounds, and no more. . . . It would be difficult, and would not compensate the trouble, to compute the number of different sounds which a good speaker gives to the different letters and combinations of letters in our language,—not including the changes of rhetorical emphasis, cadence and intonation. But if analysed, they would be found to amount to hundreds. Now how can twenty-six sounds be the elements of hundreds of sounds as elementary as themselves? Generally speaking, too, before a child begins to learn his letters, he is already acquainted with the majority of elementary sounds in the language, and is in the daily habit of using them in conversation. Learning his letters, therefore, gives him no new sound; it even restricts his attention to a small part of those which he already knows. So far then, the learning of his letters contracts his practice; and were it not for keeping up his former habits of speaking, at home and in the playground, the teacher, during the six months or year, in which he confines him to the twenty-six sounds of the alphabet, would pretty nearly deprive him of the faculty of speech. . . .

In regard to all the vowels at may be said, not only that, in the very great majority of cases, their sounds when found in words, are different from their names as letters,—so that the more perfectly the child has learned them as letters, the more certain will he be to miscall them in words,—but that these different sounds follow each other, in books in the most promiscuous manner. Were there any law of succession among these sounds, so that the short sound of any vowel should universally follow the long sound; the obscure, the broad, &c.; or were one of the sounds used twice in succession, and then another of them once, and so on, following some rule of alternation, the evil would be greatly mitigated. . . .

Did the vowels adhere to their own sounds, the difficulty would be greatly diminished. But, not only do the same vowels appear in different dresses, like masqueraders, but like harlequins they exchange garbs with each other. How often does *e* take the sound of *a*, as in *there, where*, &c.; and *i*, the sound of *e*; and *o*, the sound of *u*; and *u*, the sound of *o*; and *y*, the sound if *i*.

In one important particular, the consonants are more perplexing than the vowels. The very definition of a consonant, as given in the spelling-books, is, "a letter which has no sound or only an imperfect one, without the help of a vowel." And yet the definers themselves, and the teachers who follow them, proceed immediately to give a perfect sound to all the consonants. If a consonant has "only an imperfect sound," why in teaching children to read, should not this imperfect sound be taught them? . . . The name of the letter *b* is written *be*; but where is the sound of *be*, in *ebb, web, ebony, ebulition, abode, abound*, and in hundreds of other cases? . . . The name sound of the letter *r*, as taught in the alphabet, is *ar*; but where is this sound in all those cases where *r* precedes the vowel in the formation of a syllable or word, as in *rain, rest, rich, rock, run, rye*;—they are not sounded *ar-ain, ar-est*, &c. . . .

There is one fact, probably within every teacher's own observation, which should be decisive on this subject. In learning the alphabet, children pronounce the consonants as though they were either preceded or followed by one of the vowels;—that is, they sound *b*, as though it were written *be*, and *f*, as though written *ef*. But when they have advanced ever so little way in reading, do they not enunciate words where the letter *b* is followed by one of the *other* vowels, or where it is preceded by a vowel, as well as words into which their own familiar sound of *be*, enters? For example, though they have called *b* a thousand times as if it were written *be*, do they not enunciate the words *ball, bind, box, bug*, &c. as well as they do the words *besom, beatific*, &c.? They do not say *be-all, be-ind, be-ox, be-ug*, &c. Do they not articulate the words *ebb, web*, &c. where the vowel comes first; or the words *bet, bell, beyond* &c. where the vowel is short, or obscure, as well as they do those words which have their old accustomed sound of *b*, with the long sound of *e*? So of the letter *f*, which they have been accustomed to sound as though written *ef*. Do they not articulate the word *fig*, as well as they do the first syllable of the word *effigy*? Nay, except they are very apt, and remember in a remarkable manner the nonsense that has been taught them do they ever call *fig*, ef-ig, or *father*, ef-ather? Happy incapacity of a bright nature to be turned into a dunce![11]

[11] *Common School Journal*, VI (1844), 89 ff.

MANN'S VIEWS ABOUT READING CHALLENGED

Many of the Massachusetts teachers did not agree with the views on reading expressed by the Secretary of the Board of Education. No sooner had his Seventh Report appeared than it was replied to by a committee of thirty-one Boston grammar school masters. About a third of their nearly one hundred and fifty pages of *Remarks* were devoted to what Mann had said about reading.

The masters, having read and listened to much the Secretary had said, saw that he did not understand the relationship between letters and sounds. He thought that letters have sounds, and that when he consciously pronounced a word he was pronouncing letters. The masters dwelt somewhat at length on his confusion of letter names and the sounds for which the letters stood. They also pointed out that he had not seen while he was abroad anything to justify him in thinking that teachers in Germany were using the method of teaching reading which he endorsed. They understood that what he had seen in the Prussian classroom of beginners which he described so vividly was the first, or an early, lesson in the application of the Normal-Words method, which, as we have seen was a words-to-letters method, not a words-to-reading approach as Mann thought.

The *Remarks* by the thirty-one masters initiated one of the longest and bitterest quarrels in which Mann was involved in the course of his eleven years service as Secretary of the Board of Education. It may have contributed in no small measure to his return to the political life which he had left to become Secretary. Fortunately, in this study we are not concerned with Mann's troubles with his opponents. For us the only justification in noting this opening contribution in the pamphlet war that followed it is that the masters reported what was taking place in the teaching of reading in the Boston schools.

They were in excellent position to give competent information on this subject. They were teachers of upper grades, but they associated freely with elementary teachers and received into their classes pupils passed on by them. They were interested, on-the-scene observers of what had been going on in the Boston schools for the six or seven years during which a new method of teaching reading had been in effect.

The following is their analysis of the plan that was being used:

The plan of teaching, as developed by the publication of the Secretary, by Mr. Pierce's 'Lecture on Reading,' and by various other publications, is substantially as follows: whole, but familiar words, without any reference to the letters which compose them, are first to be taught. The alphabet, as such, is kept entirely concealed. Some three or four words are arranged on a single page of a primer prepared for the purpose, or are written on the black-board several times, and in various orders, as follows: cat-dog-chair; dog-cat-chair; chair-cat-dog. These are pointed out to the child, who is required to utter them at the teacher's dictation, and to learn them by a careful inspection of their forms, as whole objects. After these are supposed to be learned, new words are dictated to the pupil, in the same manner as before. This process is repeated, till the child has acquired a sufficient number of words to read easy sentences in which they are combined. To what extent this mode of learning words should be carried, is, no where, definitely stated. Mr. Pierce says, 'When they are perfectly familiar with the first words chosen, and the sentence which they compose, select other words, and form other sentences; and so on indefinitely.' He then proceeds to recommend several books, as containing suitable sentences for this purpose. Of these, one prepared by Miss Peabody, now Mrs. Mann, contains, he says, 'a full illustration of the whole method, with words and sentences.' Since this book is also recommended, by the Secretary, as containing the best exemplification of the whole plan, it may be taken as a standard, by which to form an estimate of the extent to which the friends of the new system would carry this process of teaching words.[1]

The masters then gave a somewhat detailed description of the book which Mrs. Mann had written, and concluded:

It appears then, that at some period in the child's progress, after learning seven hundred, a thousand, or two thousand words, he is to commence the laborious and unwelcome task of learning 'the unknown, unheard and unthought-of letters of the alphabet.' Here, if ever, it is supposed he begins to learn how to combine letters into words; that is, learns how to spell.[2]

The masters reported the results obtained by this new method as they had observed them and as they had learned about them from teachers engaged at that level of instruction: "Primary school teachers, who have tried the system, testify, that when children have learned a word in one connection, they are unable to recognize it in another, especially if there be a change of type." After pointing out that teachers in the upper grades were having to take time to do what those in the preceding grades had not done, the masters continued:

We do not say this to the disparagement of the primary school teachers, or from the belief, that there is a want of fidelity on their part. We believe it to be, in part, at least, owing to the system of teaching, or rather want of system, in the primary schools. The books used in these schools, according to the author's own account of them, are adapted to either system. This is equivalent to saying that they are adapted to neither; for it is impossible to see how two methods, so entirely different from each other, as those under consideration, can be embraced in one series of books. After repeated inquiries made in many of the primary schools of the city, we are persuaded, that the teachers have taken the full amount of license allowed them, by the author of the books which they use. Some begin with the alphabet; others require the children to learn eight or ten words from which they teach the several letters, though not in the order in which they are arranged in the alphabet. Some carry the process of teaching words to a greater extent, yet require the child to learn to spell, before teaching him to read. Others, as will appear, teach the children to read, without making them at

[1] *Remarks on the Seventh Annual Report of the Hon. Horace Mann* (Boston, 1844), p. 59.
[2] *Ibid.,* p. 60.

all acquainted with the letters. One evil, resulting from this want of system, is a great neglect of spelling. It is the opinion of those masters who have been longest in the service, and can therefore compare the results of the two systems, that in respect to spelling, among the candidates for admission [to the grammar schools] from the primary schools, there has been a great deterioration during the trial of the new system; a period of about six years.[3]

Mann made an eloquent and impassioned objection to this part of the masters' criticism, condemning it as "an arrant misrepresentation of the system it professes to impugn. I have never advocated, or known, or heard of, nor have I met any person who has ever advocated, or known, or heard of, any such mode of teaching the English language to children, as the 'Remarks' assail."[4]

One of the dissident Boston masters was Samuel S. Greene, Principal of the Grammar Department of the Phillips School. In August, 1844, he spoke before the American Institute of Instruction in reply to what Professor Peirce had said before the same organization the year before. Professor Greene made it clear that he was heartily in favor of any plan of teaching the ABC's as interestingly as possible, and he suggested some ways this might be done. He emphasized the desirability of teaching the sounds along with the letters. In this connection, and no doubt with Mann particularly in mind, he said:

These three things, the power, the character, and the name should be kept entirely distinct from each other. . . . The name sound is as unlike the elementary sound, as the visible representative of the former is unlike that of the latter. Now, if any one has assumed the position, that the names of the letters are elements in the sounds of words, he alone must defend it. Those who favor the usual mode of teaching, are not responsible for such an assumption. . . . How the idea originated, that the names of letters were elements in the sounds of words, it is not easy to conceive.[5]

In commenting on the horrible, unspeakably ugly, repulsive, skeleton-like appearance of the letters that caused the

[3] *Ibid.* p. 98.

[4] Horace Mann, *Reply to the "Remarks"* (Boston, 1844), p. 96.

[5] Samuel S. Greene, "On Methods of Teaching to Read," in *American Institute of Instruction, Lectures*, XV (1845), 210–11.

cheeks of children to blanch when confronting them, Greene said it seemed an odd way to "relieve children from such painful emotions by teaching them to examine these shapeless characters, when taken in whole groups, i.e. whole clusters of deformity."[6] His reference here was clearly to Mann's lecture on spelling books.

He commented on the excessive emphasis placed on making everything easy and pleasant for the child by those in favor of the new method. He too favored making children happy, "But if a great principle is to be sacrificed simply to promote the child's pleasure, it becomes every practical teacher solemnly to protest. . . . All attempts to make easy and simple, that which is already as easy and simple as the nature of the case will allow, serve to retard, rather than promote the progress of the child. . . . To *gratify* the child should not be the teacher's aim, but rather to lay a permanent foundation, on which to rear a noble and well-proportioned superstructure."[7]

In listing his objections to the new plan, Greene stressed the following points: (1) The letters with all their imperfections and hideous deformities have to be learned eventually. If any success attends the child's learning of words, the teacher may be sure of encountering added resistance when she endeavors to teach letters to a pupil who is succeeding already without knowing them. (2) The new method reduces English to the status of Chinese and deprives the child of all the advantage which English possesses by virtue of its being a language written in letters. (3) The learning of words alone affords the child no means of mastering others. (4) The new method makes spelling, a grievous burden at best, still more difficult.[8]

While Mann was in Europe in the summer and autumn of 1843, his friend George B. Emerson, a locally well-known educator, served as the editor of the *Common School Journal,* in which capacity he received an unusually well-written article on the reading controversy. The editor pro

6 *Ibid.,* p. 217.
7 *Ibid.,* pp. 219–20.
8 *Ibid.,* pp. 224 ff.

tem could not at the time find space for the article, but
when Mann returned about the middle of November, it was
shown to him. Mann thought highly of it, so he and Emerson
got it ready for the February, 1844, issue of the *Journal*.
They made it clear that they did not agree with the views of
the writer. Mann wrote:

> While, however, we are cordially disposed to give the advo-
> cates of that side of the question full and fair opportunity of
> being heard, we must avow our conviction of the unsoundness
> of the arguments which the writer uses to establish his opinion,
> and our entire dissent from the conclusion to which he comes.
> We believe in the expediency of giving children words before
> letters in teaching them *to read,* not less than in teaching them
> *to speak.*

Along with this statement of his own, Mann included in
his foreword to the article an expression of opinion by
Emerson:

> Less than twenty years ago we held firmly all the opinions
> which are here advanced. To quarrel with his arguments would
> be to quarrel with what were lately our own. We have gradually
> yielded to the force of what has seemed to be the truth, and
> have abandoned, one after another, all our former positions and
> arguments. We know that many of our readers have done the
> same. We have no doubt that others will follow; and we should
> not be surprised, at any time, to find the author of this defence
> among the number.

In addition to preparing a foreword to the article, Mann
and Emerson annotated it so that as it appeared in the
Journal it had the advantage of setting forth the views of an
intelligent opposer of the new teaching method and the
comments of its leading endorsers. The result is a piece of
unusual interest, but much too long for inclusion here. The
author apparently asked that his name not be used and
signed himself "Q."

At the outset he explained what his position was and why
he wrote: "Having taught the alphabet for about twenty
years, in a school where those who began generally finished
their school education, I have had some opportunity of
judging how the old system worked; and having taken
some pains to watch the progress of the new plan, I feel

called upon, as a friend of the Common Schools, to caution the public against too ready a reception of its specious promises."

He referred to the invention of the alphabet as a great gain over the system of writing with hieroglyphics which preceded it. And he regretted the tendency on the part of those who favored the new method of teaching reading to revert to this earlier procedure.

The chief reason, and almost the only one given, for the proposed retrogression to barbarism, is the fact that the *name* of a letter is not always indicative of its *sound*. This objection strikes at the root of *spelling*, of course, and, in estimating the advantage gained in reading a little earlier or a little easier, it will be prudent to consider the disadvantage of not learning early to spell. But is this objection a sound one?—is it founded in reason and in truth? I think not in either. Few children are so simple as this objection supposes them to be, and I have rarely met with any so dull as not to perceive the difference between the name and the power of a letter, after very little practice. . . . Is it true, however, that the names of our letters are no help to the pronunciation of words? It does not require much courage to deny the position, and I think it will not be difficult to show that the evil has been greatly overrated. . . . It is very common for those who would discourage the learning of the letters and elementary sounds, to thrust forward the irregular words *plough, rough, thought, cough,* and such like, to show the absurdities of pretending to spell by using the letters; but is it fair to produce such extreme examples? Is it even fair to produce exceptions, when they are, compared with regular words, hardly as one to a thousand?* Any careful classification of the words of our language must demonstrate the fact that the anomalies are few; and the *abs,* destitute of meaning as they may be, are full of power, and a key to the pronunciation and orthography of innumerable syllables in the language. Let us concede that there are some and perhaps many irregularities of orthography in our language, but let us not, to support a questionable novelty, forget that these irregularities are few compared with the whole number of words; and the worst of them, when ranged in one column, can very easily be mastered by a child of common capacity. I think I may appeal to every experienced teacher when I assert that very irregular words are often as easily learned as those which present no difficulty, and such words as *catarrh* and *phthisic* are the first to be mastered and remembered forever.

At the point marked by the asterisk above, Mann replied in a footnote: "In regard to this, we think our correspondent to be in great error. The exceptions exceed the rule, immensely."

Drawing on his own twenty years' experience in teaching the alphabet, Q considered the difficulties of the task in the light of the objections being made by those in favor of the new method:

We are told, then, by the friends of the new system, that teaching the alphabet consumes too much time, and is an irksome task to children. We doubt whether these are ever good reasons for omitting to teach children anything they ought to learn. It often takes a good while to teach a child obedience, and the lessons are often irksome and painful; but shall they be slighted on this account? It seems to me, however, that the time consumed in learning the letters is over-stated, and the pain inflicted altogether a mistake. Most children learn the alphabet in infancy, at home; and both they and their parents find a pleasure in the exercise. Many intelligent parents have assured me that they have taught the alphabet to their children in three days. My pupils have sometimes required as many months; but then it must be recollected that, in Common Schools, an abecedarian may think himself fortunate if five minutes a day are devoted to him. As there are seventy-eight working days in three months, the child, at this rate, receives six hours and a half of instruction; and, allowing him ten minutes a day, he will receive but thirteen hours' instruction in a quarter, or one hour a week. This is not an alarming amount of time; the greater concern should be about the employment of the rest of the quarter, when the child is not engaged upon the alphabet. Then, as to the irksomeness of the lessons, this depends greatly upon the manner in which the letters are taught. If the letters are pointed at with a pin, and nothing is said or done to fix the attention of the child upon them, he may well complain; but, if he is required to make the letters,—and any child can do this; if he is asked what they look like, that he may associate ideas with them; if he is told what they stand for, or associates them with some amusing rhyme;— my word for it, he will never take so much delight in any future lesson, as in achieving this first victory over written language. Almost any child can make a letter five hundred times every day on a slate or blackboard, and call it by name as many times. Next day he can make A and B, and name them repeatedly. Then A, B, C, and so on, adding one letter a day. If there is not excitement enough in this process, he may be taught to use such letters as he has learned, in forming easy words. Thus, of the first eight, he may form B E D, B A D, B A G, C A B, A C E, A G E, H A G, H A D, H E A D, F A C E, &c., which the teacher may make, one at a time, on the slate, and leave him to imitate and sound as many times as he pleases. He may teach the child, what probably was his own first lesson, that "A was an Archer, who shot at a Frog," and "B was a Butcher, who kept a great Dog." Or, he may resort to the New England Primer of our ancestors, and teach the child that "In *Adam's* fall we sinned all;" "Thy life to mend, this *Book* attend;" "The *Cat* doth play, and, after, slay." Or, he may describe the letters as we are told Will Shakespeare's mother described them to him: "First there is A, that ever standeth a-straddle; next to him is B, who is all head and body, and no legs; then cometh C, who bulgeth out behind like a very hunchback; and after him cometh D, who doeth the clean contrary, for his bigness is all before." In these, and many other ways, the alphabet may be made a very interesting lesson to very young pupils.

I have not been able to find Q's source for the part Shakespeare's mother played in her son's learning his letters. At one point in his discussion, Q objected to "natural order" as it had been used in the *Journal* by the author of one of the books prepared for those using the new word method. The author had said, as quoted in the *Journal,* "All that is insisted on is, that the learning of the word should precede that of the letters, and for this plain reason, it is the natural order, and therefore, must be incomparably easier than the reverse." Q thought the writer had confused reading with speaking, it being natural for a child to speak, but not for him to read. Emerson came to his assistance on this point with a footnote:

The new mode of reading is properly called the "natural order," because it is obviously the very mode which every child pursues in learning to recognise every object presented to his senses. He does not begin with analyzing his mother's face, and learning the features, one by one; but he sees and recognizes the face and person of his mother, as a whole, before he learns to know her or to pronounce her name. So it is with every person and object with which he forms an acquaintance. He knows them only as *whole objects,* and it is not till he has become familiar with them, that he is led to observe and name the parts of which they are composed. A child's first vocabulary consists, as all the world knows, of the names for father, mother, brother, sister, pussy, cradle, and so on. Afterwards he learns to name eyes, nose, and ears, paws and rockers, and dear, pretty, &c. Quere,—whether it would be an improvement on the present mode, to hold out a rattle, and, instead of saying, pretty, pretty, to say,—p, r, e, t, t, y,—pretty?

Q discussed at some length other texts to be used in teaching according to the new method. In dealing with one of these he showed that his years with abecedarians had not left him entirely destitute of humor:

We are told to avoid the alphabet, because it is a hindrance, and because it is irksome and painful to the child to learn it; and then we are told that, "by way of variety,"—that is, to please the child, who has become tired of the new way,—"it may be well to select a short word, and teach him *to read its letters!*" The whole quotation implies that it is impossible to teach whole words without also teaching the letters; and the author adds, "Teachers will find that, with hardly any direct effort on their part, the knowledge of the letters will come." In the first treatise on human physiology that we write, we shall direct the parent to teach her infant to run at once, and not to crawl or walk, which are irksome and tardy methods of going ahead; for *"parents* will find that, with hardly any direct effort on their part, the knowledge of *creeping* and *walking* will come.

What he said here caused Emerson to come to his help with another footnote: "Children usually learn to 'run at once' of themselves. A close observer, Dr. Paley, says, 'Nor is it (the child) less pleased with its first successful endeavors to walk, or rather to run, which precedes walking.' "

Q closed his essay with a weighty objection to the new method:

When I have urged my objections against the new method, I have uniformly been met with the remark, that the best proof that the system was what it pretends to be, is the success that has attended the experiment. Success is assuredly pretty good evidence that the means are suitable, but I do not think it is certain that any success has crowned the experiment, nor, in fact, that the experiment has been or can be tried. Let us see. The object is, to teach children to read without previously learning the letters, or pronouncing them or the syllables. Children may have learned a few words in this way, but I have been assured by teachers that the progress is slow and unsatisfactory, until, as the preface has it, "with hardly any *direct* effort on the part of the teacher," but with constant effort on the part of the poor child, the original error is repaired, and "the knowledge of the letters has come." This belief that the advocates of this new plan are deceived as to the extent of the aid afforded by pronouncing a few words before teaching the letters, and my conviction that ere long the teachers would honestly say so, has prevented me, and others, hitherto, from making any attempt to defend the old plan. We believe,— and we should rest quiet in the belief, were not experiments in education more important than those in any other department of human concerns,—we believe that the new plan is a mistake, engendered no doubt by the purest benevolence, and the sincerest concern for the wel-fare of our race, but still a mistake that will soon pass away.[9]

To this recording of his observation neither Mann nor Emerson saw fit to write a footnote.

[9] *Common School Journal*, VI (1844), 33–45.

READING FROM HORACE MANN TO FRANCIS PARKER

There is no need to go further into the quarrel between Mann and his critics. The most significant fact about the bitter dispute is that what is now called the word method or the look-and-say method of teaching reading failed to make much headway when it was first proposed in this country. In chapter 5 attention was called to the confusion in terminology which resulted from the simultaneous appearance of a method of teaching children to read by having them memorize words and a method of teaching them the ABC's by pointing out the letters in simple words. In an effort to distinguish between the two procedures I have used the expressions "words-to-reading" and "words-to-letters," the meanings of which appear obvious. Teachers who favored teaching the child letters and their sounds as quickly as possible were careful not to employ many words. Gallaudet used about fifty in working with his children. Some of the teachers who followed his primer and method used only enough words to include all the letters. The well-worn old sentence: *The quick brown fox jumps over the lazy dog,* with a total of eight different words, might have served them very well. How many words the Boston elementary teachers used in teaching the alphabet in the new manner is not known. But the tendency was decidedly to restrict the number of words shown the child. A teacher reported in 1842: "The experience of several years, during which I have tried both ways, has convinced me that the best mode is to teach a small vocabulary of words first, and *then* the letters. The length of this vocabulary must vary with the age and aptitude of the children."[1]

Mann, and others as well, regarded this new way of introducing a child to the letters as a new way of teaching him to read. In his lecture on spelling books, Mann mentioned that the books of J. F. Bumstead had been in use for a year or two in all of the primary schools of Boston. In the forematter of one of the Bumstead books, where there were suggestions to help the teacher, this sentence occurred: "The scholar may learn the whole fifteen different words on pages 7–10, before anything is said to him about the letters; or, if the teacher prefers, he may begin with the letters earlier."[2]

Those teachers who used words to teach letters recognized quite clearly that they were employing the old conventional ABC method. All they had was a new and better way to teach the letters. Once the child had mastered these, he proceeded in the usual manner to read. The teacher just cited as favoring teaching the child a small vocabulary at first, said: "This mode applies, of course, only to the first steps, which it is of the greatest importance to make easy and agreeable, while the child's eye is becoming familiar with the cabalistic characters called the alphabet."[3] Those teachers who enlarged upon the number of words shown the child before they said anything about the letters or sounds, did not, according to the Boston grammar school masters, teach their children very well. Professor Q said teachers had told him that it was not until the child had mastered the letters that he made much progress. Increasing the number of words shown the child and having him memorize them was what aroused protest.

Keagy, of course, advised that words be taught the child just as if they were Chinese symbols. In this he was following Gedike's much earlier proposal. Palmer agreed with Keagy in thinking that words should be memorized by the child at first, and that a good deal of easy reading should be

1 *Common School Journal,* IV (1842), 90.
2 *Ibid.,* V (1843), 361.
3 *Ibid.,* IV (1842), 90.

done before the letters were undertaken. (Note his sentence, "And, finally, we have formed a long vocabulary, before we know anything of syllables and letters.") Horace Mann, in explaining to the masters just what he thought the "new method" was, set the upward limit of the words to be learned at "less than a hundred."[4] Contrast this modest approach with Colonel Parker's plan of having the child learn from one hundred and fifty to two hundred words before making the transition from script to print, and postponing until the third year his learning the names of the letters.

Still another aspect of this early agitation over reading was the fact that before Mann left office in 1848, the now familiar expression "word method" had come into use to replace the earlier "new method." Like the term it replaced, "word method" for a long time had a variable meaning: it might refer to the words-to-reading system or to the words-to-letters method of teaching the alphabet.

Andrew J. Rickoff, Superintendent of the Cincinnati Public Schools, in his Annual Report for 1857 said:

> The *Word method* requires that the pupils be taught to recognize and call *words* at sight, without spelling them, or even learning the names or sounds of the letters. . . . Those who have adopted it, differ materially with each other, as to the extent to which it should be carried before the names, or sounds of the letters, should be introduced. Some would have the letters of every word taught as soon as the word is learned. Others would have this deferred till one or two of the first reading books are completed. Almost all well informed Teachers have adopted the word method, followed more or less immediately by the alphabetic or phonic.[5]

A little further on the Superintendent explained how reading was taught in his schools:

> The process of teaching the first lessons of reading, generally adopted in the Schools of this city, during the last year or two, differs from that which is pursued in the Prussian Schools in this regard, that, after the word is learned, the names of the

---

[4] Horace Mann, *Reply to the "Remarks"* (Boston, 1844), pp. 102–3.
[5] Common Schools of Cincinnati, *Annual Report* (Cincinnati, 1957), pp. 43–44.

letters are taught, and then their sounds, instead of the sounds first and then the names.[6]

To make this process entirely clear, he then explained in detail how a single word was taken, such as *ax, top, ball,* and printed on the blackboard. The class was well drilled on it for their first lesson. They then returned to their seats and amused themselves by copying the word on their slates. They were later called for their second lesson, reviewed on the word, and taught its letters, the teacher printing each one separately on the board.

William Harvey Wells, City Superintendent of the Chicago Schools, in his report to the Board of Education for the school year 1858-59, devoted considerable space to pointing out what an improvement it would be if all the schools adopted the word method. After mentioning the diversity of methods used in teaching the first lessons in reading, Wells said:

> There is, however, at the present time a very decided tendency to what is called the *word method.* Words have meaning; letters have none. Words are as easily learned as letters, and they naturally precede letters. . . . The exact point at which the names of the letters are to be introduced is not a matter of much importance. . . . If any teacher prefers to teach the names of the letters as fast as they occur in the words learned, no harm can result in such a course.[7]

In a *Manual of the Graded Course of Instruction in the Primary Schools* adopted by the Board of Public Education in Philadelphia, February 12, 1884, these explanations came first:

> READING. First Grade—*Time, five months.* . . . The reading to be taught by the word and phonic method. Begin by using simple words of one syllable—names of things within the experience of the pupils. . . . One or two words will suffice at first. . . . Analyze the first word taught into its phonic elements, and use the elements thus obtained in forming new words. For instance, the substitution of other initial letters in the word cat will give the words rat, hat, fat, without further change. This

[6] *Ibid.,* p. 47.
[7] *In Memoriam* (Chicago, 1887), pp. 25–26.

brings the great law of association into play, and illustrates also the important principle of economy, both of which should be made available in all the instruction.[8]

When Dr. Joseph Mayer Rice made his remarkable survey of what was going on in the classrooms of many of the cities in this country around 1890, he reported that in New York City the word method was in use but that the pupils were "taught to spell the words as they learn to read them."[9] In Buffalo he found that "Reading is taught by the word method, a method which, when used without the aid of phonics (as is the case in Buffalo), does less to develop power and more to waste time than any that I know of—except *perhaps*, the alphabet method."[10]

The point needs no further belaboring that "word method" during the first half-century of its use referred to any method of teaching reading in which the teacher began with a word. The term was applied to those methods where the teaching of the letters immediately followed the learning of the word, as well as to those where the mastering of the letters was deferred until a great many words had been learned and some reading had been done.

The attack upon the conventional method of teaching to read which broke out in the 1820's with the work of such men as Keagy, Gallaudet, Palmer, Peirce, and Mann, precipitated a struggle that continued throughout the century. In this time of great confusion, the ancient ABC method, although it had suffered a setback, continued in use, either in its old unadulterated form or slightly modified by those who taught letters by means of simple words. Webster's "Ole Blue-back" continued to sell in numbers which no man knows but which must have approached the hundred million mark.[11]

---

[8] Philadelphia Public Schools, *Manual of the Graded Course of Instruction in the Primary Schools* (Philadelphia, 1884), p. 5.

[9] J. M. Rice, *Public-School System of the United States* (New York, 1893), p. 38.

[10] *Ibid.*, pp. 74–75.

[11] Robert Keith Leavitt, *Noah's Ark* (Springfield, Mass., 1947), legend to Plate 1, opposite p. 6; Harry R. Warfel, *Noah Webster, Schoolmaster to America* (New York, 1936), p. 395.

With the spelling books went the McGuffey readers, largely following in the old tradition.[12] As in the case of the spellers, accurate figures for gross sales cannot be made out for this remarkable series of readers, but a well-informed guess is that between 1836 and 1920 one hundred and twenty-two million McGuffeys were sold. To arrive at the number of pupils who used these readers one would have to multiply this figure by perhaps four or five, as they were treasured and passed on from older to younger members of families as they were needed.[13]

No fault was ever found with the McGuffey readers by those who studied them. Pupils loved and respected them, which is one reason why they are still being published. These old books praised such virtues as hard work, economy, honesty, truthfulness, kindness, reverence. Their pallid successors are praised by few and ridiculed by many. But in the latter half of the nineteenth century, currents of change were beginning to stir. Philosophies of education were being modified. For a long time the rural schools were not affected, but in the larger centers influences were being felt that would later reach the hinterlands.

In the forefront of those sensitive to the imperative need for change in the schoolrooms was Francis Wayland Parker (1837–1902). He was born in very poor circumstances in the village of Piscatauquog, Town of Bedford, in southeast New Hampshire, near Manchester. When he was six years old he lost his father and went to live with an uncle who had become his guardian. At sixteen he thought he would try to teach, and he secured a position in a country school with seventy pupils, many of them older than he was.

He continued teaching and working on his uncle's farm between sessions until about 1859 when, through a friend, he found work in a school at Carrollton, Illinois. He was there at the outbreak of the Civil War and promptly enlisted. An excellent soldier, he received a severe neck wound, but survived, and by the time the war was over he held the rank of colonel. Despite inducements to remain in

12 Charles C. Fries, *Linguistics and Reading* (New York, 1962), pp. 20–21.
13 W. W. Livengood, *Our Heritage* (Cincinnati, 1947), p. 23.

the service, he hurried back home and again took up teaching.

His greatest ambition was to teach small children. Finding a job in Manchester, New Hampshire, he taught there for three years, but somehow he became involved in local politics and lost his position. His desire to teach small children increased with his experience. In the account of his life, which he dictated to a friend, he said: "I had been down in the school at Manchester and had seen the little children studying their A B C's, and doing their work, and they did not seem happy in it as I thought children should, and my question was, Did God intend that this mournful process, that this mournful plan, should be the way of developing the embryonic man?"

By this time he had a reputation as an oddity, an innovator, and it was not easy for him to secure employment, but by going as far away from home as Dayton, Ohio, he succeeded. There he tried to work with little children, but he said his first efforts were "so crude" that the papers "poured out their vials of wrath against me." He more than held his own, however, and around 1869 he became the principal of a new normal school in Dayton. At about the same time he tried out the word method of teaching reading, though he gave no details of how he administered it.

Adversities of all kinds came upon him at Dayton. He suffered so much from being regarded an ignoramus that he determined to go to Germany and get all the information he could about kindergarten methods and to secure the status which he badly needed. A small legacy enabled him to spend two years at the university in Berlin and to travel extensively abroad. His efforts to secure a position in Boston failed, however; the job he sought went to a man with far less qualification. Fortunately, he was given the superintendency of the public schools in Quincy, and in 1875 he began a remarkable career there.[14] Within a few years what

---

[14] I have followed mainly the account of his life which Parker dictated, given in William M. Giffin, *School Days in the Fifties* (Chicago, 1906). Minor discrepancies occur between this and accounts given elsewhere, including that in Paul Monroe (ed.), *Cyclopedia of Education* (New York, 1911–13). The best of the shorter accounts is that in the *DAB*.

was known as the "Quincy System" became even more famous than the Oswego Movement[15] had been earlier. How much the later spectacular innovation depended upon the earlier need not concern us. Colonel Parker's "crackpot" period was behind him; he was now an educational leader, the most outstanding figure in elementary education in the country.

Writing in 1930, John Dewey said that Francis Parker "more nearly than any other one person was the father of the progressive educational movement."[16] Parker was also the first widely known practitioner of the words-to-reading method. Although Horace Mann is commonly regarded as having played a decisive role in the initiation of this movement, what he said was far less significant than what Parker and his teachers did.

One should not lose sight of the fact that reading was merely one aspect of the revolution which Parker headed in elementary education. He and his friends enlarged the curriculum of the primary grades to such an extent that the traditional three R's shrank tremendously in relative impotance. The limits of the present investigation demand concentration on one phase of a tremendously significant and inclusive program in which the aim was not only to instruct children thoroughly in the conventional subjects, but also to see that they knew at least a little about botany, zoology, physiology, geography, history, drawing, clay modeling, games, grammar, rhetoric, and the like.

In Parker's school those preparing to teach children to read spent hours learning to draw and to write on the blackboard. They planned each lesson as carefully as a general plans a military campaign. They began with a clearly expressed purpose for each lesson and ended with a summary

15 The fullest account of the Oswego movement is by Andrew Phillip Hollis, *The Contribution of the Oswego Normal School to Educational Progress in the United States* (Boston, 1898). Nothing new in teaching reading was essayed there; the phonics system was used.

Dr. Edward A. Sheldon (1832–97), inspired chiefly by Pestalozzianism, initiated the movement in the Oswego Normal School which he founded in 1861. How much inspiration Parker might have received from what went on there cannot be determined, but it may have been considerable.

16 "How Much Freedom in New Schools?" *New Republic,* LXIII (1930), 204.

of details of just what was to be done to attain the object sought.

After the children had been in school for about six weeks and had been treated with unfailing kindness, they began to memorize words which the teacher wrote on the board. Nothing at all was said at first about the letters. Nor was there any haste manifested in getting the children acquainted with a great many words in a very short time. At the slightest sign of weariness or lack of interest on their part, their attention was directed to some other subject. Partridge reported: "When one hundred and fifty or two hundred words have been taught *thoroughly,* when the children can read from the blackboard as rapidly as the teacher can write, when they can grasp promptly and give fluently the thought contained in sentences fifteen or sixteen words long, they are ready to make the change from script to print." At some point in this process, though the exact time is not specified, sounds of the letters were taught by the slow pronunciation of easy words. The names of the letters were withheld for at least the first two years to prevent the child from becoming confused about the names and the sounds of the letters.[17]

Every effort was made by the teacher to arouse so much interest on the pupil's part in some subject or object that he would be driven to devote attention whole-heartedly to reading. Only in this way could he attain what he desired in the way of information about whatever had excited his interest. Those who taught reading in the Quincy schools were given a philosophy by which to operate. The conception of what reading is and how it can best be taught is well expressed by the following, written either by Colonel Parker himself, or by someone under his influence:

Reading may be defined as the act of the mind in getting thought by means of written or printed words arranged in sentences.

[17] Lelia E. Partridge, *"Quincy Methods" Illustrated* (New York, 1885), p. 162; George A. Walton, *Report of Examinations of Schools in Norfolk County, Massachusetts* (Boston, 1880), p. 174, Table A; Board of Supervisors for the Public Schools of Boston, *Method of Teaching Reading in the Primary Schools* (Boston, n.d.), p. 15.

This act of the mind may or may not be followed immediately by the oral expression of the thought. In the former case it is oral reading, in the latter it is silent reading or study; but in neither case is there any real reading unless the reader's mind grasp the thought. The mere pronunciation of words, however correctly and readily done, is not reading as here defined. The teacher who concentrates effort upon the vocal utterance only, or upon the vocal utterance first and the thought afterwards, is leading her pupils astray. Her teaching is formal, and not real. The all-important habit for the child to form is that of never supposing that a sentence has been read before the thought is clear in his mind.

The main point, therefore, to which the attention of the teacher should be directed at every step, from first to last, in the teaching of reading, is this: *Are the pupils led to get the thought?* . . .

A written or printed word is used to recall an idea; it has no other use. A word which has been associated with a particular idea in the mind will, when seen, recall that idea, faintly if the association is weak, vividly if the association is strong. An association grows stronger by repetition of those acts which first produced it. A word is learned only when this bond of association has grown so strong that the word instantly at sight recalls its appropriate idea. It follows that the teaching of reading consists essentially in acts of association between written or printed words and their appropriate ideas. *That teaching which assists these acts of association assists the child in learning to read; that which does not assist these acts is useless.* If this be so, the best method of teaching reading will include all those devices, and only those, which aid efficiently in causing associative acts between ideas and written or printed words.[18]

The fame of the Quincy schools should not blind one to the fact that there were at least twenty-three other schools in Norfolk County which were not under Parker's control. Nor should the acclaim lavished on the achievement of Parker and his teachers create the impression that everybody was in accord with their method. Many parents feared that the schools were giving inadequate training in the basic subjects. Accordingly, in the fall of 1878, those in charge of the county's schools arranged for an examination to see how well the children were doing in reading, writing, and arithmetic. This testing was limited to children who had been four and eight years in the county system. By restrict-

[18] Board of Supervisors, *op. cit.*, pp. 3, 4.

ing the tests to those in the fourth and eighth grades, the examination left untouched those pupils in Quincy who had begun school under Colonel Parker. The examinations began with the fourth grade because there was not at that time any way to test the reading ability of children earlier. In those days a child had to attend school three or four years before he could read sufficiently well to have his attainments evaluated.

The examinations that were given were under the direction of George A. Walton, Agent of the Massachusetts Board of Education, a friend of Parker and an endorser of his expanded and enriched program for children. In his account of the examination of the schools in Norfolk County, Walton gave in some detail information about the methods being used to teach children to read. He found in the county what he called the ABC method, the word-and-object method, the phonic method, and the object-word-phonic method. The old ABC method, formerly the only one in use, had by 1878 declined in popularity so much that only five out of the twenty-four school systems tested still used it. In Quincy it had prevailed before Parker came but had then given way to the object-word-phonic method. In schools where a word method of some kind was used, naming the letters was deferred for different lengths of time varying from "early" in many of the schools to "never" in the case of four. In the six Quincy schools under Parker's administration, teaching of letter names was postponed until after the first two years.[19]

It may be of interest for those who imagine that children of a former time spelled much better than those of today to see what Walton reported on the spelling he found prevailing in the schools of Norfolk County. In their written work, pupils in the primary grades spelled *whose* in 108 different ways; *which* in 58; *depot* in 52, and *scholar* in a grand total of 221.[20] Walton found on the whole that "the results, in these and other towns that pursue the same plan in whole or in part, confirm the theory long held by the most experi-

19 Walton, *op. cit.*, p. 174.
20 *Ibid.*, pp. 151–52.

enced educators, that the object and word method of teaching beginners to read, with the constant exercise in writing, is the best means of making good spellers."[21]

About the time the report of this extensive and extended examination of the county's schools took place, Parker left Quincy and became a Supervisor, that is, an Assistant Superintendent, in Boston. Perhaps this advance came as a result of the good showing in the examination made by the Quincy schools: both the primary pupils and those in the grammar grades representing six schools in Quincy scored noticeably higher than did pupils from the other schools.[22] The experiments at Quincy passed into history with the departure of Parker.[23] He was destined to attain his greatest fame elsewhere.

[21] *Ibid.*, p. 155.
[22] *Ibid.*, pp. 187, 197.
[23] There is no lack of material on what Parker did at Quincy; the most helpful book is Partridge's *"Quincy Methods" Illustrated*, which contains 660 pages.

THE READING SCENE AS
VIEWED BY DR. RICE

The interest in the public schools of Norfolk County,
Massachusetts, is suggestive of the increased interest being
taken in elementary school instruction in many other
places in this country at that time. Great changes had taken
place and were continuing to take place in all aspects of
American life. The nation was becoming more and more
urbanized. For those living east of the Mississippi River
the frontier was disappearing in the direction of the Far
West. The physical struggle to live was less severe; greater
leisure for more people meant more time for thinking.

Not much time was needed for anyone who thought at all
to realize that conditions inside the elementary schools
were not keeping pace with the changes going on beyond
the limits of the school grounds. The course of elementary
instruction had certainly not changed much. The traditional
three R's still dominated the scene. The physical equipment
provided for the pupils was scanty or entirely lacking.
Elementary teachers were often poorly trained and paid
accordingly for presiding over crowded rooms of children
who would much rather be elsewhere. The idea that the
schools should devote attention to the health of the pupils
was scarcely known.

It was under such circumstances that Joseph Mayer Rice
began his medical practice in New York City in 1881. His
work brought him into closer contact with the elementary
schools than he had ever been before and he became greatly

interested in and appalled by what he saw. He soon resolved to give up his practice and devote his full time to remedying the situation. First he went to Europe and studied for two years at Jena and Leipzig, becoming familiar with the educational philosophies taught there. In addition, he traveled widely on the continent and observed all he could about what was actually being practiced in the schools.

When he returned to this country in 1890, his suitcase was full of notes and his head full of ideas about elementary education. He began to write articles on the subject, some of which were published in a New York weekly. He sent an article to the *Forum*, then edited by Walter Hines Page. The response to this contribution was so encouraging that the magazine engaged him to travel over the country and report on conditions in various large American cities. The articles he wrote aroused so much attention that they were collected into a book, *The Public-School System of the United States*, which appeared in 1893.[1]

This book is one of the most significant and interesting ever written on the subject of elementary education in this country. The spirit of it can be seen in this excerpt: "As experience has taught me to place no reliance whatever on reports published by school officials regarding the condition of their schools, such reports being frequently no more than purely political documents . . . I relied, in studying the conditions of the schools, only on personal observations of class-room instruction."[2]

Scattered through Rice's book there are many interesting and instructive comments on the methods being used to teach reading in the schools he visited. Here is part of his account of what he observed in New York City:

In reading, the word method is followed. The pupils are taught to read the number of words prescribed for the grade and no more, and they are taught to spell the words as they learn to read them. They are not encouraged to acquire the ability to read

1 Lawrence A. Cremin, *Transformation of the School* (New York, 1961), devotes considerable attention to Rice and gives an excellent background for appreciating his work. See also the account of Rice in the *National Cyclopedia of American Biography*, XII (New York, 1904), 203.

2 J. M. Rice, *The Public-School System of the United States* (New York, 1893), p. 2.

new words, each new word being developed before it is shown to the child, which means practically that the child is told what the word is before he is allowed to name it. But this method is typical of the New York primary schools. I asked the principal whether the children in the highest grade (third-year class) were not able to read new words without being told what they were. She answered in substance: 'How can they know what a word is when they have never seen it before? Could you recognize a thing that you had never before seen?'[3]

Boston with its twelve hundred teachers, a city superintendent, and six assistant superintendents, disappointed Rice. "The Boston schools belong, in my opinion, to the purely mechanical-drudgery schools," he said. In one of the schools he pronounced the concert drill in phonics "ludicrously mechanical."[4] In another school he found the children drilling in concert on the long sounds of the vowels in such words as *name, here, fine, bone.*

The drill was carried on thus: Beginning with the word "name," the pupils (this time pronouncing the letters instead of the sounds) recited together in perfectly rhythmical singsong: "N-a-m-e, n-a-m-e, name; e at the end of the word makes the a say its own name, e at the end of the word makes the a say its own name; h-e-r-e, here; h-e-r-e; e at the end of the word makes the e say its own name, e at the end of the word makes the e say its own name."[5]

In Buffalo, Rice found it difficult to tell whether the teachers were not learning more from the pupils than the pupils were from them. The language of the pupils was atrocious, but so was that of the teachers. "Do it like you done it yesterday," was a typical direction to a pupil. The pupils were taught to spell in a singsong concert that fell into a rhythmic pattern, the melody of which Rice wrote out.[6] Here he found the word method without phonics and condemned it as time wasting. Some of the teachers discussed spelling with him and expressed a desire to return to the alphabet method "because those children who know their alphabet progress most rapidly in spelling."[7]

[3] Ibid., p. 38. On a previous page (p. 101) we referred to Rice's observations in New York; we quote him more fully here.

[4] *Ibid.*, pp. 123, 127.

[5] *Ibid.*, p. 128.

[6] *Ibid.*, p. 71.

[7] *Ibid.*, pp. 74, 75.

In Cincinnati, Rice found the Board of Education proud of the excellent condition of their schools and the high quality of work done by the students. Some of his observations on conditions in this city should be given at length:

The most striking peculiarity of the Cincinnati schools exists, in my opinion, in the fact that so much time is devoted to concert recitations,—a form of instruction than which there is none so preëminently fitted to deaden the soul and convert human beings into automatons. These recitations are heard, as a rule, as soon as a district (primary) school building is entered, and in tones so loud that the uninitiated might readily mistake them for signals of distress.

My experiences of this nature were frequent. In one of the schools I heard on entering the building sounds unusually shrill coming from one of the class-rooms, and being prompted by my desire to know the true cause of so much commotion, I entered the room whence they came.

What did I see? Only this: a teacher and about a dozen pupils standing before a black-board covered with lists of words, spelling the word "Quail" at the top of their voices, and in melodious tones, thus:

Quail q - u - a - i - l   quail, Quail q - u - a - i - l   quail.

When the teacher found occasion to take a moment's rest, she said to me:

"These are my poorest spellers; they always need an extra drilling. *Quail* appears to be a very difficult word for them to remember. I must give them a little more drill upon it."

She then returned to the blackboard and told the children to continue. As a signal for them to start, she pointed with her stick to the letter Q, and after they had begun she swept the stick from left to right along the word "Quail," endeavoring in this manner to keep them in time while they were spelling the word. To keep them in time was, however, no easy matter. They kept together fairly well until they had spelled the word two or three times, but after that their voices became ever more independent, so that soon a regular medley ensued, some calling out the word "Quail," while others had only reached the letter "l," and still others had gone no further than "i."

The "mystery of the strange sounds" was solved.

When the word "Quail" had been earnestly, thoroughly, and

conscientiously studied, the word "Market" was begun. Although the spelling of this word was carried on upon the same principles as those which governed the spelling of the word "Quail," nevertheless the monotony was broken, for the reason that both the melody and the *tempo* were changed. While "Quail" was sung rapidly and with much spirit, "Market" was sung slowly and plaintively, thus:

After a few more words had been studied in this manner, the teacher said that she would let me hear the whole class read.

The sentence, "Is it a quail, John?" had previously been written upon another blackboard, and the teacher asked the children to read it together.

"Read it backward first," she said.

The children then read the words as the teacher pointed to them with her baton, and after they had read the sentence backward and forward, they spelled all the words contained in it. The teacher endeavored to keep them in time by sweeping her stick across each word while the children were spelling it, as she had done in the other case. The effect, as near as I can reproduce it, was as follows:

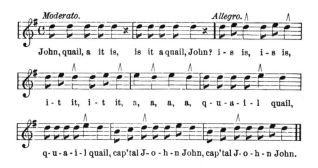

"You don't spell 'John' very well yet," the teacher now remarked. "Let us try it over again, but don't sing it."

She then spelled the word for the class, immediately, however, falling into the sing-song which she had told the children to avoid. After she had sung it alone two or three times, the voices of the children began to chime in, but she continued to spell with them. While teaching the children to spell the word "John," she adopted a different plan of leading them. She now beat time, and this she did most comically, by bringing her hands (with the backs upward) as near to her shoulders as possible, when she pronounced the word "capital," and thrusting them forcibly forward when she uttered the "J."

"I do have such trouble in getting these children to recite together," the teacher afterward said to me.

If such teaching represents education upon psychological principles, it is not at all surprising that so many persons should be opposed to modern methods.

In one of the other classes that I visited in this school, some of the children were reading while others were writing. After hearing some of them read, the teacher said to me:

"Now I will let one of those engaged in writing read for you. I always like to see whether they can read what they write. They copy the words from the board, you know, and so I am not always sure that they can read what they write." She then said to one of the children:

"Lucy, read what's on your slate for that *there* gentleman."

Lucy then came forward courageously and read this thrilling tale: "The cows feed on the grass. At night they come to the barn."

c - o - doub-le - u - s cows,   c - o - doub-le - u - s cows,

f - doub-le - e - d feed,   f - doub-le - e - d feed.

It must not be supposed that the above-described method of teaching spelling is confined to this one school. Indeed my observations led me to believe that this was the method commonly used in the schools of Cincinnati.

A reading-lesson that I attended in the third-year class of another school presented some special features, though the method in itself was typical.

The lesson was announced soon after I entered the room. When all the children had placed their books upon the desks, the teacher said:

"Position! Books in your left hands; right hands behind your backs!"

The lesson was conducted as follows: One child was called upon to read a paragraph, then another pupil was told to read the same paragraph over again, and lastly, this paragraph was read by the class in concert. The same course was pursued in all the paragraphs read. Taken all in all, this reading sounded like a piece of music consisting of a solo, an echo, and a chorus. How interesting the story must have been to the children!

In one of the pieces read the word "merchant" appeared.

"What is a merchant?" the teacher inquired after one of the children had read the word.

"A merchant is a tailor," answered one.

"A merchant is a man what keeps dry-goods stores," said another.

"A merchant is a man what buys cheap and kin sell dear," remarked a third.

At last a little boy, with a triumphant air, cried out, "A merchant is a man what sells goods."

The teacher corrected none of these mistakes in language; but when one of the children had read the sentence, "I broke the glass, and I will pay for it," the teacher said, "What mistake did he make?"

"Teacher," answered one, "he said 'glass' and he ought 'a' said 'glars.' "

"Right," said the teacher.

It is teaching of this nature that the president of Cincinnati's Board of Education calls magnificent. But what this teaching shows beyond the fact that the teachers are not illiterates it is difficult to perceive.[8]

In the Chicago public schools Rice observed that "the methods employed in teaching reading vary in the different schools. In some instances the pupils are taught by the word method, in others by the sentence method, and in still others by a variety of methods, including phonics and word-building."[9] In some of the Chicago schools he found examples of the most perverted forms of reading he had ever observed, and he devoted considerable attention to what he saw in one of these schools.[10] The principal told him that her school was celebrated for its reading and that she would show him how the method they used was carried out in all the grades. First she led him to a primary room:

After entering the room containing the youngest pupils, the principal said to the teacher, "Begin with the mouth movements and go straight through." Complying with the request of the

8 *Ibid.*, pp. 84–89.
9 *Ibid.*, p. 170.
10 *Ibid.*, p. 174.

principal, the teacher directed her attention to the class, and said, "Now let us see how nicely you can make the mouth movements." About fifty pupils now began in concert to give utterance to the sounds of a (as in car), e, and oo, varying their order, thus: a, e, oo, a, e, oo; e, a, oo, e, a, oo; oo, a, e, oo, a, e; oo, e, a, oo, e, a; etc.

The mouth movements made by the pupils while uttering these sounds were as exaggerated as the mouths would permit. While uttering the sound "a" the mouth was stretched open as far as it would go; in "e" the corners were drawn as closely as possible to the ears, and in "oo" the lips were pointed. The facial expression of the pupils while performing these mouth movements was grotesque; to see fifty pupils thus occupied at once presented a scene that beggars description.

When some time had been spent in thus manoeuvering the jaws, the teacher remarked, "Your tongues are not loose." Fifty pupils now put out their tongues and wagged them in all directions. The principal complimented the children on the superiority of their wagging. What an idea these pupils must have received of the purpose of a school, when from the start they were taught systematically how to make grimaces and wag their tongues![11]

These mouth exercises were followed by equally ridiculous head exercises, about nine in number, followed by another set of facial expressions indicative of various emotions. Breathing exercises came last, at the conclusion of which the pupils were prepared to go on with their reading lesson. Rice thought the method he had seen was founded on the Delsarte system[12] and that it "had been introduced in a large number of Chicago schools."[13]

Dr. Rice found three places that proved that it was "possible to educate the child without robbing him of his happiness," and he devoted the ninth chapter[14] of his book to his approval of what he found in Minneapolis, Minnesota, La Porte, Indiana, and the Cook County Normal School at Englewood, Illinois. Here he found schools of a new kind, with teachers of a progressive type who read educational literature and followed systems from which everything of

11 *Ibid.*, pp. 176–77.

12 *Ibid.*, p. 176. François Delsarte tried to revolutionize dramatic expression by intensive training of different parts of the body to reflect various shades of emotion. See the article about him in Paul Monroe (ed.), *Cyclopedia of Education* (New York, 1911–13).

13 Rice, *op. cit.*, p. 174.

14 *Ibid.*, pp. 193–216.

a purely mechanical nature had disappeared. Progressive superintendents and progressive corps of teachers were working together to enlarge the curriculum far beyond the traditional three R's, and yet were by no means neglecting these. The students' interest was being enlisted at the start; botany, drawing, modeling in clay, nature study—all these and more—were receiving attention. He found that the Cook County Normal School had for ten years been under the direction of Colonel Parker. The last six pages of Rice's ninth chapter are devoted to Parker's work there. He found the Colonel a man of marked inspirational powers and pronounced his faculty "one of the most enthusiastic, earnest, progressive, and thoughtful corps of teachers that may be found anywhere, and they are continually growing."[15]

As we have seen, Rice found the sentence method in use in some Chicago schools. This method had some vogue in American schools at that time, and some of the views about reading and teaching to read set forth in connection with it have lived on. In a previous chapter mention was made of the fact that German educators, in their efforts to take advantage of the "philosophy of the Whole" enunciated by Jacotot, experimented with sentences as units for instructing beginners. Their efforts were unsuccessful. It may be that George L. Farnham, a superintendent of schools in New York, had heard of these much earlier attempts in Germany, but whether he had or not, in 1881 he brought out a small manual for teachers, *The Sentence Method of Teaching Reading*. The second edition (1887) was somewhat modified, and similarly the third and last (1895).

Farnham believed that the "first principle to be observed in teaching written language is 'that things are cognized as wholes.' Language follows this law. Although it is taught by an indirect process, still, in its external characteristics, it follows the law of other objects. The question arises, what is the whole? or what is the unit of expression? It is now quite generally conceded that we have no ideas not logically associated with others. In other words, thoughts, complete

15 *Ibid.*, p. 211.

in their relations are the materials in the mind out of which the complex relations are constructed. It being admitted that the thought is the unit of thinking, it necessarily follows that *the sentence is the unit of expression."*

Farnham defined reading as "gaining the thoughts of an author from written or printed language." He explained that as a rule reading was done silently, and he analyzed this process as one in which the reader either pronounced the words to himself or thought of the pronunciations. The thought was not "formed in his mind directly through the language but indirectly after the written words have been changed into oral expression." He pronounced this process "slow and laborious" and even painful if long continued. The practice of it, he thought, accounted for the fact that not many people read anything. The better plan, he felt sure, was for every pupil to become trained as an "eye reader," that is, he should have the ability "to look directly through the written expression to the meaning." He regarded it as most important in teaching a child to read "to make the eye perform the office of the ear."

It was at this point, he thought that education often failed. The slow difficult translation of what was written, first into speech and then from sound to meaning condemned many pupils to ignorance, because words as they appear on the printed page "have no meaning to them." He thought "one who has acquired the power of directly receiving thought from the printed page, is endowed with a new intellectual faculty." Oral reading he regarded as of secondary importance in comparison with "correct eye reading." Once the pupil was able to take in thought, directly from the printed page, oral expression of that thought would take care of itself.[16]

Edmund Burke Huey discussed the sentence method and the work of Farnham. The method itself, he said, had been "suggested by Comenius" but "was scarcely used in America until popularized through the experiments of Farnham in the schools of Binghamton, New York, about 1870, and

[16] I have seen only the second (1887) edition of Farnham's book. The passages quoted are from pp. 11 ff. and 15 ff. of that edition.

was not widely adopted until 1885–1890." Although a good deal had been done with it, Huey regarded Farnham's manual as "still a very fair presentation of the method."[17]

This method has apparently prospered better abroad than here. A valuable contribution to the movement was made quite inadvertently and unintentionally by Henry Bradley, a famous scholar and lexicographer. In 1913 he read a paper of considerable length at the International Historical Congress on the subject of "Spoken and Written English." He spoke at a time when spelling reform was of great interest in England and in this country. What he said has been printed more than once, and has become a classic on the subject with which it deals.[18]

In counseling that great care be exercised in renovating English spelling, Bradley in the opening paragraph of his lecture reminded his hearers that writing is not entirely concerned with reproducing sounds: "Many of the advocates of spelling reform are in the habit of asserting, as if it were an axiom admitting of no dispute, that the sole function of writing is to represent sounds." He explained this aspect of writing at some length and with great clarity.

The entire article is well worth reading, bringing out carefully, as it does, the well-known fact that English writing is well sprinkled with what Bradley called "ideographic devices," having at present no value at all in terms of sound. Spellings which were once phonetically significant have often ceased to be so, with the result that written English, involving as it does, these "devices," often makes clear distinctions which have disappeared from spoken English. Bradley illustrated this situation with such sentences as these: "The hair of the hare is commonly called fur"; "The knight spent the night in prayer"; "We rode to the side of the lake and then rowed across."

Bradley's article made a great impression upon J. H. Jagger, an English student who later became well known in connection with his advocacy of the sentence method. In 1929 he published a book with the same title as Farnham's

---

[17] Edmund Burke Huey, *Psychology and Pedagogy of Reading* (New York, 1908), pp. 272–73.

[18] See *Collected Papers of Henry Bradley* (Oxford, 1928), pp. 168–93.

much earlier work, *The Sentence Method of Teaching Reading.* About this identity of subjects he wrote: "In 1887 a pamphlet bearing the same title as this book was published by A. B. Farnham at Syracuse, New York State. As far as the author is aware, no copy of this pamphlet reached the shores of England, and it does not appear to have exercised any influence on English education." Jagger explained that "The Sentence Method has arisen spontaneously in some London schools, as a reaction against the mechanical tyranny that phonetic teaching has imposed."[19]

Jagger quoted Bradley's introductory paragraph, but disregarded the main portion of the essay. This was unfortunate, for Bradley might have saved him from saying: "Our system of written words, in structure and in the way that it is used by us, is mainly indicative of the sense; it is indicative of sound in a secondary degree. The written form of each word is associated directly with its meaning, and indirectly with its sound. . . . To teach reading ideographically, without the interposition of sounds between written sign and meaning, is therefore in accord with the present character of English spelling as well as in accord with the historical development of writing."[20]

Dr. Jagger apparently never lost the impression made upon him by Bradley's introductory paragraph, nor did he assimilate the remainder of the article. In April, 1953, he wrote: "English writing today is an ideographic system— or, as those who regard it as a system intended to represent sounds would say, it is perfectly irregular. As a means of representing ideas it is unequaled; as a means of representing sounds, as a phonographic system, it is useless."

Jagger pointed out that "it might be an assumption" to think children of five to seven possess the ability "to learn to read by means of any spelling system, consistent or inconsistent. . . . if this assumption be conceded, it draws with it the remarkable conclusion that in the process of learning

[19] J. H. Jagger, *Sentence Method* (Glasgow, 1929), p. 5. He was, of course, in error about Farnham's initials.
[20] Jagger, *op. cit.,* p. 58. Hunter Diack, *In Spite of the Alphabet* (London, 1965), pp. 76–92, discusses "Sentence Methods" and comments, with generous excerpts from their work, on both Farnham and Jagger.

to read the ordinary direction of acquiring knowledge and skill is reversed." He repeated the arguments used in Germany in the first part of the nineteenth century, such as: "Ordinarily, the mind proceeds from the . . . whole to the part." He explained that "Reading is getting the meaning of printed and written symbols." And he said that if the child should make "the strenuous effort to learn in reverse —if it is at all possible for him to do that"—it would be the most intelligent and docile that would succeed. For those not so gifted "the reverse method will lead towards failure."[21]

[21] *Journal of Education*, April, 1953, pp. 161–62.

THE WORDS-TO-READING
METHOD SECURES A
BEACHHEAD AT CHICAGO

While Colonel Parker was an assistant superintendent in Boston, Albert G. Lane, who had "through former labors, proved himself progressive and liberal-minded,"[1] was serving his second term (1877–91) as superintendent of the schools in Cook County, Illinois. No doubt through Lane,[2] Parker became the Principal of the Cook County Normal School in 1883. He set out at once to repeat what he had done in Quincy, and he succeeded. The Normal became as celebrated as Quincy had been; educators came from foreign parts to learn and be amazed. But some, of course, doubted.

On Sunday morning, November 22, 1891, dissatisfaction with what Parker was doing boiled over on page three of the *Chicago Tribune*. Charles S. Thornton, a member of the County Board of Education, reported what he had found at the Normal, and the *Tribune* published it under the heading: "It Is A Merry War." One of the things Thornton did at the Normal was to learn what he could about the way pupils who had been there a long time expressed themselves in writing and how well they spelled. He had some of the pupils write a little essay on "The Horse." One boy who had been six and a half years at the Normal wrote: "A horse

[1] J. M. Rice, *Public-School System of the United States* (New York, 1893), p. 168.
[2] See *Who's Who in America*, Vol. I (Chicago, 1899–1900), for a good account of Lane.

has a tail." Another who had attended an equal length of time did better: "A horse has one tail and four feet."

We cannot go into the details of the "war" launched against the Colonel. In 1891 Lane moved into the superintendency of the Chicago Public Schools. Five years later the Cook County Normal was taken over by the city and became the Chicago City Normal.[3] Lane's influence, however, could not save Parker from his enemies, who became more eloquent than ever in their attacks on his "fad factory" and "glorified mudpie making."

In June of 1899, Parker and most of his faculty resigned from the Normal; the Colonel and the cause for which he battled had been saved in an unusual manner. One of his patrons at the Normal had been Mrs. Emmons Blaine, a daughter of Cyrus McCormick. She became a great admirer of the Colonel and a devoted supporter of the "new" system of education which he demonstrated in his school. She well knew the trouble he was having with his board employers, and just when his fortunes were darkest, came forward with one million dollars to build for him the "Chicago Institute" for the training of teachers. In the Institute, Parker would be forever free of board members and politicians. As he and Mrs. Blaine planned this bright future, they were both neatly caught in the very wide loop of the lariat President Harper of the emerging University of Chicago carried for roping in benefactors of great wealth.

As the matter ended, the Francis Parker School rose on the city's Near North Side, with Flora J. Cooke, one of Parker's best teachers, in charge; and Emmons Blaine Hall, the initial building of the School of Education at the University of Chicago, appeared on the Midway campus. The bill of two million dollars went to Mrs. Blaine. As the century closed, Colonel Parker and some of his teachers came from the Normal to the University of Chicago where the Colonel was the Director of the School of Education.[4]

---

[3] Robert L. McCaul, "Dewey's Chicago," *School Review*, Summer, 1959, pp. 258–80. See also Ida B. De Pencier, *History of the Laboratory Schools* (Chicago, 1960), pp. 18–19.

[4] De Pencier, *op. cit.*, pp. 2–23, tells of Dewey's arrival in Chicago, and brings into her account Colonel Parker, Mrs. Blaine, and President Harper.

Parker's new position at the University was fortunate for him in more ways than one. He was an internationally famous practitioner of the principles of the new educational movement, but he was unable to make a logical, coherent presentation of the principles themselves. Ida B. De Pencier expressed it well when she said of him: "He could not tell in any intellectual way why he thought as he did."[5] At Chicago, Parker became a neighbor of John Dewey, a man of similar educational views who was as articulate as Parker was not. Dewey had arrived at the University in the summer of 1894 as the head of the departments of Philosophy, Psychology, and Pedagogy. He and Parker became good friends; the talents of each supplemented those of the other.[6]

Dewey realized, as did all the other educators of the time who thought seriously about the matter, that radical changes were long overdue in elementary education. The articles by Rice in the *Forum* and in the book which resulted from them had aroused widespread concern about the schools. When Rice's findings were confirmed by those of Adele Marie Shaw a decade later, this concern increased.[7]

The problem which Dewey and those who thought as he did confronted was that of determining the direction which this inevitable new departure in education should take. Dewey was as full of ideas on the subject as Parker was full of tender emotion toward children, but he badly needed a school in which he could test his theories. He soon obtained it. In January, 1896, Dewey opened a school at 5714 Kimbark Avenue, in a building still standing near the University. It consisted of about a dozen pupils, two teachers, and an appropriation of a thousand dollars from the University. The community was an exceptional one, made up largely

5 *Ibid.*, p. 17.

6 *Ibid.*, p. 17: "Colonel Parker once said that he and Dewey were agreed on educational theories but Dewey could express it in educational philosophy while he, Parker, could not."

7 The ten articles by Miss Shaw, a teacher and writer, appeared in *World's Work*, VII (November, 1903–April, 1904), 4204–21, 4317–30, 4460–66, 4540–53; VIII (May–October, 1904), 4795–98, 4883–94, 4996–5004, 5244–54, 5405–14; IX (November–April, 1905), 5480–85.

of well-to-do people, many of them connected with the University—some scholars of distinction in various fields.

Interest in what Dewey was about increased as soon as his school opened. Parents and friends came to see what was going on. What they found was more puzzling than informative. Children were going freely about various activities, talking and laughing, under no control at all; some were preparing lunch, others were carding wool or spinning it into thread, and still others were busy sawing and hammering and nailing. The fact is that a new day had dawned for the child.

Superintendent Glenn of Atlanta in his keynote address before the National Education Association meeting at Charleston in 1900 took for his text a passage from Luke 1:66: "What Manner of Child Shall This Be?" His speech was an eloquent panegyric on the child. The following excerpt indicates its sentiment and flavor:

If I were asked what is to be accounted the great discovery of this century, I would pass by all the splendid achievements that men have wrought in wood and stone and iron and brass. I would not go to the volume that catalogs the printing-press, the telegraph, the wireless telegraphy, the telephone, the phonograph. I would not go among the stars and point to either one of the planets that have been added to our solar system. I would not call for the Roentgen ray that promises to revolutionize the study of the human brain as well as the human body. I would pass over all the labor-saving machines and devices by which the work of the world has been marvelously multiplied. Above and beyond all these the index finger of the world's progress, in the march of time, would point unerringly to the little child as the one great discovery of the century now speeding to its close. . . .

What the American child of the future is to be no man can prophesy. . . . We have begun to shift and readjust the paths that lead to and from the schoolhouse. We have quit trying to fit the boy to a system. We are now trying to adjust a system to the boy. The American boy is praying the prayer of the psalmist as he never prayed that prayer before: 'Set thou my feet in a large room.' We American teachers are trying to obey the command of the Great Teacher when he said at the grave of Lazarus: 'Loose him and let him go.' If we might reverently change this command to fit our day and time, the change would be: 'Loose

him and let him grow.' The demand of the hour is that we shall
take away, not only the grave-clothes, but all the deadly cere-
ments from the minds and bodies of our children.[8]

The sentiments which Glenn so eloquently voiced at this
meeting were shared by forward-looking educators everywhere. Among them was G. Stanley Hall, the intellectual
Goliath among the proponents of the "New Education,"
teacher of John Dewey, and admirer of Colonel Parker. In
an article in 1901, speaking reverently of the child, he said:

> The guardians of the young should strive first of all to keep
> out of nature's way, and to prevent harm, and should merit the
> proud title of the defenders of the happiness and rights of chil-
> dren. They should feel profoundly that childhood, as it comes
> fresh from the hand of God, is not corrupt, but illustrates the
> survival of the most consummate thing in the world; they should
> be convinced that there is nothing else so worthy of love, rever-
> ence, and service as the body and soul of the growing child.[9]

It was with this reverential attitude toward the child, this
desire to see his actions as manifestations of heavenly will,
that such men as Parker and Dewey and Hall set about
fashioning a new educational program that would prevent
harm to the child and would merit for its promulgators the
proud title of "defenders of the happiness and rights of
children." And it was in this spirit that John Dewey talked
to his patrons and neighbors about what he was trying to
do in his school.

Among other things, he explained to them that their devotion to the three R's went back to the sixteenth century
when, as a result of the invention of printing and the growth
of commerce, the ability to read, write, and figure "gave
access to careers in life otherwise closed."[10] But times had
changed most radically during the intervening centuries.
The highest duty of the schools now was to train children
for membership in such communities as those in which they

[8] *Proceedings, National Education Association*, XXXIX (1900), 176–77.
[9] G. Stanley Hall, "The Ideal School as Based on Child Study," *Forum*,
XXXII (1901), 24.
[10] John Dewey, *School and Society* (Chicago, 1899), p. 82. The commercial
influence on the rise of the primary school applies particularly to the situation in Germany and is duly noted in German histories of education. But
generally speaking, the religious inspiration was more powerful. The practical aspect of what took place in Germany suited Dewey's purpose here,
and the religious drive did not.

lived. When a school so trains a child, "saturating him with the spirit of service, and providing him with the instruments of effective self-direction, we shall have the deepest and best guarantee of a larger society which is worthy, lovely, and harmonious."[11]

Following out this idea of adjusting the child to his society, Dewey, the scholar, the academic, the intellectual, reported to his neighbors: "The merely intellectual life, the life of scholarship and learning, thus gets a very altered value. Academic and scholastic instead of being titles of honor, are becoming terms of reproach. But all this means a necessary change in the attitude of the school, one of which we are as yet far from realizing the full force. Our school methods, and to a very considerable extent our curriculum, are inherited from the period when learning and command of certain symbols, affording as they did the only access to learning, were all-important."[12]

Turning his attention to the curriculum, Dewey proposed to present the child, in place of the old poverty-stricken three R's, a vastly enriched program including such subjects as drawing, manual training, cooking, sewing, weaving, carving, archaeology, modeling, chemistry, physics, geology, biology, music, art, physical culture. In this welter of so much that was new what did he think should become of the old stand-bys, reading, writing, arithmetic? In facing this question he cited statistics to show that in the older dispensation from seventy-five to eighty per cent of the first three years of a child's time in school was "spent upon the form—not the substance—of learning, the mastering of the symbols of reading, writing, and arithmetic." "There is not much positive nutriment in this. Its purpose is important—is necessary—but it does not represent the same kind of increase in the child's intellectual and moral experience that is represented by positive truth of history and nature, or by added insight into reality and beauty."[13]

Dewey admitted that he did not have a definite program

11 *Ibid.*, pp. 43–44. These views do not associate Dewey with the much later (1945—) life-adjustment program in high schools.
12 *Ibid.*, p. 40.
13 *Ibid.*, pp. 117–18.

for teaching the older basic subjects, but he did feel quite definitely that they should not be permitted to usurp the amount of time formerly accorded them. As we have just noticed, he distinguished between "symbol learning" and gaining "added insight into reality and beauty." The latter he valued highly, but he thought of the former as not having much "positive nutriment" in it, stating the problem in this manner:

How can instruction in these formal, symbolic branches—the mastering of the ability to read, write, and use figures intelligently—be carried on with everyday experience and occupation as their background and in definite relations to other studies of more inherent content, and be carried on in such a way that the child shall feel their necessity through their connection with subjects which appeal to him on their own account? If this can be accomplished, he will have a vital motive for getting the technical capacity. It is not meant, as has been sometimes jocosely stated, that the child learn to bake and sew at school, and to read, write, and figure at home. It is intended that these formal subjects shall not be presented in such large doses at first as to be the exclusive objects of attention, and that the child shall be led by that which he is doing to feel the need for acquiring skill in the use of symbols and the immediate power they give. In any school, if the child realizes the motive for the use and application of numbers and language he has taken the longest step toward securing the power; and he can realize the motive only as he has some particular—not some general and remote—use for the symbols.[14]

Somewhat earlier, on October 31, 1896, after his school had been in operation nine months, Dewey had expressed his sentiments about these traditional subjects:

Reading, writing, and spelling are usually taught too soon, since the brain centers called into exercise by these studies are not sufficiently developed to make their use pleasurable and profitable. It is one of the great mistakes of education to make reading and writing constitute the bulk of the school work the first two years. The true way is to teach them incidentally as the outgrowth of the social activities at this time. Thus language is not primarily the expression of thought, but the means of social communication. By its use the child keeps track of his work from day to day; by it he gives to others the results of his own special activity, and his own consciousness is widened by knowing

14 *Ibid.,* pp. 118–19.

what others have thought and done in the same lines. If language
is abstracted from social activity, and made an end in itself, it
will not give its whole value as a means of development. When
the same reading lesson is given to forty children and each one
knows that all the others know it, and know that the teacher
knows it, the social element is effectively eliminated. When each
one has something individual to express, the social stimulus is an
effective motive to acquisition. It is not claimed that by the
method suggested, the child will learn to read as much, nor perhaps as readily in a given period as by the usual method. That
he will make more rapid progress later when the true language
interest develops, and that the break in the continuity of the
child's life will be prevented, can be claimed with confidence.[15]

To appreciate the views expressed here by Dewey, the
disciple, it is instructive to place beside them a brief excerpt from the master, G. Stanley Hall, who had taught
Dewey at Johns Hopkins.

Before we let the pedagogue loose upon childhood, not only
must each topic in his curriculum give an account of itself, but
his inroads must overcome the fetishism of the alphabet, of the
multiplication table, of grammars, of scales, and of bibliolatry,
and must reflect that but a few generations ago the ancestors of
all of us were illiterate; that the invention of Cadmus [i.e. the
letters] seemed the sowing of veritable dragon's teeth in the
brain; that Charlemagne and many other great men of the world
could not read or write; that scholars have argued that Cornelia,
Ophelia, Beatrice, and even the blessed mother of our Lord knew
nothing of letters. The knights, the elite leaders of the Middle
Ages, deemed writing a mere clerk's trick beneath the attention
of all those who scorned to muddle their wits with others' ideas,
feeling that their own were good enough for them.

Nay more: there are many who ought not to be educated, and
who would be better in mind, body, and morals if they knew no
school. What shall it profit a child to gain the world of knowledge
and lose his own health? Cramming and over-schooling have
impaired many a feeble mind, for which as the proverb says,
nothing is so dangerous as ideas too large for it. We are coming
to understand the vanity of mere scholarship and erudition, and
to know that even ignorance may be a wholesome poultice for
weakly souls; while scribes, sophists, scholastics, and pedants
suggest how much of the learning of the past is now seen to be
vanity, and how incompetent pedagogues have been as guardians
of the sacred things of culture.[16]

[15] "The University School," *University Record,* I (1896), 417–22.
[16] Hall, *op. cit.,* pp. 24–25.

THE WORD METHOD SUITS
THE NEW EDUCATION

There is no evidence that Dewey was ever interested in working out a methodology of teaching a child to read. In his broad vision of the needs of the times, teaching to read occupied a relatively unimportant place. He said it was "not the primary purpose of this [i.e. his] school to devise methods with reference to their direct application to the graded school system."[1] Mastering the letters and the multiplication table was merely learning symbols, and he felt that there was not much value in it. Learning to take a piece of wool and convert it into a thread and weave it into a piece of cloth was to him real learning, dealing with objective facts and realities. In addition, he stressed the need of arousing the child's motivation so that his enthusiasm for reading would enable him to learn quickly. This view he shared with Parker and all the other progressive teachers of the time. Parker was positive that properly situated, skillfully guided, wisely motivated children would "learn to read as they learn to talk, and we know they talk when they have something to say. Instead, then, of a child's being plunged into a labyrinth of empty words, his mind is aroused and quickened by vital, interesting thoughts in science, geography, and history, and out of these in a perfectly natural manner come the learning to read and the reading."[2]

1 "The University School," University Record, I (1896), 417.
2 Course of Study, I (1900), 13.

Enrollment increased steadily in Dewey's "Laboratory School," as Ella Flagg Young, one of his assistants, called it. By February, 1899, ninety-five pupils were in attendance, and the school moved into larger quarters at 5412 Ellis Avenue, still quite close to the University of Chicago campus.

It was about this time that Colonel Parker came to the University as the first Director of its School of Education.[3] Clara Mitchell, one of his graduates who had remained with him to teach, was on Dewey's faculty by October, 1896, and may have juined the group at the beginning of January of that year. Dewey must have welcomed a teacher who had studied and taught with a man whose educational philosophy so closely agreed with his own. He frankly admitted that he was able to provide his teachers with "question marks, rather than with fixed rules."[4]

Not having worked out any system of his own for teaching beginners to read, and thinking highly of what Parker, the practitioner, was doing, Dewey, with one of Parker's teachers on hand, apparently took over the word method in some such form as it was used in the Colonel's work. The quotation above (pp. 128 ff.) giving his sentiments about reading at the elementary level indicates that he was in agreement with the pedagogical philosophy behind the word method.

It does not lie within the province of this investigation to give in detail the steps by which Dewey's Laboratory School and the projected Chicago Institute of Colonel Parker and Mrs. Blaine merged into one institution. The account of this "merger" has been given by McCaul;[5] here we will merely note that it took place. The death of the Colonel may have prompted the consolidation. One of Parker's last public appearances was at the ground-breaking ceremonies for Emmons Blaine Hall on June 28, 1901.

---

[3] Ida B. De Pencier, *History of the Laboratory Schools* (Chicago, 1960), p. 19, says that Parker and most of his faculty resigned from the City Normal in June, 1899. Since there was not yet a building for the Chicago Institute, the faculty was given a year's leave of absence with pay, to study or to travel abroad.

[4] John Dewey, *School and Society* (Chicago, 1899), p. 116.

[5] See Robert L. McCaul, "Dewey and the University of Chicago," *School and Society*, LXXXIX (1961), 152–57; April 8, 179–83; April 22, 202–6.

He officially broke the ground on that occasion and delivered an address which ended with a quotation from Froebel: "Come let us live with the children."[6] In the fall of the same year he became ill and died on March 2, 1902. His friend and colleague John Dewey succeeded him as Director of the School of Education.[7]

By the time of Parker's death the model elementary school in which students in the School of Education did their practice teaching had attracted wide and favorable notice. When the National Council of Education met at Charleston, S. C., in 1900, Dr. B. A. Hinsdale of the University of Michigan said: "More eyes are now fixed upon The University Elementary School at Chicago than upon any other elementary school in the country and probably in the world."[8] Soon after Parker's death and Dewey's succession to his office, Dewey's school and The University Elementary School were merged into the present Laboratory Schools of the University of Chicago.

As a part of a new university, rising rapidly to national and international prominence, the School of Education was in a fortunate position. Three great men—President Harper, Colonel Parker, and John Dewey—had participated in its founding. It drew students from all over this country and from abroad. Wherever elementary teachers trained in the school went, the fame of the "New Education" went too, and took with it as one of its features the word method. In this way, a method of teaching reading which had been first tried out in Germany under the inspiration of Gedike, followed in this country by Keagy and others, and put into practice by Colonel Parker, among others, came to occupy a prominent place in a new system of education to which the adjective "Progressive" was applied.

None of the other so-called methods of teaching reading then in vogue fitted so well into the pattern of the new educational program. Such leaders as Dewey and Hall, and others whose names are not so well known, endorsed the

---

[6] De Pencier, *op. cit.,* p. 23.

[7] McCaul, *op. cit.,* p. 179, describes the circumstances under which Dewey succeeded Parker.

[8] Quoted in De Pencier, *op. cit.,* p. 16.

educational philosophy of the word method. Among those who approved it, G. Stanley Hall stood out because of the quality of his scholarship and the effectiveness of his teaching and writing. Moreover, unlike many of his contemporaries, Hall examined, to some extent at least, the modern history of the teaching of reading. His study in this area had left him with some ideas that may appear startling to one who comes upon them for the first time.

In 1886 Hall brought out a forty-page brochure: *How to Teach Reading, and What to Read in School.* In 1911 he drew heavily upon, and more than doubled the size of, this earlier effort in the ninth chapter of Volume II of his *Educational Problems.* He had read extensively about the teaching of reading as it had been investigated and practiced in Europe, notably in Germany. This approach was natural for a man who held a German Ph.D. degree. At the outset he named and discussed the two methods of teaching reading —the synthetic and the analytic. He gave in some detail an account of the work of Ickelsamer and his efforts to have the child analyze words into their sounds. He mentioned the efforts that had been made to help the child over the stumbling block of learning the ABC's and their sounds by using raisins, candy, and nuts as rewards. All kinds of things, such as ABC blocks, pictures, songs, and reading machines, were used in this connection. But he felt the child's difficulty with letters had been exaggerated: "That the letter-names are themselves far easier than is commonly thought for bright children has been often illustrated by good pedagogic methods; as, e.g., in the case of Mrs. John Wesley, who, after exciting high expectations and interest, dressed her children in their best clothes, and taught them the alphabet in a day."[9]

Nowhere in this chapter, however, or anywhere else, did Hall give any clue to what he considered the fundamental nature of the reading process, nor did he pinpoint precisely the child's first task in learning to read competently. Omissions of this kind suggest that perhaps Hall had not thought his way through these problems. In studying him one gets

[9] G. Stanley Hall, *Educational Problems* (New York, 1911), II, 403.

the impression that the only kind of reading he was interested in was "true reading," that is, reading done "when the
act has become so secondarily automatic that it can be forgotten and attention be given solely to the subject matter.
Its assimilation is true reading and all else is only the whir
of the machinery and not the work it does."[10]

He felt that the sooner the mechanical features of learning to read were mastered, "so that reading is rapid, sure,
and free, the sooner the mind can attend to the subject-
matter. . . . There appears to come to many children a
period, lasting perhaps many months, between the age of
five and eight, when both interest and facility in learning to
read culminate; and if this period passes unutilized, they
learn it with greater difficulty and at a certain disadvantage."[11]

This last sentence should be kept in mind in reading the
following:

> The best pedagogues are now drifting surely, if slowly, toward
> the conclusion that instead of taking half the time of the first
> year or two of school to teach reading, *little attention should be
> paid to it before the beginning of the third year,* that nature
> study, language work, and other things should take the great
> time and energy now given to this subject. Huey collected nearly
> one hundred primers, and classifies reading methods as alpha-
> betic, phonic, phonetic, word, sentence, and combination meth-
> ods. The true teacher will not entirely neglect any of these
> methods, and psychology has little respect for or even recogni-
> tion of the absurd stress laid upon petty variations by the mod-
> ern primer maker. Their analysis in this field has fallen far
> behind practical needs, and has brought methods into too great
> prominence. We can agree with Huey that the home is the natural
> place for a child's learning to read, and intelligent children of
> intelligent parents, will almost do so of themselves sooner or
> later. Primary reading should no longer be made a fetich. This
> should always be secondary and should have a purpose—that is,
> there should be no reading for the sake of reading, for this is
> never an end, but should always be a means of gratifying an

[10] *Ibid.,* p. 445.

[11] *Ibid.,* p. 408. In connection with what Hall says here, compare recent
evidence on the phenomenon known as "imprinting" and discussions of
"the critical period hypothesis." See A. C. Ramsay and E. H. Hess, "A
Study of Imprinting," in D. E. Dulany, Jr., *et al., Contributions to Modern
Psychology* (New York, Oxford, 1963), pp. 10–18, and J. P. Scott, "Critical
Periods in Behavioral Development," *Science,* CXXXVIII (1962), 949–58.

interest. There should be much practice in silent reading, and there should be more oral work until speech habits are well developed. Most primers should vanish and so should mere exercises. The vacuity of the content of primers is deplorable, and the matter of most of them should be radically reviewed. . . . Patrick would have books, pens, and pencils kept away from children until they are ten, and all instruction come directly from objects and the voice of the teacher.[12]

It is certainly strange and inconsistent that Hall should approve, or at least condone, the postponement of the child's learning to read until "both interest and facility in" acquiring the art had culminated, and he could master the skill only "with greater difficulty and at a certain disadvantage."

Hall apparently never had any experience as a teacher of reading, but he reported impressively the results of experiments that had been made in this field, saying:

This is not the place to analyse in detail the many *psycho-physic processes involved in the act of reading,* which in recent years has been made the subject of manifold and fruitful investigations, but we must briefly résumé the pedagogical results of this work, which have established a number of approximate norms and given such a wealth of educational suggestions despite the fact that but relatively few of these studies have been made upon children. . . .

Nearly all reading methods now start from the word and sentence rather than from the letter, and these are more often chosen for their form value than for their thought value. Becker shows that words are *first recognized as wholes* from their gross forms rather than from the letters that compose them, and Messmer showed that in the tachistoscope long words may be recognized as rapidly as short ones, but that they tend to be analysed into small groups of letters. Cattell and Sanford showed that certain letters and combinations in ordinary small type are recognized far easier than others, and there are many indications that the consonants are more important than vowels for recognition.[13]

This paragraph should be taken in connection with one on a preceding page:

In fine, the growing agreement that there is no one and only orthodox way of teaching and learning this greatest and hardest

12 Hall, *op. cit.,* II, 417–18.
13 *Ibid.,* pp. 409, 414.

of all the arts, in which ear, mouth, eye, and hand must each in turn train the others to automatic perfection, in ways hard and easy, by devices old and new, mechanically and consciously, actively and passively, by things familiar and unknown, and by alternately resting and modulating from one set of faculties to another, tends to secure mental unity and school economy, both intellectual and material—and this is a great gain, and seems now secure. But there is still very much to be learned, which only long and painstaking pedagogical experiment and observation can reveal, respecting the most sanative and normal sequence and proportion of all these ways, respecting which there is still much difference of opinion and practice. Not merely the native powers of children, but those of teachers should be studied and given free scope. The natural tact for some special and partial method which so many teachers have should be encouraged and not suppressed by the printed official course or program.

While a good pedagogic method is one of the most economic— of both labor and of money—of all inventions, we should never forget that the brightest children, and indeed most children, if taught individually at home, need but very few refinements of method like the above.[14]

Hall knew that illiteracy was abroad in the land. He cited the census of 1900 to the effect that "the percentage of illiterates over ten years of age in this country ranged all the way from 2.3 per cent in Nebraska which led, to 5.9 per cent in Massachusetts, the twenty-fifth state, and ending with Louisiana, the forty-ninth [sic], with 38.5 per cent— all this as against .16 per cent in Prussia." The figures he cited did not unduly discourage him. He went on to point out:

Very many men have lived and died and been great, even the leaders of their age, without any acquaintance with letters. The knowledge which illiterates acquire is probably on the whole more personal, direct, environmental and probably a much larger proportion of it practical. Moreover, they escape much eye-strain and mental excitement, and, other things being equal, are probably more active and less sedentary. It is possible, despite the stigma our bepedagogued age puts upon this disability, for those who are under it not only to lead a useful, happy, virtuous life, but to be really well educated in many other ways. Illiterates escape certain temptations, such as vacuous and vicious reading. Perhaps we are prone to put too high a value both upon the ability required to attain this art and the discipline involved in

14 *Ibid.,* pp. 408–9.

doing so, as well as the culture value that comes to the citizen with his average of only six grades of schooling by the acquisition of this art.

When we reflect how long it took the race to invent script and printing and realize the many intricate stages by which all the processes involved were developed historically, and when we learn again from analytic laboratory psychology how complex all the processes are, it seems almost a marvel that children learn it so quickly and easily, even with the worst methods of teaching, and the question may naturally arise whether the experience of the relatively few generations of readers through which we have descended may not have contributed some degree of facilitization. There is, of course, no answer possible to this problem. Wits have suggested that as the inheritance of stressed qualities gets in its work ever earlier in the individuals as generations pass, the time may come when children will be born with ability to talk and that yet later they may learn to read and write by innate and untaught instinct. Now, perhaps, too, familiar acquaintance with the experimental laboratory work on the reading processes may tend to make elementary teachers feel that read-writing is harder than it really is for children, and also incline them to hyper-methodical teaching. We must not forget that for school work both processes are arbitrary and utterly without reason and so must be inculcated chiefly by pure mechanical drill and incessant practice with little attempt at explanation. It comes by blind habituation in which even logical arrangement of steps has only a rudimentary place. Learning to read and write, however we look at it, is thus an almost purely mechanical product of drill, with almost nothing rational or even educational about it. Teaching it is a breaking-in process. Save historically (which is a far cry for children) there is no reason why one letter should represent a given sound any more than any other. A Morse code, numbers, pictures of the hand in making the deaf mute alphabet, or any other form of letter e.g., Arabic, a cypher would be no more and no less reasonable. Hence most time spent in explaining is lost and in fact usually worse than lost, for it is farfetched and adds to the confusion in the child's mind. *Per se*, too, it is anti-educational because it does not develop but constrains both sense and mentation. But for the content to be got at or imparted by mastering the process, the necessity of read-writing would be an almost unmitigated curse to the human race. It is a psycho-physiological absurdity. All is form, capricious and fantastic, and there is no content. It is almost literally mind-breaking, as we break colts to the harness that they may by its use render more valuable service. Hence the less we appeal to consciousness the better. . . . If the teacher followed a fully perfected method which involved a logical sequence of every step that scientific analysis reveals, it is doubtful if any pupil could ever learn to read or write.[15]

This brief glance at Hall's attitude toward reading prepares one for his hearty endorsement of Colonel Parker and of Parker's elementary program of education, including reading instruction. It was for a time his custom to visit Cook County every year, "to set my educational watch," as he said in one of his letters to Colonel Parker.[16]

At the time Colonel Parker's word method was getting the firm support of those enthusiastic about the "New Education," the teaching of reading in the public schools was in a state of great confusion. An indication of how great this confusion was has been seen in the comments made by Dr. Rice. Amid this bedlam, the work Colonel Parker and his teachers were doing had many things to commend it. It did not make a fetish out of reading. This subject, which had exercised virtual rulership in the older dispensation, had now to share attention with a host of other subjects. The ability on the part of the pupil to read fluently had formerly been regarded as an accurate indication of how well his education was progressing. In the new order of things, reading was no longer used as a measuring stick.

Educational leaders of the time were convinced that Hall was correct about the error of exalting reading. This excellent scholar had cited notables of ancient times who could not read, mentioning the medieval knights, Charlemagne, and even the Mother of Jesus. He praised the "learning" of the unlettered and thought that in not a few respects they had the advantage of their literate brothers. He was convinced, and sought to convince others, that a person might be very well educated indeed and not know a letter in the book. These educational leaders knew very well that in reducing the stress on reading they were initiating a program which would delay a child's learning to read. But they were sure this delay was one of the most advantageous things about the "New Education." They felt sure that the child's mental equipment, and his physical development as

[15] *Ibid.*, pp. 443–44, 445.
[16] Lawrence A. Cremin, *Transformation of the School* (New York, 1961), p. 135.

well, were not up to the demands of reading before he was eight or ten years old. They did not mention just which educational experiments they relied upon to document this view, but of its accuracy they had no doubt.

Educators were also favorably impressed by the argument that a word is as easy to learn as a letter, and that it makes a far more pleasant impression on a child than a letter could possibly make. They carefully observed the desirability of so arranging things that at every point the pleasure of the child was served. Formerly the child's happiness had played no role at all. He took what instruction was offered him and did at least passably well with it, or he was thrashed. But now the pendulum, which never stops in the middle of its swing, went to the other extreme. The school was to be centered about the growing child; his wishes were to be of paramount concern. It would certainly be rash to attribute this new attitude to teachers alone; parents were also inclining to this view. The teachers could not have stemmed the tide of permissiveness that was setting in.

PUBLIC EXCITEMENT
OVER READING

In the manner briefly traced in the preceding chapters, the word method, as it is at present understood, received the favorable notice of leaders in the comprehensive elementary program known at first as the "New Education" and later as "Progressive Education." During the first two decades of the present century, the new reading method enlarged and firmly secured the beachhead it had established by 1900.

As has been emphasized, the method was suited to the spirit of the times. The much older ABC method, on the other hand, was entirely contrary to the philosophy rapidly coming to prevail in elementary education. The major objection to having children learn the letters and their sounds and proceed thus to reading and spelling through a long continued and montonous routine was that this way did not please the child. As never before, the child had come into his own. His pleasure must now be consulted; his endorsement of anything done for him had first to be obtained.

As a pleasant pastime for children, the old method of teaching reading had a miserably poor record. Involved in this record were long tedious hours of doing nothing on the child's part, and, even worse, the generous application of tough switches to his innocent back—a program not at all calculated to endear learning to the little man. But all that was behind him now; his sufferings were over; his wishes were urgently sought and carefully observed.

During the two decades or more that the "New Education"—and the word method with it—was solidifying its position in American elementary schools, treatises on the subject of reading and the teaching of reading poured off the presses in a steady stream. To examine and digest even a major portion of them would greatly exceed the limits of the present undertaking. The literature is largely repetitious, so it is possible to get the essence of what was said without attempting a comprehensive reading.

At the very beginning of the century, Dr. Rudolf R. Reeder, an instructor in the theory and practice of teaching at Columbia University, wrote a small but influential book on *The Historical Development of School Readers and of Method in Teaching Reading.* In this work, Reeder devoted some space to the various methods and devices used to master the mechanics of reading, "after the breaking away from the alphabet routine." To show the thoroughness with which he went into this aspect of his subject, it is sufficient to list the elements he enumerated as entering into the problem of reading. He divided them into those that were "Fundamental" and those that were "Accessory." Under the first heading he listed: the idea; the sign or graphic symbol; the sound or spoken word. The "Accessory" elements involved were: the object; the picture; the group— or the relation of the ideas; the writing of the word; the psychology of the process; the physiology of the process. Reeder concluded this enumeration with the remark: "It will be observed that there are enough factors involved in the problem to offer a very wide range of permutations."[1]

In Reeder's treatment of reading this sentence occurred: "The earliest proposed substitute for the alphabet method was the word and picture method suggested by Comenius."[2] Nothing could be further from the truth than that Comenius for a moment thought of setting aside the traditional ABC method for teaching a child to read his own language; but this misleading statement by Reeder has been responsible for including Johann Amos Comenius (1592–1670), the cele-

[1] Rudolph Rex Reeder, *Historical Development of School Readers* (New York, 1900), pp. 74 ff.
[2] *Ibid.*, p. 68.

brated Moravian educator, among the endorsers of the word method.

This erroneous attribution came about in a peculiar way. In 1887, C. W. Bardeen, an editor and publisher in Syracuse, New York, brought out *The Orbis Pictus of John Amos Comenius*. This little volume was a reproduction of a translation of the *Orbis Sensualium Pictus* ("The World of Sense Objects Pictured") of 1657 by Comenius. He wrote his *Orbis* primarily to assist students of Latin, but he hoped it might also help a child learn to read his own language more readily. It contained about one hundred and fifty composite pictures, showing all kinds of objects of everyday life. Each object pictured was named in both German and Latin.

As soon as the *Orbis* appeared, Charles Hoole, then in charge of a Latin school in London, translated it for the use of students of Latin. In rendering Comenius' preface to the reader, Hoole wrote:

> First it will afford a Device for learning to read more easily than hitherto; especially having a Symbolic Alphabet set before it, to wit, the Characters of the several Letters, with the Image of that creature, whose voice that letter goeth about to imitate, pictured by it. For the young Abc-Scholar, will easily remember the force of every Character by the very looking upon the Creature, till the imagination being strengthened by use, can readily afford all things. And then, having looked over *a Table of the chief Syllables* also (which yet was not thought necessary to be added to this Book) he may proceed to the viewing of the Pictures, and the Inscriptions set over them. Where again the very looking upon the thing Pictured, suggesting the name of the thing, will tell him how the Title of the Picture is to be read. And thus the whole Book being gone over by the bare Titles of the Pictures, Reading cannot but be learned; and indeed too, which thing is to be noted, without using any ordinary tedious spelling, that most troublesome torture of wits.

Dr. Reeder, coming upon this passage in Bardeen's volume of 1887, selected most of the last part of it, beginning "The very looking upon the thing"; and ignoring what Comenius had said about the alphabet and syllables "For the young Abc-Scholar," he concluded that Comenius in 1657 had advocated a word method of teaching a child to read his own language. The most notable of those who have recently cited Reeder as authority for crediting Comenius with "recommending a 'word recognition' or 'look-and-say' method" is Dr. Arthur I. Gates of Columbia.[3]

As was shown in chapter 7, it was Dr. Reeder who found that Bulwer-Lytton favored a word method approach to teaching to read.[4] This attribution has also become a part of the orthodoxy of the modern word method and has gained wide currency both here and abroad.[5]

Dr. Reeder wrote at a time when methods, so called, of teaching reading were very numerous. Edmund Burke Huey, in 1908, listed the methods "that are in common use today" as the "alphabetic, phonic, phonetic, word, sentence and combination method." A little further on in his discussion of methods, Huey virtually withdrew the alphabet method from consideration. He said: "The alphabet method, used almost universally in Greece and Rome, and in European countries generally until well into the nineteenth century, and which was nearly universal in America until about 1870, is now chiefly of historical interest."[6]

Thus, according to Dr. Huey, the "methods-competition" at the time he wrote and for a decade or more later did not involve the ABC method, but, rather, different applications of the look-and-say method. Huey concluded his thirty-five page chapter on "Present-Day Methods" with an endorsement of that method by Flora J. Cooke of the Francis Parker School who wrote him that she had had "nearly twenty years' experience" with it.[7]

There is no question but that the one man most responsible for the triumph of the word method was Colonel Francis Parker. Among the means he employed for advancing the cause must be reckoned his ardent love for children and the tears he so often shed in their behalf. A teacher left this testimonial of him:

---

[3] See *School and Society*, November 3, 1962, pp. 370–75.

[4] Reeder, *op. cit.*, p. 78.

[5] William Murray and L. W. Downes, *Children Learn to Read* (London, 1955), pp. 27–28. These scholars also accepted what Reeder said about Comenius (see p. 31).

[6] Edmund Burke Huey, *Psychology and Pedagogy* (New York, 1908), p. 265.

[7] *Ibid.*, p. 300.

I had a class with Colonel Parker (Summer, 1901) in the Kozminski School. Often have I said his lectures changed completely my teaching career. He'd hold his dear, broad, fat hands out in gesture and the tears would slip down as he would plead with us for consecration to teaching—especially for understanding the children.[8]

One of the Colonel's most experienced teachers was Flora J. Cooke. Her third-grade children, she said, could "read, with ease, fluency, and pleasure, almost anything one can put into their hands." The success which she had with the method in the Francis Parker School on the Near North Side of Chicago was not being duplicated on the South Side of the city in the Laboratory School of the University of Chicago.

Ida B. De Pencier pointed out that "In spite of the outstanding program in reading in the Elementary grades, there were always pupils who were in need of additional instruction, over and above what the teacher had time to give." This condition continued in the Laboratory School, with the result that in the autumn of 1944 The University of Chicago Reading Clinics were set up.[9] They have fulfilled a continuing need, and now have a waiting list of parents anxious to enroll their children.

The thought on the part of the instigators of the new program of elementary education was that reading should take its turn with many other subjects just as important for the child's educational development. They were convinced that the new program which they had worked out would so please a child and so inspire him with a zeal to learn to read that the acquisition of the skill would come easily. Arousing the child's desire, his intense interest, his determination to read was the crux of the situation. Flora J. Cooke expressed it well: "In the use of any of the so-called successful methods, the teacher invariably fails until she discovers some stimulus which reacts upon the will power of the children. They must first desire to read; after the desire is awakened the child will learn by any method, with or without a school. He will find a teacher."[10]

[8] Ida B. De Pencier, *History of the Laboratory Schools* (Chicago, 1960), p. 17.

[9] *Ibid.*, p. 154. Such clinics had, of course, been needed for centuries.

[10] *Course of Study*, I (1900), 111.

While teachers and educators were thinking and writing in this vein, there lived on among the people an ancient belief that the ability to read was a reliable index of how well a child had been taught in school. Parents understood from what little they read and heard about how reading was being taught in school that a much easier and better method had been found. They at once equated "better" with "faster" and felt comfortable about the matter.

Many people were thus entirely unprepared for the startling situation uncovered during World War I. At that time, when tests were given 1,522,256 American soldiers, 24.9 per cent proved unable to read and write well enough to perform the simple tasks assigned them.[11] These results were explained by May Ayres Burgess. She said, "this deficiency was not caused by their [the soldiers'] never having learned to read." She explained that the overwhelming majority of the soldiers had learned to read in the primary grades but had forgotten the skill before they reached early manhood.[12] This forgetting on a large scale will be discussed later.

It was not long until other disturbing discoveries about reading came to the attention of the public. Only a few of these can be touched upon here. About 1936, according to Florence C. Coyle, Associate Editor of *Speech Magazine,* "a survey of the reading ability of children in the Chicago area showed that a high percentage in the seventh grade was only on the third-grade level in reading. The teachers seemed to think that they were up against a local problem. Mrs. Henderson pointed out again and again in *Speech Magazine* how urgent it was to recognize the condition as nation-wide rather than local. But ours was just a tiny voice whispering in the wilderness."[13]

Ten years later, in 1946, Professor George H. Henry, the principal of a high school in Dover, Delaware, wrote an article, "Can Your Child Really Read?" which appeared in *Harper's Magazine.* At the outset he spoke of how

[11] William S. Gray, *Summary of Investigations Relating to Reading* (Chicago, 1925), p. 14.

[12] May Ayres Burgess, *Measurement of Silent Reading* (New York, 1921), pp. 11–12.

[13] Ellen C. Henderson, *You Can Teach a Child That Reading Can be Fun* (New York, 1956), p. 7.

"sobered" educators were by the "human material with which they work." He said:

When educators write for one another they envelop their statements in a cloak of pedagogic lingo in order that as public servants they may not be charged with lack of faith in democracy. Yet it is common gossip inside the profession that at least a third of the entire secondary school population—grades nine to twelve—are incapable of mastering the stock tools of learning (reading and writing) well enough to profit from textbook instruction. . . .

The pupils who compose this lower one-third are not to be confused with the mentally backward. . . . The great majority of them are normal, wholesome, even talented, responsible youth. They are, to put it simply, non-verbal. Of the six and two-thirds million on the high school rolls in 1940, easily two and one-half million belong to this group.[14]

Professor Henry's suggestion was that the taxpayers dig deeper into their pockets and provide the needed funds for the high schools to secure pictures and to build up film libraries for these non-verbal millions. He concluded his article with a warning to Americans to "recognize that because of the pressure of this non-verbal third on an educational system which is helpless to deal with them, precious little education, even for the others, is now going on."

Dr. William S. Gray (1885–1960), the greatest of the reading experts of his time, has been cited as having found that one half of the adult population of this country is "functionally illiterate," that is, they are not able to read with ordinary comprehension books and magazines addressed to the general public.[15] Dr. Rudolf Flesch brought out his most disturbing book, *Why Johnny Can't Read,* in 1955. Public alarm at what seemed to be going on in the elementary and high schools spread more widely. School people shared in the discontent with things as they were. The Progressive Educational Association expired the year Flesch's book appeared, and two years later its official journal also died. Lawrence A. Cremin said that the mourners at both funerals were a "pitifully small group."[16]

14 *Harper's Magazine,* CXCII (January, 1946), 72–76.
15 Cited in James D. Koerner, *The Case for Basic Education* (Boston, 1959), p. 106.
16 Lawrence A. Cremin, *Transformation of the School* (New York, 1961), p. vii.

The decline of faith in Progressive Education involved the new analytical look-and-say method of teaching to read which came in with it. This radical departure had been suspect by many from the beginning. As illiteracy among adults, as well as among high-school seniors and college students, became more widely known the number of critics of the "look and guess" method increased. Reading experts were not in the least disposed to forsake the modern way; but as a rule they did not explain to parents that the new elementary education program was not designed to teach children to read more quickly but to give them better and broader training. There was certainly no lack of material and arguments, as has been shown in chapter 12. Perhaps many parents would have been reassured by G. Stanley Hall's kind words in behalf of illiteracy and illiterates and with his endorsement of the plan to have children pay little attention to reading before their third year in school.

At least one educator, the principal of a junior high school in Champaign, Illinois, proceeded along sound historical lines in justifying what the schools were doing when he wrote:

Through the years we've built a sort of halo around reading, writing and arithmetic. We've said they were for everybody—rich and poor, brilliant and not-so-mentally-endowed, one who liked them and those who failed to go for them.
We shall some day accept the thought that it is just as illogical to assume that every boy must be able to read as it is that each one must be able to perform on a violin, that it is no more reasonable to require that each girl shall spell well than it is that each one shall bake a good cherry pie.

This educator, harking back to the principles of the earlier leaders in Progressive Education, must have anticipated that the task of persuading modern parents would be difficult, for he went on to say: "A lot of us are going to have to do the best job of our lives in the matter of public relations. We shall need to make a sale to many of our classroom teachers and to John Q. Public. It will not be easy."[17]

The author of this article was entirely correct in thinking

[17] Albert Lynd, *Quackery in the Public Schools* (Boston, 1953), pp. 45–46. Lynd gives this as coming from A. H. Lauchner in *News-Gazette* (Champaign, Ill.), February 14, 1951.

it would not be easy to sell the view of reading he endorsed and that education's "greats" had approved orally and in writing at the beginning of the century. No matter what the parents who sent their children to John Dewey's experimental school thought sixty years ago, those who are concerned about their children's education today regard the ability to read as an absolute prerequisite to an education. They are convinced that there is a hierarchy in school courses, and that reading heads all the others. The educator who tries to reconcile them to any other view is merely shaking hands with the east wind. And those who, with Professor Henry of Dover, tell the parents that a third of their children do not have what it takes to learn to read need not expect to convince anybody except their colleagues. The fact is that the whole attitude toward the elementary school program is today quite different from what educational leaders at the beginning of the century thought it should be.

Those who have maintained the superiority of the word method as a way of teaching a child to read quickly have often succeeded in promoting themselves professionally, but they have not always enhanced their reputations as scholarly persons in the estimation of scholars in other disciplines. The fact is that the method, prior to its adoption, had never been scientifically tested in competition with any other. This assertion will be challenged by many devoted practitioners. All anyone has to do to refute it, however, is to give the details of the experiment: who conducted it, for how long, involving how many children, how many teachers, and so forth.[18]

In response to public pressure, the best informed of those interested in the reading problem in the public schools twenty years ago realized that modifications would have to be made in the word method, that in its unadulterated form it had weaknesses of a kind that could no longer be tolerated. One of the most glaring of its defects was that it did not provide the child with any way of mastering words independently; he had to be told what every new word was.

[18] Gray, *op. cit.*, did not refer to any such testing.

This meant that children in higher grades were handicapped by their limited reading vocabularies. One way around this difficulty was to rewrite the things the children needed most to read in the small number of words which they knew. Some work of this kind was done, but what may have been the most stupendous undertaking of this sort ever conceived, has never, so far as I know, been undertaken. In the heyday of this fervor for rewriting everything down to the level of the average child's vocabulary, I was approached by an educator who wanted to rewrite the *Encyclopaedia Britannica,* not once but three times! The first of his projected versions was to be in a vocabulary of 3,000 words, the next in one of 7,000 words, and the third in a 10,000 word version. He hoped that I might assist him by recommending his project to the press where I was then employed.

By 1948, on the basis of what he knew was being felt by schoolmen and parents, Dr. William S. Gray set forth such auxiliary helps as, in his opinion, should be used with the word method to overcome the objections made to it. The foreword of his book, *On Their Own in Reading,* was written by Dr. Artley, Associate Professor of Education and Director of the Child Study Clinic in the University of Missouri. In this foreword, Dr. Artley said:

> For a generation the teaching of word-attack skills was almost a lost art. During this period some educators, in their anxiety to modify the false emphasis of the past, openly challenged the necessity of any word-attack skills at all—in particular, phonetics. Reading instruction in general gradually deteriorated at this vital point. As a result, children came from our schools poorly if not totally unprepared for independent attack on new words in their reading on their own.
>
> Public pressure finally forced a re-evaluation of word-perception skills and demanded a properly balanced reading program that included them. Fully aware of this great need, Dr. William S. Gray developed such a program.

We cannot concern ourselves with Dr. Gray's treatise here. Perhaps the most arresting statement in his book is this: "The recent trend toward reinstating the purely mechanical word-perception programs of the old alphabetic or phonic method is viewed with alarm by educators who are interested in promoting growth in reading power."[19]

The Harvard University Graduate School of Education recently undertook to find out what preparation is being given to teachers of reading and to make recommendations for improving this preparation. Mary C. Austin in *The Torch Lighters* (1961) gives the report of those detailed to make the investigation. The investigators secured the assistance of six hundred and thirty-eight faculty members, in the education departments of seventy-four institutions distributed over the country. It is surprising that in an investigation of this nature, those under indictment, as it were, for bearing considerable responsibility for existing conditions, should be the ones invited to pass judgment on their own shortcomings and to suggest remedies for improving upon their own performance. The report makes it clear at the outset that public pressure had no small part in calling for such an investigation. "That such improvement must take place is obvious. Professional educators and the general public are demanding better instruction in reading in the elementary schools in order that children may cope with the challenges of the coming decade."

The foreword supplies an expansion on this theme:

> Whether Johnny learns to read is no longer a matter of concern only to him, to his teacher, and to his parents. The national interest is now involved, and the subject has even come to Presidential attention. In the chapter on Goals in Education, printed with the Report of the President's Commission on National Goals, John W. Gardner pointed out that, 'Some subjects are more important than others. Reading is the most important of all.'
>
> Nor is Mr. Gardner the only observer of the educational scene to reach this conclusion. James B. Conant, whose reports on American schools have been read from coast to coast and whose judgment reflects the views of many educators and interested laymen, puts heavy stress on the need for a sound program in the teaching of reading if the high school program is to succeed. Teachers and parents alike are agreed that if a child does not learn to read well, many doors will be forever closed to him. Everyone says that something ought to be done about it. . . .
>
> At long last, the public has become interested in what is, with-

19 William S. Gray, *On Their Own in Reading* (Chicago, 1948), p. 32.

out any doubt, one of the key aspects of a good system of schools.[20]

To one acquainted with previous attitudes in this troubled area, these statements are most remarkable. The idea that some school subjects are more important than others and that reading is most important of all is positively ancient. The last sentence quoted above about the public's having "at long last" become interested in having its children taught to read is a surprising and obvious twisting of the facts. The public has never doubted "that if a child does not learn to read well, many doors will be forever closed to him." Educational leaders, especially Dewey and Hall, the David and Jonathan of Progressive Education, had long ago departed from the ancient concepts.

Another remarkable part of the report of this investigation shows the sentiment of those questioned about the use of the ABC's in teaching beginners to read. The report says:

An issue of some controversy appears in the question: Should beginning readers be taught the names and forms of letters apart from simple words? If so, when? Before the words, or simultaneously with the words (sight vocabulary)?

In the present survey, only a few persons . . . endorsed the method of teaching names and forms of letters before the sight vocabulary. The majority of the respondents, or 61 per cent, held that it should be a simultaneous process. A large minority of 171, or 27 per cent, on the other hand, maintained that the beginner should have no formal training in the names and forms of letters.

One instructor of the majority group stated that letters should be taught simultaneously with a sight vocabulary, provided that the child also learned 'other word recognition and attack skills (phonetic and structural analysis) along with meaningful story content.' Still another said that 'because of the importance of phonetic analysis for the attainment of independence in reading, it is advisable to teach the child not only the letters of the alphabet, but also their sounds and simple combinations as needed.'[21]

The view of sixty-one per cent of the respondents that words and letters should be taught simultaneously is particularly interesting in view of the fact, as was shown in chapter 5 above, that this is precisely what Taylor said was

[20] Mary C. Austin, *The Torch Lighters* (Cambridge, Mass., 1961), p. xi.
[21] *Ibid.*, pp. 124–25.

being done with excellent results in the district schools of New York by 1834. It was the technique endorsed by the county superintendents of New York in their convention at Syracuse in 1845, whose approval of it secured for them the lyrical praise of Horace Mann. It was the method which Superintendent Rickoff said was used in the schools of Cincinnati in 1857, and Superintendent Wells of Chicago, a short time later, hoped could be introduced into the schools of his city.

Because of the widespread dissatisfaction in this country with the reading results following from conventional approaches, a number of what are usually referred to as "phonic systems" are now being tried out. All of these are akin in that they provide for teaching letters and sounds at the beginning of the child's instruction in reading. Walcutt listed and discussed such of these systems as had been used with success up to the time he wrote.[22] Others have since appeared. Two systems of a distinctive kind are coming increasingly into public notice and merit attention in the following chapters. We shall consider first what is often referred to as the Bloomfield method or linguistic approach to reading.

[22] Charles C. Walcutt, *Tomorrow's Illiterates* (Boston, 1961), pp. 141–63.

READING REGULARLY
SPELLED WORDS FIRST

Joseph Neef was an Alsatian disciple of the great educator Pestalozzi. In 1803 he opened a Pestalozzian school in Paris, and three years later came to this country at the request of an American philanthropist who wished to introduce Pestalozzianism into the educational system of the United States.

In 1813 Neef brought out in Philadelphia a book on teaching children to read. In this work he tried to develop an idea that had come to him in his efforts to learn English. He had observed in his study that while much of English is spelled irregularly—that is, unalphabetically—much of it is not. In his book on reading he proposed that the child in learning to read should have to deal only with words spelled in a regular manner. Once the child had gained confidence by grappling successfully with words spelled as they sound, he should be advanced little by little to words not alphabetically spelled. Neef was unsuccessful in his efforts to work out an orderly progression of lessons for the child because he did not know enough about the sounds of English or the range of its vocabulary. His book appears to have failed utterly in arousing either interest or understanding.[1]

This same idea of beginning reading instruction with regularly spelled words was suggested in two articles that appeared in 1844 in the *Common School Journal*. Russell's

[1] Joseph Neef, *Methods of Instructing Children Rationally in the Arts of Writing and Reading* (Philadelphia, 1813), pp. 95 ff.

Primer and Primary Reader were there said to have been constructed on this plan. But again the seed somewhat timidly sown fell on stony ground.[2]

The same fate attended a more competent and determined effort to distinguish between good and bad, logical and illogical, spellings in teaching children to read. This effort was made by A. Sonnenschien and J. M. D. Meiklejohn, whose *English Method* appeared in 1869. From what appears to be a competent and flattering review of it, it is clear that the authors proposed to start the child with the regularly spelled words and later to introduce him to those spelled in irregular ways.[3]

The work of these two scholars did not gain the attention of influential educators. In 1879 Meiklejohn continued his efforts in a book called *The Problem of Learning to Read.* In this he pointed out that the beginner should be made familiar with only one function of each letter; his experience in learning to read should never contradict itself. The result would be a steady gain of competency in reading. Dr. Reeder, an advocate of the New Education, pronounced Meiklejohn's method entirely erroneous, saying "English must be learned and read as it is from the start." He further said, "The view presented by Meiklejohn is one-sided and partial. It follows the general tendency of human nature to notice and emphasize exceptions."[4] We shall see later whether Meiklejohn had been led astray by exceptions.

As the nineteenth century advanced, the study of linguistics made progress in many different directions.[5] As scholars became more and more familiar with the English language, they became less and less impressed with the inconsistencies of its spelling. And as for the twentieth century, Sir William Craigie said in 1944: "In many ways, in fact, the usual spelling is much better, phonetically con-

---

2 *Common School Journal,* VI (1844), 271–73, 287–90. The author of these articles identified himself only by the letter R.

3 The reviewer was the Rev. F. W. Farrar, Fellow of the Royal Society, writing in *Macmillan's Magazine,* XXI (November, 1869–April, 1870), 445–48.

4 Rudolph Rex Reeder, *Historical Development of School Readers* (New York, 1900), pp. 70 ff.

5 For an excellent account, see Holger Pedersen, *Linguistic Science in the Nineteenth Century* (Cambridge, Mass., 1931).

sidered, than it is commonly supposed to be. A very large proportion of the words of one or two syllables . . . are written in a way which can leave no doubt whatever as to their pronunciation." G. H. Vallins, in a book published in 1954, said: "Even if we assume a necessary relationship between the spoken and the written word, our spelling is not, in fact, so crazy as we sometimes pretend (or like) to think." Sir James Pitman said in 1961: "English spelling is misleading but it is not all that misleading. One does not fail to be carried along by the context." And in 1962, Professor C. Dean of Queen's University, Kingston, Canada, wrote: "English spelling is a traditional joke, like mothers-in-law. But in each case the mental image that provides the humour does not necessarily have any counterpart in actuality. It is easy, but hardly fair, to cite such words as *plough, cough, rough, bough, though,* and *through* for by the side of these words one could just as easily cite much longer lists such as *bet, bit, bat* and *hat, hit, hot, hut* where the equation of sounds with letters could not be improved."[6]

In 1959 Jean S. and Paul R. Hanna published a remarkable article, *"Spelling As a School Subject."* In this the authors reviewed a century of research undertaken to improve the teaching and learning of spelling. They found that by 1882, if not before, studies of word-frequencies had begun to appear. Within a little less than fifty years, six hundred and twenty-four such investigations were published in the United States. At least 50 of them were concerned with finding out what words are of most frequent use in everyday written communication. From these studies there resulted a basic list of about three thousand words which comprise ninety-eight per cent of those used by children, and by adults in writing.

The Hannas subjected these words to careful phonetic

[6] *Some Arguments For and Against Reformed English Spelling* (Kingston, Ont., 1962), pp. v, vi. Students of English spelling agree that its more illogical features have been exaggerated. At the vocabulary level at which beginners learning to read may well encounter it, English spelling is remarkably alphabetic. Spellings that are not alphabetical constitute a fruitful field for study and appreciation. See G. H. Vallins, *Spelling* (London, 1954), especially pp. 13–49. Also see Robert Hall, Jr., *Sound and Spelling in English* (Philadelphia and New York, 1961). This booklet should be read in its entirety by all those interested in teaching children to read.

analysis. They found that eighty per cent of them are spelled alphabetically. That is, in the spelling of them there is observed a one-letter-one-sound / one-sound-one-letter relationship. Furthermore, the remaining twenty per cent of these words, the authors found, lend themselves very well to grouping into classes of irregularity so that they may be mastered more easily by the pupil. The scholars who made these findings properly regarded them as being "a startling revelation in spelling."[7] With equal justification they might have called attention to the bearing which their work could have on teaching children to read.

Recently the Hannas participated with other educators in directing a research project at Stanford University, sponsored by the United States Office of Education. Their report was given in an article called "The Teaching of Spelling" in the *National Elementary Principal* (November, 1965, pp. 19–28). The object of the investigation was to study in detail, with the aid of computers, "American-English phonemes and the graphemes used to represent them," a phoneme being "the smallest practical unit of speech sound that can serve in a particular language to distinguish one utterance from another," and a grapheme being the "technical name for a phoneme's representation in written or printed form."

In this study seventeen hundred words were subjected to a depth analysis. Among other things, it was discovered that "the correct graphemic option can be predicted for a given occurrence of a phoneme . . . approximately 90 per cent of the time *when the main phonological factors of position in syllables, syllable stress, and internal constraints underlying the orthography are taken into consideration.*" The authors thought that so much stress has at times been laid upon the irregularities of spelling "that we tend to overlook the very high degree of uniformity with which the phonemes of our language are represented in writing." They reported that "today, more and more pre-school children are discovering the delight of using letters to write the

[7] Jean S. and Paul R. Hanna, "Spelling As a School Subject," *National Elementary Principal*, XXXVIII (1959), 8–23.

words they speak and, upon entering the first grade, are already in command of a sizable volume of words they can write (spell) correctly."

Dr. Leonard Bloomfield (1887–1949), an outstanding linguist at the University of Chicago, began in the late 1930's to devote study to the problem of teaching to read. The more he studied the matter, the more he became convinced that the word method or look-and-say was not soundly based on either linguistic or psychological principles. He thought the prevailing method had resulted from (1) the inability of educators to cope with the illogical nature of English spelling and (2) confusion about the basic nature of reading.

With respect to the first of these two aspects of the problem, he prepared, initially, seventy-six lists of monosyllabic words in which there were no inconsistencies of spelling. For example, he had in one group words involving short *a* arranged by initial consonants as *bab, bad, bag, ban, bat,* etc., and by final consonants, *bat, cat, fat, hat,* etc. He listed here perhaps as many as seventy-five words, leaving it to the teacher to use as many as the pupils could master at a time. Reading exercises were interspersed among the word lists. Bloomfield used these lists and readings to teach his two sons, and he was pleased at the ease with which they learned to read. The confusion he thought existed about the nature of reading, and the consequent uncertainty of teachers as to what they should teach, he discussed in an essay which we will consider presently.

Not long after Bloomfield had completed the initial drafts of his lists and essay, one of his students, Clarence L. Barnhart, became interested in teaching his own son to read. Bloomfield thereupon turned over to him his manuscript, suggesting that he not teach his son in the conventional manner but in accordance with a linguistic system. On the basis of the experience Bloomfield had with his sons, he thought it should not take more than six months for a child, properly instructed, to learn to read.

The association between Bloomfield and Barnhart thus begun continued as long as Bloomfield lived. With Barnhart's help, the lists of words Bloomfield had compiled were broken up into units of more manageable length, and more sentences and stories were written. By the summer of 1939 the system, in two hundred and fifty-four lessons with over two hundred and fifty pages of reading material, was available in multigraphed or dittoed form in sufficient quantity to be used in experimental work. But Barnhart was unable to interest authorities at institutions such as Columbia and Johns Hopkins to venture on experimentation. In talking with a friend, Father Stanley Stoga, Assistant Superintendent of the Catholic Schools of Chicago, he spoke of the difficulty he was having. Father Stoga was interested, and after learning more about the method agreed to test it in three or four first-grade classes in one of the schools under his jurisdiction.

The modest test began with perhaps a hundred first-graders in one of the chiefly Polish parishes of Chicago. It proceeded under difficulties. The teachers were not able to depart entirely from their instructional habits, and were also, in the other work of the first grade, compelled to use words not regularly spelled, in violation of the cardinal principle of the reading system they were following. Assisted by coaching from Barnhart and suggestions from Bloomfield, they were soon pleased with their results and especially encouraged by the interest the children were taking in the work.

After this experiment had been going on for a year or two, Barnhart tried to get the University of Chicago Press to sponsor experimental and developmental work with the Bloomfield System. In this connection the Press was invited to send representatives out to the school where work with the system was in progress. A group from the Press, together with Dean Gray from the School of Education, visited the school in question. Father Stoga and Barnhart were also present.

They were taken into a classroom of perhaps forty children who had been taught for a year by the linguistic method. On the teacher's desk were elementary books from various grades. The visitors were invited to select a book and ask any of the children to read from it. The readiness with which the children read was unusual. One of the guests happened to pick up a sixth-grade science book and asked one of the boys to read a passage from it. In doing so the child encountered and read the word "satellite." Father Stoga asked him what the word meant and the child said it meant a big object in the sky. Dean Gray found this answer unsatisfactory, showing that the child was reading, that is pronouncing, quite beyond the vocabulary appropriate to his age, and not getting the sense of what he read. He explained to the other visitors that what the children were doing was in no sense remarkable. He said that reading experts had long known that children could rather quickly be taught to pronounce words with remarkable glibness, but that real reading with understanding of what was read was another matter entirely. He pointed out that these children were mere word-callers, that they were pronouncing well beyond their mental ages, and that they were heading straight for serious trouble later in their reading development.

Experimentation involving the Bloomfield System continued in the Catholic schools of Chicago for ten or twelve years, being used in such parishes as St. Mary of Perpetual Help, St. Romans, and St. Simeon, among others. Over ten thousand pupils learned to read by this linguistic approach, using conventional readers as suppplementary material. The system as applied was never pure Bloomfield, but Bloomfield taught along with other systems. Although irregular words were not introduced into Bloomfield, the other readers containing irregular words were used after the child had started with Bloomfield. Even so this introduction of some regularity into the mass of irregularity resulted in superior reading.

In 1958, an educational foundation helped Barnhart sufficiently to enable him to write new stories, expand the word lists, and edit the whole for publication. About the same time Dr. Harold A. Basilius, Director of Wayne State University Press, became interested in publishing the Bloomfield System. Dr. Basilius had been associated with

Bloomfield at Ohio State University and felt sure that what he said about teaching to read deserved to be widely known. In 1961, a dozen years after the death of Dr. Bloomfield, Barnhart was able to bring out the Bloomfield System in a handsome volume, *Let's Read: A Linguistic Approach.*

Since the publication of this volume Barnhart has arranged the material in units suitable for classroom work. The result is an "Experimental Edition" of nine readers together with workbooks and an ABC book for the use of the child before he begins to read. There are no pictures in the series, as the authors felt they tended to draw the child's attention away from the task at hand. Horace Mann spoke approvingly of omitting pictures from elementary texts.

In the readers used first there are no irregular spellings. At the outset the child is able to rely with confidence on regularity in the symbol-sound relationship in the words with which he deals. Nonsense syllables are provided to enable the teacher to test readily the child's mastery of the symbol-sound pattern he is studying. After regularly spelled words, those that exhibit irregularities are taken up. The most common of them are given first, grouped in a way to facilitate the child's mastery of them.

The system contains about five thousand words. Having mastered such a basic vocabulary the child can read anything he wants to. On the basis of the experimenting done thus far it is estimated that bright children can complete all nine books in a year or a year and a half. Even below-average children get through them in about three years. Under the present system, teachers testing the Bloomfield approach are handicapped by having to introduce in their language arts, spelling, and arithmetic courses, words not regularly spelled. Were it not for this situation, children could complete the nine books of this system in a much shorter time.

In the 1961 volume, *Let's Read,* Bloomfield's essay "Teaching Children to Read" is given in its final form. It is likely to remain for a long time the best exposition of the views of an eminent linguist on the fundamental nature of writing by means of letters and teaching to read what is thus written. The essay is here summarized and generous excerpts given.[8]

Bloomfield thought a consideration of writing was an essential step in understanding how reading is done and how to teach one to read. He described briefly picture writing, word writing, and alphabetic writing. Of this last development he said, "The letters of the alphabet are signs which direct us to produce sounds of our language. A confused and vague appreciation of this fact has given rise to the so-called 'phonic' methods of teaching children to read." He then discussed the phonic method at some length, calling attention to its weaknesses.

The method as he described it is no longer in use, but early in this century various applications of it were employed. Those interested in such approaches to reading tried to do much more than they should in instructing the beginner in phonetics. As Bloomfield said, they went about their work "as though the child were being taught to pronounce—that is, as if the child were being taught to speak." A second error was that of trying to teach the child speech sounds in isolation, when as a matter of fact some of them never occur except in words. The sound which *t* has in such words as *two* or *ten*, for example, is one never occurring alone in English utterance. Bloomfield said, "We intend to apply phonetics to our reading instruction; this does not mean that we are going to try to teach phonetics to young children."

He dealt at some length with "the *sentence method* or *ideational reading.* This method attempts to train the child to get the 'idea' or content directly from the printed page." He explained how this misconception of what the child should be taught to do arose from observing adult professional readers and concluding that the child should be taught to do the same thing. He said:

Even the most elementary understanding of systems of writing suffices to show the fallacy of 'ideational' reading. The kind which can be read ideationally is picture writing. . . .

[8] These excerpts are taken by special permission from *Let's Read: A Linguistic Approach*, by Leonard Bloomfield and Clarence L. Barnhart (© 1961, by Clarence L. Barnhart, all rights reserved).

In word writing and in alphabetic writing, the visible marks are tokens for speech forms and not for "ideas." The visible word marks tell the Chinese reader to speak (out loud or internally) such and such words of his language. The visible letters of alphabetic writing tell us to speak (out loud or internally) such and such phonemes of our language. . . . In short, the black marks on paper which represent an English word, say, h o r s e do not represent the shape or smell or any other characteristics of a horse, or even the "idea" (whatever that may be) of a horse; they merely direct us to utter the speech sounds which make up the English word *horse*. These speech sounds, in turn, are connected for us as a kind of signal, with the animal, and it is only through these speech sounds that the black marks h o r s e on the paper have any connection with the animal, or, if you will, with the "idea" of the animal. The adult's instantaneous step from the black marks to the "idea" is the result of long training. To expect to give this facility directly and without intermediate steps to the child is exactly as though we should try to teach the child higher mathematics (which solves complicated problems with power and speed) before we taught him elementary arithmetic.
. . .

The extreme type of ideational method is the so-called "non-oral" method, where children are not required to pronounce words, but to respond directly to the content. They are shown a printed sentence such as *Skip round the room,* and the correct answer is not to say anything, but to perform the indicated act. Nothing could be less in accord with the nature of our system of writing or with the reading process such as, in the end, it must be acquired.

He pointed out that in spite of special methods which had been advocated at various times, the conventional way of teaching a child to read was the word method:

The most serious drawback of all the English reading instruction known to me, regardless of the special method that is in each case advocated, is the drawback of the word method. The written forms for words are presented to the child in an order which conceals the alphabetic principle. For instance, if near the beginning of instruction, we present the words *get* and *gem,* we cannot expect the child to develop any fixed or fluent response to the sight of the letter *g.* If we talk to him about the "hard" and "soft" sounds of the letter *g,* we shall only confuse him the more. The irregularities of our spelling—that is, its deviation from the alphabetic principle—demand careful handling if they are not to confuse the child and to delay his acquisition of the alphabetic habit.

After examining and showing the linguistic weaknesses of these various approaches to reading, Bloomfield wrote: "It is not easy for a student to speak patiently of such vagaries, in which educationalists indulge at great cost to thousands of helpless children. It is exactly as if these same educationalists should invent their own guesswork system of chemistry and introduce it into our schools."

So much for what Bloomfield disapproved. Of the plan he had worked out in accordance with linguistic principles, he explained:

The first step, which may be divorced from all subsequent ones, is the recognition of the letters. We say that the child *recognizes* a letter when he can, upon request, make some response to it. . . . The conventional responses to the sight of the letters are their names, *aye, bee, see, dee, ee, eff,* and so on, down to *zee* (which in England is called *zed*). There is not the slightest reason for using any other responses.

The letters have queer and interesting shapes; their interest is enhanced if they are presented in colors. Begin with the printed capitals in their ordinary simple form. When these have been mastered, take up the small printed letters. The written forms of the letters should not be taught until reading habits are well established; the early introduction of writing is a cause of delay.

The child should be familiar with all the letters, capital and small, of the printed alphabet before reading is begun. Not all of them will be used in the first reading work, but we do not want the reading work, at any stage, to be upset by the appearance of unfamiliar shapes. . . .

When the letters and the left-to-right order have been thoroughly mastered, we are ready to begin reading. In the words to be read during the first stage every letter must represent only and always one single phoneme. The great task of learning to read—one of the major intellectual feats in anyone's life—consists in learning the very abstract equation: *printed letter = speech sound to be spoken.* This equation is all the more difficult because it never occurs in simple form, but only in the complex shape where several letters in left-to-right order serve as the signal for several speech sounds in the corresponding soon-to-later order. If we try to simplify this by presenting single letters as signals for single speech sounds, we only make matters worse, since the isolated speech sounds are foreign to our language. This task is sufficiently difficult; we must not make it even more difficult by introducing irregular spellings before the basic habit is set up, or by asking the child to attend to the meaning of what he reads. . . .

Our first material must show each letter in only one phonetic value; thus, if we have words with g in the value that it has in *get, got, gun,* our first material must not contain words like *gem,* where the same letter has different value; similarly, if we have words like *cat, can, cot,* our first material must not contain words like *cent.* Our first material should contain no words with silent letters (such as *knit* or *gnat*) and none with double letters, either in the value of single sounds (as in *add, bell*) or in special values (as in *see, too*), and none with combinations of letters having a special value (as *th* in *thin* or *ea* in *bean*). . . .

The best selection of value of letters to be used in the first materials for reading is the following:

Vowel Letters

a   as in *cat*   o   as in *hot*
e   as in *pet*   u   as in *cut*
i   as in *pin*

Consonant Letters

b   as in *bit*   n   as in *net*
c   as in *cat*   p   as in *peg*
d   as in *dig*   r   as in *red*
f   as in *fan*   s   as in *sat*
g   as in *get*   t   as in *tan*
h   as in *hen*   v   as in *van*
j   as in *jam*   w   as in *wet*
k   as in *keg*   y   as in *yes*
l   as in *let*   z   as in *zip*
m   as in *man*

Note that this list contains one duplication: c and k both designate one and the same English phoneme. This will be a difficulty later, when the child learns to write, but it need not trouble us now, since he has merely to read words as they are presented to him.

Our first reading material will consist of two-letter and three-letter words in which the letters have the sound values given in the above list. Since the vowel letters *a, e, i, o, u* are the ones which, later on, will present the greatest difficulty, we shall do best to divide this material into five groups, according to the vowel letter contained in each word. Within each of these five groups, two arrangements are possible; we can form groups by final consonants (e.g. *bat, cat, fat,* etc.) or by initial consonants (e.g. *bad, bag, bat,* etc.). . . .

If the child has learned the pattern in the list of actual words, he should be able to read nonsense syllables using the same pattern. . . . The nonsense syllables are a test of the child's mastery of the phoneme. Tell the child that the nonsense syllables are parts of real words which he will find in the books that he reads. For example, the child will know *han* in *handle* and *jan* in *January* and *mag* in *magnet* or *magpie*. The acquisition of nonsense syllables is an important part of the task of mastering the reading process. The child will learn the patterns of the language more rapidly if you use the nonsense syllables in teaching. However, the lessons may be taught without teaching the nonsense syllables, if you so desire.

Reading is so familiar to us that we are likely to forget how difficult it is for the beginner. The child has so hard a time forming a connection between visual marks and speech sounds that he cannot attend to the meaning of what he reads. We must help him to establish this connection, and we must not bother him, for the present, with anything else. We can best help him by giving him the most suitable words to read, and these are short words in which the letters have uniform values. We present as many as possible of these, without regard to their meanings. The child will get the meanings only when he has solved the mechanical problem of reading.

Although Bloomfield died before the reading system he had worked out was published, it seems likely that his influence in the field of reading may have been considerable. As will be shown in chapter 17, today even educationalists of national reputation speak and write openly on behalf of the child's learning, even in kindergarten, letters and the sounds for which they stand. Thirty years ago, when Bloomfield turned his attention to reading, this was not so. At that time professionals in the reading field were much more inclined to retain their orthodoxy.

BEGINNING READING WITH TEMPORARY ALPHABETS

In chapter 3, attention was called to the conviction on the part of John Hart and others that teachers and children were having a difficult time teaching and learning to read because the letters and sounds of the English language had fallen out of phase with each other. Hart with his proposed new alphabet and Richard Hodges with his suggested diacritical markings failed to accomplish anything.

Efforts to improve English spelling have been made for over four hundred years and will probably never cease.[1] In 1837, however, Isaac (later Sir Isaac) Pitman (1813–97) invented a system of phonetic shorthand which he set forth three years later in a twenty-four-page pamphlet entitled: *Phonography, or Writing by Sounds; Being a Natural Method of Writing Applicable to All Languages, and a Complete System of Short Hand.* This shorthand was a success from the beginning. In 1843 Pitman met Alexander John Ellis, a young man of his own age, and soon, with his friend's help, he set to work to do for printing what he had already accomplished for writing. He undertook to prepare a phonetic alphabet suitable for use by printers.

Pitman was particularly fortunate in his helper. Ellis was a wealthy and well-educated young man, whose major inter-

---

[1] Histories of the English language, such as that by Albert C. Baugh, give accounts of English spelling and attempts to reform it. H. L. Mencken in *American Language Supplement* (New York, 1948), II, 271–331, wrote interestingly and competently on American spelling, spelling reformers, and the simplified spelling movement. Abraham Tauber's *Spelling Reform in the United States* (Ann Arbor, Mich.: University Microfilms, 1958) is of great value.

est was philology. By January, 1844, Pitman and he had devised a phonetic alphabet composed of characters which they called *phonotypes*. In this new alphabet each speech sound had its phonotype. Printing which employed these phonotypes was called *phonotypy*.

Even before they completed their first alphabet, the inventors must have thought of two aspects of what they were doing. They were reasonably certain that anyone could learn to read material printed in their alphabet much more readily than he could read that printed in the usual manner. Second, they felt sure that anyone skilled in reading phonotypy could likewise read material printed in the traditional manner. Ellis taught his young daughter to read material written in the new alphabet. He found that she did it readily and went on without difficulty to reading ordinary printed matter. Before their alphabet was a year old, Ellis set to work on *A Plea for Phonotypy and Phonography* which appeared in 1845. In this work Ellis said, "The phonotyper . . . having acquired a habit of reading phonotypy . . . will soon be able to read heterotypy with ease."

This new system of "sound-printing" aroused immediate and, on the whole, favorable comment. Inspired by a vision of phonotypy's eventually supplanting the traditional method of printing, Pitman set to work with a devotion seldom equaled to improve his first alphabet of 1844. In the meantime, his disciples, including two of his brothers, went far and wide setting up wherever they could reading and writing schools—"Phonetic Schools," as they were called. In workhouses, in prisons, in the Edinburgh Ragged School, in the Preston House of Correction, and in the Glasgow Bridewell, children and adults learned to read phonotypy in a remarkably short time and were able to transfer without difficulty to reading matter in ordinary print.[2]

[2] Maurice Harrison, *Story of the Initial Teaching Alphabet* (New York, Toronto, London, 1964), pp. 29–92. This book is of unusual interest and value. The author is Director of Education in the County Borough of Oldham, England. The "Phonetic Schools" Harrison mentions on pp. 34–36 continued for years. The earliest certificate awarded to Joseph Wright, later Professor of Comparative Philology at the University of Oxford, was from one of them. His certificate was dated April 22, 1875, and signed by "Ysak Pitman." See the *Life of Joseph Wright* by Elizabeth Mary Wright (London, 1932), I, 40.

News of what was being done in England quickly spread to this country. At a meeting of the American Academy of Arts and Sciences (Boston) in the early part of 1846, a committee was appointed to consider phonotypy and phonography. Undoubtedly Ellis' book inspired the appointment of this committee. A report was made before the Academy at its quarterly meeting, August 12, 1846, by George B. Emerson, whom we have met before as a friend and helper of Horace Mann, whose views on teaching to read he endorsed.

In his thirteen-page report Emerson heartily approved Pitman's work and gave special attention to phonotypy. He described the forty-two-character alphabet involved: "After exhausting the letters of the present alphabet, excluding *k*, *q*, and *x*, it became necessary to adopt nineteen new letter-signs for the unrepresented or misrepresented sounds. These have been chosen with great care and after very numerous experiments. The present form of the phonetic alphabet being as high as the seventeenth of those which have been successively proposed." He reproduced the alphabet—twenty-four consonants, fifteen vowels, and three "compound vowels."

Emerson next dealt with four objections that had been made to this departure from conventional printing:

It is feared by many that if the new mode of printing should prevail, all the libraries now in existence would become useless. This fear is entirely groundless. When a knowledge of the language, or facility in reading, is once acquired through phonotypy, it will be perfectly easy to read books printed in the common type; far more easy than it is for us to read old black-letter English, or the English of the times of Chaucer. It will probably take less time,—I have no doubt myself that it will take much less time,—to read phonotypically first and heterotypically afterwards, than to learn to read by the common mode alone; inasmuch as, when one has learnt the phonotypic alphabet, he may learn to read of himself without farther assistance, the letters giving necessarily the true sounds of the words, and, the knowledge of the words of the language once acquired, one may, afterwards, soon read them with ease, however disguised by a barbarous heterography.

The other objections Emerson discussed were based, just as this first one was, upon the fear of the objectors that the initial use of phonotypy to assist children in reading was merely the entering wedge in the overthrow of conventional spelling and printing. And to this they were opposed.

Emerson concluded his report by giving eight advantages he thought would follow the adoption of the reformed alphabet. The first one he listed was that a child could learn to read in phonotypy "in one fifteenth part of the time necessary for the present." To this estimate he added a footnote: "A writer in *Chamber's Edinburgh Journal* says one twentieth the time. A child has now, instead of the mere alphabet, to learn nearly all the words of the language, as if they were represented by separate hieroglyphics."[3] Emerson said nothing about his former devotion to the word method.

About the time Emerson made his report, Stephen Pearl Andrews of Boston brought to that city some of the Pitman type. Soon experiments were being made with phonotypy in the State Normal School of Massachusetts. Dr. James W. Stone was instrumental in getting the system into some of the Massachusetts schools. On July 3, 1851, Horace Mann wrote him and praised him highly for his good work.[4] From 1852 to 1860, an experiment involving eight hundred pupils was made with the new method in the schools of Waltham, Massachusetts. The chairman of the Waltham Committee responsible for the test was Thomas Hill, later President of Harvard University.[5]

The result of these experiments was that children read much more quickly and with greater pleasure than was customary. After seven or eight months they were able to read so well in material printed in the new alphabet that they shifted without difficulty to material printed in traditional orthography. Those in this country interested in approaching reading through phonotypy were soon joined by Benn Pitman, one of Sir Isaac's brothers, who in 1855

[3] For the entire report, see *Proceedings of the American Academy of Arts and Sciences* (May, 1846–May, 1848), I, 23–35.

[4] Tauber, *op. cit.*, p. 73, gives Mann's letter, which is brief.

[5] These experiments, especially the ones at Waltham, have often been described. See Tauber, *op. cit.*, pp. 73–75; Thomas Hill, *True Order of Studies* (New York, 1882), p. 107–9; John Downing, *Experiments With An Augmented Alphabet* (London, 1962), pp. 11 ff; Francis A. March, *Spelling Reform* (Washington, 1893), pp. 7 ff; Harrison, *op. cit.*, pp. 42–50.

brought out in Cincinnati his *First Phonetic Reader*. Some of the experiments in Massachusetts used this book as a text.

News of what was being done in Massachusetts spread widely. As early as 1853 a memorial was presented to the legislature of Michigan on the subject of using phonotypy in the elementary schools of that state. A committee appointed to investigate and report found from endorsers of the new plan that children started on phonotypy learned to read material printed in the new alphabet in about one-fourth the time ordinarily required to read conventional matter. They found phonotypy was then used in one hundred and sixty schools in Massachusetts, and that the State Normal of New York had already taken it up for testing. The system had spread to about five hundred schools in this country, and to about two hundred in England. In view of its excellent record, the committee recommended its adoption in their state.[6]

The success of phonotypy inspired the production of competing alphabets. The best known of these was one devised by Dr. Edwin Leigh (1815–90), a New England minister and physician. In 1864 he brought out in St. Louis an eight-page pamphlet entitled *Pronouncing Orthography*. In this he gave his alphabet consisting of some seventy or seventy-five characters. In departing from the phonetic alphabet principle Leigh had done a significant thing. He had moved away from strictly phonetic spelling to ease the pupil's transfer from reading matter printed in his temporary alphabet to that printed in the traditional manner. He had not done his work very skilfully, but that he had done it at all is worthy of notice. There were a primer and a first reader in the Leigh type, both of them containing about twice the amount of material usually found in such books.

In 1866, one hundred and fifty primary teachers in St. Louis began testing the Leigh System. In ten weeks they all reported that their pupils had studied the primer in a

---

[6] *Documents Accompanying the Journal of the Senate and House of Representatives of the State of Michigan at the Regular Session of 1853* (Lansing, Mich., 1953), Document No. 7.

thorough manner. During the second ten weeks they completed the first reader with similar thoroughness. In the second half of the first-grade year, many pupils completed the second reader, although it was printed in ordinary type. Those who did not get through it finished at least half of it.

With reference to a particular school Maurice Harrison gives the following account:

Under the St. Louis Board experiments were conducted in 1868 in the Clay School. The Superintendent reported: "Its [Simplified Spelling's] introduction has been followed by far greater results than were at first anticipated; not only has it tended to the eradication of defects in enunciation, but there has been a saving of time to the extent of a whole quarter in the course of the first half year." In 1869 the School Board officially reported: "A given standard of good reading can always be reached in about one half the time. . . . They make better arithmetic and grammar scholars, and are more wide awake, attentive and discriminating." In 1870 the Superintendent wrote: "Each year increases our admiration of the work. Gain in time—quite one half—distinct articulation, and better spelling represent the undoubted advantages."[7]

After an extensive period of testing it was found that bright pupils under the Leigh System could in one year's time complete the primer, the first reader, the second reader, and one-hundred pages in the third reader even though in mid-career they had switched from material in the Leigh type to that ordinarily used. From such a good beginning the system spread to all the schools of St. Louis, where it remained in use for twenty years.

W. T. Harris, the Superintendent of the St. Louis schools, summed up the advantages of the Leigh alphabet as an introductory teaching medium for beginners:

1. Gain of time—a saving of one year out of the two years usually occupied in learning to call off easy words at sight.
2. Distinct articulation, the removal of foreign accents and local and peculiar pronunciations.
3. The development of logical power of mind in the pupil. He can safely be taught to analyze a word into its sounds and find the letters representing them, whereas with the ordinary orthog-

[7] Harrison, *op. cit.*, pp. 44–45.

raphy it is an insult to his reason to assure him that a sound is represented by any particular letter.[8]

Maurice Harrison gives the following report by Boston teachers of the use of the Leigh System in their city.

> The system was introduced in February 1873. The results were immediate, and to me wonderful; none of us entertains the slightest doubt about the advantage of the system. The children learn to read in half the time it formerly took and do not contract that old habit, so hard to eradicate, of reading one word at a time, as though they were pronouncing a column of words from the speller. The teachers find no difficulty about spelling.[9]

Harrison goes on to say that the Board of Public Instruction of New York reported in 1871 that "Much time is saved in teaching to read by this method, and the children are better trained by it for other instruction. It is, therefore, recommended to all the schools."[10]

From the accounts available of the successes obtained with these temporary alphabets one is justified in concluding that the teachers involved taught pretty much in the manner then most usual. Presumably they taught their pupils the letters and the sounds for which they stood. They could not have taught the names of all the letters, for there is no evidence that in the temporary alphabets all the letters had names. Only those borrowed from the traditional alphabet were thus provided.

If the teachers who employed the new alphabets and were pleased with the results they obtained used, in addition, a new method of teaching to read, there is no record of this. Besides, it is not easy to see how such modifications of the traditional alphabet as were then made could have been of any help to pupils instructed by an analytical or whole word method. The quite successful alphabet devised by Dr. Leigh would certainly not have contributed much to helping a child taught by the latter method.

During the twenty years of experimentation with differ-

---

[8] March, *op. cit.*, devotes two pages (pp. 37–38) to what was done in St. Louis. I have disregarded the phonetic spelling used by Harris in the excerpt given from his report.
[9] Harrison, *op. cit.*, p. 45.
[10] *Ibid.*, p. 46.

ent temporary alphabets in this country, testings of like
kind were going on in England, with similarly satisfactory
results. As Harrison points out, these tests were uncon-
trolled, since objective testing was at that time unknown;
nevertheless, the reports of classroom teachers and administrators are valuable. The results allegedly achieved
parallel to a remarkable degree those of the 1920's and
1960's in England.[11]

In spite of the excellent results obtained from these introductory alphabets, experimentation with them declined
in this country well before the end of the century. Competing systems using the same principle, the scarcity of
suitable books, competition from Webster's Blue-back
speller, and the wide use of the McGuffey readers, were
among the causes.

Another enthusiasm that undoubtedly did much to bring
about a decline in interest in introductory alphabets for
beginners was simplified spelling. By 1870 the best phil-
ologists in both Europe and the United States were realizing
more and more clearly that "the foundation of the science
of language is laid in the science of vocal sounds. Every
student of the modern science studies phonology. The
means of representing sound by visible signs are also part
of his study, and the spelling of the English language,
among other things."[12]

Every philologist was now more than ever a devoted student of phonetics. To attest their competence they all
wished to prepare alphabets, especially of an introductory
kind for the use of beginning readers. This desire led into
and merged with a desire to assist everybody by radically
reforming English spelling. In August, 1876, an international Convention for the Amendment of English Orthography was held at Philadelphia, inspired by the work of the
American Philological Association and other educational
associations in this country and in England. On the fourth
day of the meeting, the convention resolved itself into the
Spelling Reform Association. The making of phonetic

---

11 *Ibid.*, p. 47.
12 *American Institute of Instruction*, XLIX (1879), 139.

alphabets took on new life. By 1879 a Spelling Reform Alphabet was ready, in which thirty-two sounds were distinguished. It was claimed that by means of this introductory alphabet a child could be taught to read in three months, passing in that time from the use of the phonetic alphabet to that ordinarily employed. Following closely on the heels of this alphabet came another in which all the speech sounds were distinguished. It too promised to bring the child from phonetic material into the conventional alphabet in three months—"aye, often in twenty hours of thorough instruction." Scores of alphabets accompanied by sets of rules, often with voluminous expositions of their special merits, swamped the Association.[13]

Simplified spelling would, of course, obviate any need for a temporary alphabet. Also, the fear in some quarters that these temporary alphabets might result in the displacement of the conventional one made them suspect. Then too the work being done by Colonel Parker, heartily endorsed by G. Stanley Hall and John Dewey, drew attention away from the use of such alphabets. Under the circumstances, it is not surprising that interest in introductory teaching alphabets subsided in this country as quickly as it had arisen.

Interest in introductory alphabets and in simplified spelling persisted longer in England. At least one experimenter there carried his work into the present century. W. H. Winch, Chairman of the Committee of the Education Guild of Great Britain and Ireland, spent about twenty years testing carefully (though in only a few schools) look-and-say, phonic, and phonoscript methods. The last of these he found gave the best results. It made use of an introductory alphabet, from which the children later changed with little difficulty to the use of traditional orthography. He found the look-and-say the least effective of the methods tested.[14]

[13] March, *op. cit.*, pp. 17, 23, 29.
[14] See especially the following pages in W. H. Winch, *Teaching Beginners to Read in England* (Bloomington, Ill. 1925), pp. 38, 50, 58, 59, 174.

The Simplified Spelling movement developed differently in this country and in England. In 1906 the Simplified Spelling Board was organized in New York. Two years later, on September 10, 1908, the Simplified Spelling Society was founded in London. The S.S.B. in this country, expending its energy in behalf of simplified spelling without attention to its use in teaching children to read, accomplished very little in the end. The English S.S.B., on the other hand, maintained a lively interest in the use of simplified spelling in schools as a means of getting children over the initial difficulties of reading. A number of beginning readers were printed in "Simplifyd Speling" and experiments were arranged in many schools in Scotland. Despite the dislocations brought about by World War I, these experiments met with remarkable success, and their scope was extended to schools in London, Hereford, and the north of England, as well as to other schools in Scotland.

In chapter 8 Maurice Harrison gives in some detail the successes achieved with introductory phonetic alphabets in at least a dozen of the schools engaging in these experiments from 1914 to 1921. Everywhere the story was the same; children who started out with an alphabet upon which they could rely moved ahead in reading considerably faster than those who did not. The changeover from phonetically spelled introductory material to that expressed in traditional orthography presented no real difficulty. The absence of drudgery for both teacher and pupil made reading a pleasure.

Fluency in reading engendered greater fluency in speech. After a few months children wrote with confidence and enthusiasm, often revealing by their spelling inaccuracies in pronunciation. Teachers, headmasters, inspectors, and Education Committees were delighted with what was being done. Better reading was accompanied by improvement in spelling, writing, and arithmetic. This progress all along the line justified the pronouncement that "scientific study in any branch of knowledge prepared the way for rapid advance in any other branch of knowledge."

Impressed by the success of such experiments as these[15] and feeling sure that what was being accomplished in individual attempts at instructional improvement should not be allowed to go for naught, the Spelling Society was continuing its efforts on behalf of beginning readers when World War II broke out. During the war the military authorities— in the selection procedures they used to secure the type of personnel needed for particular assignments—discovered a surprisingly large number of men who either could not read at all or who read too poorly for practical purposes; that is, they were "functional illiterates." The findings at this time in the British Services closely paralleled what had earlier been found to be the case among American soldiers. Even the percentages—twenty-five or thirty per cent—were virtually the same.

This state of affairs received wide publicity, with the result that during the decade following the war, learning to read and teaching to read aroused great public interest in England. Out of this increased concern, a Spelling Reform bill was introduced in the House of Commons early in 1949. It failed of passage, but in 1953 a bill was passed which authorized a properly selected association or institution "to institute researches with a view to reading and, if possible, eliminating the widespread inability of the children of Great Britain to read their own language." The bill authorized an investigation into "the assistance to children likely to result from the use (in the earlier stages of teaching reading) of matter printed in a spelling which uses the letters of the alphabet consistently and from a transfer, in due course, to the reading of matter printed in the existing orthography." Sir James Pitman, grandson of Sir Isaac, had a prominent part in securing the passage of this bill. The speech which he made in the House of Commons on Febru-

[15] There were no doubt many more of these local experiments than were recorded. See Robert Jackson, "Phonetics and Phonetic Texts in the Teaching of Reading," in *Miscellanea Phonetica* (International Phonetic Association, 1914), pp. 33–37. Jackson was Lecturer in Phonetics at Dundee Training College. In 1915 he prepared *A Ferst Reeder in Simplifyd Speling* which was published by "The Simplifyd Speling Sosyeti" (London, 1915). This forty-nine page booklet was of great help to teachers interested in using simplified material at the outset in teaching their children to read. See Harrison, *op. cit.,* pp. 53, 58 n., 59–60, 64, 200.

ary 27, 1953, is of unusual interest. The following selections are typical. With respect to the need to do something about the reading situation, he said:

The present results are so deplorable that this House and the Minister must take notice of them. Some 400,000 to 500,000 five-year-olds begin their schooling every year and some 120,000 to 150,000 are destined to come out of the school system at the other end unable to read properly. . . .

The same sort of figures happen in Australia and America. It seems to be connected particularly with the English-speaking world and it is, therefore, important that, since we know there is something wrong somewhere, in our insistence that we do something—and I hope the House will insist that we do something about it—we do it by a modern scientific educational inquiry which will require the co-operation of the Minister and is a matter of major educational policy for the Minister. . . .

The Chinese or picture writing has two great disadvantages. I have in my hand a book dated 1558 in which Dr. Timothy Bright, talking about the Chinese characters, says in the most lovely spelling which I can still read: "Besides, they wanting an alphabet fal into an infinite number, which is a thing that greatlie chargeth memory, and may discourage the learner." There could not be anything more apposite from 1558 to 1953 of the task we are giving our little children of five, six and seven than those words coming back to us over the centuries.

Sir James expressed the hope that the Minister of Education could secure money from the Cabinet for furthering the investigation contemplated in view of the fact that a much larger sum had been spent on basic English. He continued: "It may well be that Colonel McCormick would assist, because I know that the figures in Chicago are, if anything, worse than the figures disclosed by the Ministry in Britain. He is very interested in this subject and he might give a donation."[16]

One of the first things to be done in implementing the bill as it was finally passed was to prepare an alphabet for use in the forthcoming research. In *The Times* of London, May 29, 1959, Sir James presented the alphabet which he and his helpers had devised. After slight modifications in the light of experience, this became the Initial Teaching

[16] *Parliamentary Debates House of Commons*, DXI, 2419, 2422, 2423, 2427. Also see Harrison, *op. cit.*, p. 204.

Alphabet—often abbreviated I.T.A. or i.t.a.—now so well known.[17]

This alphabet is a remarkably clever one. It uses all the conventional letters except q and x. The additional characters devised to make up the forty-five in the alphabet are easily recognizable modifications of the usual ones. Each character stands for one, and only one, speech sound. It is not strictly a phonetic alphabet, departing from the phonetic principle in the interest of increasing the ease with which the child, at the proper time, transfers to the use of conventionally printed material. Compare this with Dr. Leigh's temporary alphabet.

From the first, emphasis was placed on the suitability of this alphabet for the beginner's use, no matter by what method he might be taught to read. Teachers who favor a word-method approach to reading at the initial stage find that i.t.a. words never vary in form. Capitals have the same forms as the small letters; they are merely larger. The pupil is saved from encountering at the outset such forms as dog, Dog, DOG. Teachers who favor a synthetic phonic approach to reading have in i.t.a. a medium that serves them much more efficiently than the ordinary alphabet. There are no silent letters; such spellings as *knife* and *gnat* never occur. The child soon discovers that every letter can always be depended upon to represent the same sound. There is never any such complexity as that afforded by *get, gem.*

We cannot go into the details of the experimentation with i.t.a. which began in 1961. Mention has already been made of the fact that the results parallelled those achieved much earlier with temporary alphabets not nearly so cleverly made or administered as the i.t.a. The best proof of the

---

[17] In this account of i.t.a. I have followed the book by Harrison and the works by Downing (see the bibliography and the footnotes in Downing's "Current Misconceptions"). The literature on i.t.a. is extensive; see Hunter Diack, *In Spite of the Alphabet* (London, 1965), pp. 156–76. A somewhat detailed account of the work being done at Bethlehem is contained in a five thousand word illustrated article by George Riemer in the *Ladies Home Journal,* October, 1964, pp. 70 ff. Joel Weinberg of Simmons College in *Harvard Educational Review,* Spring, 1965, pp. 245–49, expressed reservations about some features of i.t.a. and stressed the need for longer observation of some of the procedures followed.

excellence of the results is the tremendous increase in the number of schools making use of the medium.

In chapter 16 of his book, "Appraisals of the Infant Experiment," Harrison gives the reactions of some of his teachers in Oldham to the use of the new medium. For example:

> In one school the head-mistress very conscientiously decided that the look-and-say method used in earlier years would be strictly maintained. Apart from the stressing of individual sounds when pointing to words during blackboard reading, phonics were not taught at all. Before the end of the first term, the head-mistress told me that the children had beaten her. The brighter ones had detected the sound values of letters and were happily word-building. In the class teacher's words, "The children had extracted the phonics through the visual consistency without any definite lead."

In this chapter of "Appraisals" the things that stand out most prominently are the eagerness with which the children in the i.t.a. program read, the fluency with which they express themselves in writing, and the readiness with which they transfer to reading and using traditional orthography.

As a result of the almost instant communication possible today, this British attempt to improve reading was known about in this country from its inception, and occasionally a teacher ventured to try it out. The most elaborate testing of i.t.a. in the United States has been in progress at Bethlehem, Pennsylvania (since September, 1963), under the direction of A. J. Mazurkiewicz and H. J. Tanyzer. The success these educators have achieved is remarkable to say the least.

It is not surprising that with the exciting experiences both children and teachers are having with i.t.a., misunderstandings should arise as to its nature and purpose, and that exaggerated claims should be made for it. Mr. John Downing, Research Officer to the Reading Research Unit of the London Institute of Education, has called attention to "Current Misconceptions about i.t.a." in *Elementary English* (May, 1965, pp. 492–501). Among the misconceptions he discusses, he finds the most popular is that i.t.a. is a synthetic phonics approach to reading. As a teaching medium, not a method, i.t.a. is not identified with either a synthetic or an analytic method. Teachers who use it are urged to continue the practices to which they have been accustomed and which they understand best.

Children in England usually begin their schooling at age five, or a little before, but even so those participating in the i.t.a. experiments are able to read remarkably well. The same thing is true of American children in classes in which i.t.a. is used. Under the circumstances, the impression naturally arose that i.t.a. was a scheme for forcing precocious readers. Downing is at some pains to dispel this misconception.

Any procedure that succeeds is likely to be hailed by enthusiasts as a panacea and easy of implementation. Downing does well to call attention to these exaggerations, lest in the long run they lead to disappointment.

READING EXPERIMENTS
AND THEIR RESULTS

Before about 1920 there was no dependable way for teachers of reading to test the results of their efforts. The situation is quite different today; there are tools for testing and measuring in all kinds of elementary school subjects, including reading. In this chapter we shall look briefly at the measured results of a few typical experiments.

We shall begin by summing up what has already been shown, to the effect that there are only three ways of teaching to read. The first and by far the oldest of them is the synthetic. According to this method, the beginner in reading is, at the outset, taught letters and the sounds for which they stand. There is an increasing number of approaches making use of this principle and referred to in various ways. Charles C. Walcutt discussed a number of them in 1961, referring to them as "Phonic Systems." "Phonic" is a word frequently used in connection with them.

The second method is the analytic. This is a modern system, known since the close of the eighteenth century, but put into widespread practice about 1900. Many names have been given to its various applications. In the 1830's and 1840's, it was called the new method, later the word method, and later still the look-and-say method. It has also been called the experience method, whole-word recognition, and probably by other names as well. No matter what it is called, the method is that of starting children in reading by having them memorize words without analyzing them into letters and sounds. That comes later and incidentally.

The third method is what is known as a mixed method. It partakes of both the synthetic and the analytic approaches, predominantly the analytic in the beginning. It has been shown, especially in chapter 9 above, that in the 1830's and 1840's when the "new method," as it was then called, began to be used there were two ways of applying it, one with and one without phonics. In the phonics method of application, the child got the letters and sounds immediately after becoming familiar with the word; in the other, he was not at first, or for a considerable time afterward, given any information about letters and their sounds. This was a pure or unadulterated word method.

When Rice was making his inspection of schools in some of the larger cities, he found that in New York City the children he visited were being taught by the word method, and that they were taught to spell the words as they learned to read them. In Buffalo he found the word method in use *without phonics,* and he condemned it as doing "less to develop mental power and more to waste time than any that I know of—except *perhaps,* the alphabet method." In Chicago he found different methods in use—the word method, the sentence method, and "a variety of methods, including phonics and word-building."

Some phonic instruction was brought in to supplement the word method and has maintained its place among many other "word-attack skills" developed later, which teachers use on the basis of their judgment of the child's needs and aptitudes. The term "gradual phonics" or "incidental phonics" is sometimes used for this method of giving instruction in letters and sounds to help the beginner learn new or difficult terms. Teachers usually start their children, after preliminary reading procedures, on learning words, and later, perhaps in the second or third grades, introduce them to phonics, not to take the place of the whole-word-learning technique but to supplement it.

The most significant thing ever to occur in the history of reading is the experimenting now being done in this country and in England to find how a child may best be taught to read. For the first time large-scale, long-term tests are being conducted and the results scientifically evaluated and extensively publicized. The immediate reason for this activity is, of course, the widespread dissatisfaction with what is being achieved by the use of the conventional analytic method based mainly on word learning initially— (and for an indefinite time afterward).

An additional reason for the present experimentation is that the *principle* of the traditional ABC method of teaching to read has never been shown to be in error. Hunter Diack was correct when he wrote in 1965, "Alphabetic methods have the peculiar distinction of not having been shown by some manipulation of statistics to be inferior to all other methods or combination of methods. They went out before statistics came in—went out as a recognized modern method, I mean."[1]

What is being done by those interested in the improvement of teaching to read gives promise that the method or system which gains approval will do so by virtue of what classroom teachers are able to achieve with it. No amount of pedagogical expertizing will save any method that fails on the proving ground, that is, in the classrooms. The traditional ABC teaching gave unsatisfactory results at a time, and under circumstances, which would have doomed any method to failure. The old reading method, handicapped by short sessions, miserably poor teaching, and by public apathy, was swept aside by those ambitious to install an entirely new regime that would be in harmony with the spirit of progress then abroad in the land.

The tests being made and the results secured with synthetic, that is phonic, approaches to the reading problem are causing many parents and not a few teachers to suspect that perhaps in the laudable desire to improve upon an extremely unsatisfactory elementary program at the century's end, those then in places of leadership failed to take account of the distinction between a fundamental principle and the applications being made of it. Not just one, but

[1] Hunter Diack, *In Spite of the Alphabet* (London, 1965), p. 23.

many things were wrong with the elementary curriculum. It certainly needed a thorough overhauling. But evidence is accumulating that those who dreamed dreams and saw visions of better procedures may, so far as teaching to read is concerned, have tossed out the baby with the bath water in their zeal to be rid of the inherited setup of primary education. Some attention to what is now being done and said may justify this suspicion.

About fifteen years ago J. C. Daniels and Hunter Diack at the University of Nottingham began an intensive study of the reading problem. As a result of their study and first-hand experience, they developed a mixed method to which they have applied the name Phonic Word-Method. The two most significant aspects of any mixed method are the in-gredients that go into it and the proportions in which these are used. In the Daniels and Diack "mixture" there is some-thing of the synthetic and something of the analytic, the former dominating. They published the *Royal Road Read-ers* embodying their method, and they conducted careful tests of the efficiency of various synthetic, analytic, and mixed methods. In 1956 they brought out a brochure called *Progress in Reading,* in which the methodology and results of their tests up to that time were given in detail. They wrote: "The large measure of agreement in the experimental evidence showing the superiority of various types of phonic methods over various 'whole word,' 'sentence,' and other 'modern' methods is surprising in view of the general trend of expert and official opinion."[2]

Charles C. Walcutt in *Tomorrow's Illiterates* discussed the *Royal Road Readers* in some detail, and Irving Adler praised them highly in his *What We Want of Our Schools,*[3] concluding by saying that American specialists and pub-lishers should get acquainted with the materials and method: "The publisher who first adapts them for use with the American idiom will take the country by storm."

The leading article in a recent issue of the *Journal of*

[2] J. C. Daniels and Hunter Diack, *Progress in Reading* (Nottingham, 1956), p. 26.
[3] Charles C. Walcutt, *Tomorrow's Illiterates* (Boston, 1961), pp. 160–61; Irving Adler, *What We Want of Our Schools* (New York, 1957), pp. 215 ff.

Educational Research gives the results of comparisons between gradual and intensive use of phonics in teaching beginners to read. At the head of the article is an "Abstract" explaining what was done:

Drawing from unpublished as well as published research this review presents 22 comparisons between intensive phonics groups and gradual phonics groups. On the basis of this tabulation, 19 comparisons favored intensive phonics, three favored neither method and none favored gradual phonics. The reviewers conclude that early and intensive phonics instruction tends to produce superior reading achievement.[4]

At the end of their review the authors include among their recommendations:

1) that all the main sound-symbol relationships, both vowel and consonant, be taught intensively from the start of reading instruction, 2) that schools provide their teachers with suitable materials and in-service training for using an intensive phonetic approach, and 3) that colleges and universities offer training in the necessary technique, both in summer workshops and in regular courses.

A second recent report based upon a similar type of comparison appeared in the June, 1965, *Phi Delta Kappan*. This study, "A Comparison of Ten Different Beginning Reading Programs in First Grade," was made by Emory L. Bliesmer, Director of the McGuffey Reading Clinic, University of Virginia, and Mrs. Betty H. Yarborough, Director of Developmental Reading for the Chesapeake (Va.) Public Schools. This comparative study was carried out during the school year 1963–64 and involved ten reading programs, five of them using the conventional whole-word, delayed phonics technique and five using synthetic phonics instruction. In summing up their conclusions the authors say:

It would appear that beginning reading programs which give attention to sound-symbol relationships prior to teaching of words, or which involve a synthetic approach initially (pupils actually building words from sounds) tend to be significantly

[4] Louise Gurren and Ann Hughes, "Intensive Phonics vs Gradual Phonics in Beginning Reading: A Review," *Journal of Educational Research*, April, 1965, pp. 339–47. The first of these authors teaches at New York University, and the second is with the Reading Reform Foundation.

more productive in terms of specific reading achievement in grade one than do the analytic reading programs which involve the more conventional approach of going directly from readiness procedures (using pictures) to the reading of whole words before either letter names or the sounds the letters represent are taught.[5]

The results of these experiments are impressive, and they are typical of what is being achieved with many other reading systems similarly based upon the synthetic principle. They indicate clearly that phonics methods in which letters and sounds are taught initially and persistently give results superior to those obtained by other approaches. Selma Fraiberg, Associate Professor of Child Psychoanalysis at the University of Michigan, wrote recently: "Those systems which employ a phonics approach from the start have a very small percentage of reading failures *even among children with I.Q.'s in the eighties and nineties.*"[6]

It has been shown that the Normal-Words Method in Germany was essentially a synthetic method. Immediately after being shown a word, children learned its letters, the sounds for which they stood, and the syllables they formed. Stress was placed upon the analysis of the words into letters, sounds, and syllables. We have seen that similar results were obtained in this country with what was essentially the same method. As long as there was no delay in taking a child from the contemplation of the word that had captured his interest to the letters and sounds composing the word, he learned to read fairly easily. Horace Mann approved what was being done by teachers who employed this new way of getting children over the initial difficulty of the alphabet and then proceeded in the old manner. If any length of time elapsed between contemplation of the word and analysis into its letters and sounds, the results in terms of reading achievement became less satisfactory.

During the wave of enthusiasm for teaching children to read by the use of specially devised alphabets—that it, from about 1840 to 1880 in this country—quite satisfactory re-

---

[5] See *Phi Delta Kappan,* June, 1965, pp. 500–504.

[6] Selma Fraiberg, "The American Reading Problem," *Commentary,* June, 1965. p. 58.

sults were obtained. Among those who endorsed this practice was, again, Horace Mann. The impression one gets from a consideration of his approval of the different things being done in his time to help children to read was that he stood ready to endorse any method that was not the one under which he had suffered as a boy.

This idea that the promptness with which a child moves from words to letters and sounds may have an important bearing on how well he learns to read is suggested by what has thus far been learned about teaching to read with i.t.a. Harrison says: "Many teachers first introduce children to print by showing them the sentence affixed to the large picture, of which there may be a dozen or so. The first real step in reading is usually 'whole-word' recognition with flash cards, but almost all teachers agree that phonetics with a view to word-building comes much earlier than it used to come."[7] Downing in his account of the misconceptions about i.t.a. wrote: "Generally the i.t.a. teachers in Britain have continued to use their previous eclectic approach to reading with much success. Phonics generally was taught by most teachers, but often not until the second year (age 6 plus). With i.t.a., phonics is still postponed until after an initial look-say period, but now with i.t.a. it comes a good deal earlier—but still not *at the start.*"[8]

It is probable that after further testing with the i.t.a. in England additional light may be shed on the relationship between the promptness with which the child gets to letters and sounds and the success he has in learning to read. This point seems pertinent because it appears that in the experimenting with i.t.a. going on at Bethlehem, the children get to phonics earlier in the reading program than they do in the experiments being conducted in England.

Nancy Larrick, who spent three half-days observing the Bethlehem experiment, "watched middle and upper groups reading and writing more fluently in Pitman than any first-graders I ever saw." She was not favorably impressed by

---

[7] Maurice Harrison, *Story of the Initial Teaching Alphabet* (New York, Toronto, London, 1964), p. 197.
[8] *Elementary English*, May, 1965, p. 494.

some features of what she observed; the rooms were too quiet, the teacher was having it too easy—"All she has to to do is keep breathing"—no science projects were going on, "no rock collections were in evidence," but Miss Larrick noticed the improvement in reading. "Although early tests indicate that children taught with i.t.a. are reading far better than those using the traditional alphabet, the new alphabet is no panacea."[9]

A synthetic method of teaching to read is being used in Washington, D. C., where Superintendent Carl F. Hansen and his teachers are arousing national attention by their work in the primary schools. A part of the "Amidon Plan," as it is called from the school in which it was first tried out, involves teaching first-graders to read by what is known as the Phonovisual Method. This system was developed by Lucille Schoolfield and Josephine B. Timberlake and has been used with notable success. It was introduced into the Amidon school by Dr. Hansen and has been extended to all the schools under his jurisdiction.

In this approach to reading, children in kindergarten are taught sounds and letters in a manner suited to their age and comprehension. Before they leave kindergarten they know so much about reading that they are given to trying their skill on words wherever they come across them. By the time they are in first grade some of them do not hesitate to attack long words such as *information* and *anniversary*. Many second graders are able to go right through fourth and fifth grade reading material.[10] These children are clearly among those spoken of by Hall who make excellent progress if caught "between the age of five and eight, when both interest and facility in learning to read culminate."

A soundly based and well-executed study in reading made in Boston recently gave encouraging results. In 1957 the language arts staff of Boston University carried through a study involving about two thousand first graders.

[9] Nancy Larrick, "What Forty-Four Letters Can Do," *Saturday Review*, September 19, 1964, pp. 66–67. The author is a "former President of the International Reading Association, and a well-known writer about children and their education."

[10] Norman Poirier, "The Extraordinary Amidon School," *Saturday Evening Post*, December 19, 1964, pp. 22–23.

Dr. Donald D. Durrell wrote a paper called "First-Grade Reading Success Study: A Summary," which appeared as the February issue of the *Journal of Education* published by the University. According to the major findings of this study, early instruction in letter names and sounds contributed greatly to the prevention of most reading difficulties. Dr. Durrell wrote: "Tests of knowledge of letter names at school entrance are the best predictors of February and June reading achievement." It was found that children who knew letter names and sounds had a great advantage in mastering a sight vocabulary. "While a knowledge of letter names and sounds does not assure success in acquiring a sight vocabulary, lack of that knowledge produces failure."[11]

While it is undoubtedly true that there have recently appeared "about a dozen more primer series in current use in which pairs exactly like Dick and Jane (Alice and Jerry, for example) exhort each other to run, jump, look, and see in a controlled vocabulary of fifty words,"[12] this study made at Boston University suggests that by no means all educators are wholly committed to the type of reading instruction here suggested by Selma Fraiberg.

What Reeder wrote in 1900 is still basically correct: "The development of method in English reading has sprung from two main sources—the one having its origin in the inherent peculiarities of English notation, the other in the psychology of the process of learning to read."[13] We look briefly at these two sources and at a third which Reeder could not mention, as it was unknown in 1900.

The illogical nature of English spelling is undoubtedly an obstacle for the child in learning to read. As has been shown, however, two procedures for greatly reducing this initial hazard have been devised and shown to be effective. One is the use of temporary alphabets, and the other is a careful selection of alphabetically spelled words for the beginner. Henry Bradley commented approvingly on the

---

[11] *Journal of Education,* February, 1958, pp. 5–6.
[12] Fraiberg, *op. cit.,* p. 56.
[13] Rudolph Rex Reeder, *Historical Development of School Readers* (New York, 1900), p. 70.

first of these devices. Of the reading problem he said: "The introduction of an accurate phonetic notation into school use is a very different matter [i.e. from spelling reform], and I am inclined to believe that it is in this direction that we must look for the solution of our present difficulties. . . . Some very able teachers have given it as the result of their experience that children who are taught to read by means of a phonetic alphabet actually learn the current spelling more quickly than those who are taught in the old way; and, provided that the teacher has adequate phonetic knowledge, I see no reason why this may not be true."[14]

The second "main source" which Reeder mentioned as "the psychology of the process of learning to read" is the "Wholeness" theory already discussed. Nature teaches by wholes; we contemplate wholes and thence advance to elements. It is surprising that this theory of "Wholeness" and of Nature's approval of proceeding from "Wholes" to elements was ever brought over into the field of reading, one of the most unnatural activities in which man has ever engaged. Nature has never taught anyone to read and never will. Before Jacotot, the great exponent of the "Wholeness" doctrine, was born there was an old maxim, variously expressed, to the effect that "Words are the daughters of men, but things are the sons of God." Words are not like tadpoles or flowers or horses. Words are man-made, and it hardly seems temeritous in him to deal with them without any consideration of "Mother Nature."

In the present study no mention has been made of "Gestalt psychology," which in the 1930's made a great impression on those interested in teaching to read. Aside from the fact that educational psychologists have been accused of badly mangling Gestalt,[15] it has little to contribute to the much earlier theory of "Wholeness." In speaking of the application of Gestalt to reading, Diack says:

> To such an extent was this so that anyone who makes his first contact with reading theories through books published since

---

14 *Collected Papers of Henry Bradley* (Oxford, 1928), p. 192.
15 See Fraiberg, *op. cit.,* p. 59.

1935 is likely to form the impression that Gestalt theory provided the original basis for the theories of reading that were rapidly becoming accepted as true and proper. That was my own impression several years ago. When, however, I went into the matter more thoroughly, I came fairly quickly to the conclusion that Gestalt theory did not bring any new ideas to the teaching of reading but rather set into a more imposing framework ideas that had already been widely promulgated.[16]

Although the irregularities of English spelling and the psychological concept of "Wholeness" do, as Reeder said, form the "main sources" of the prevailing reading method, there is now another important source consisting of research studies. During this century particularly, these studies have strengthened the faith of educators in the correctness of the present analytical way of teaching to read. Daniels and Diack in 1956 said: "The number of studies of various aspects of learning and teaching reading published during this century runs well into five figures. Over 8,000 such studies were published in one decade alone and there is no sign of any abatement of the flood."[17] Sam Duker and Thomas P. Nally said that before 1900 only fourteen research studies dealing with teaching to read were recorded. From 1900 to 1920 there were 220; from 1920 to 1940 more than 1,800 were reported; and from 1940 to 1956 (the date of Duker and Nally's report) another 2,000 at least had been completed.[18]

Anderson and Dearborn devoted nearly forty pages of their *Psychology and Teaching of Reading* to these studies and from that work the following samples are taken. In 1879 Émile Javal, a French oculist, published a paper on the psychology of reading. In this he pointed out that as one reads one's eyes do not sweep smoothly along the line of print but advance by "jumps" or "fixes," a number of words being taken in at each brief pause. He made this clever observation simply by watching someone read.

The findings of Javal aroused tremendous interest among those studying the techniques of teaching to read. Anderson

---

[16] Diack, *op. cit.*, p. 93.

[17] Daniels and Diack, *op. cit.*, p. 1.

[18] Sam Duker and Thomas P. Nally, *The Truth About Your Child's Reading* (New York, 1956), p. 62.

and Dearborn, for example, wrote: "Much of what is known about the psychology of reading and of learning to read has been discovered through careful studies of eye movements in reading."[19] They then reviewed the principal studies of this kind, citing nearly fifty of them. They described the laboratory equipment necessary for studying eye movements and gave pictures of some of it. They discussed the electrical recordings of eye movements, with the subject's head held in a rigid position with chin rests, head clamps, and biting boards.

On the basis of the statistics that soon began to pile up, much of it secured by skilful use of the Metronoscope and Ophthalmograph, as well as the Harvard Reading Films and a triple-shutter tachistoscope, students were encouraged to read each line of a selected text with only three fixations. Experiments were made in over three hundred colleges and universities that were doing remedial work with their own students. The authors' report contained the following statement: "Unfortunately, research has not conclusively demonstrated that any lasting benefit is derived from eye-movement training as such. The whole approach requires reexamination."[20] Although it produced nothing that could be utilized in a training-to-read program, Javal's discovery made a lasting impression on reading experts, who regarded it as a telling indictment of the earlier ABC method.

In the midst of the eye-movement excitement, another paper appeared in a foreign publication, *Ueber die Zeit der Erkennung und Benennung von Schriftzeichen, Bildern und Farben* ("Concerning the Time Involved in Recognizing and Naming Letters, Pictures, and Colors"), which greatly strengthened the hand of those opposed to teaching children letters at the beginning of their reading instruction. This fifteen-page paper, published in 1885, was written by James McKeen Cattell, one of the earliest and most renowned students of psychology this country has produced.

By experimenting with fluent adult readers, Cattell found among other things "that the time required for

19 Irving H. Anderson and Walter F. Dearborn, *The Psychology and Teaching of Reading* (New York, 1952), p. 101.
20 *Ibid.*, p. 131.

recognizing and pronouncing letters is a little, but only a little, shorter than that for words." In this same connection he reported: "The words and the letters were of course not perceived one after the other, but at one mental operation, as an entire group." Reading specialists, following a common practice with them of securing guidance for teaching children by watching the performance of expert adult readers, saw at once that if an entire word can be recognized by an adult reader about as quickly as a single letter, it is unreasonable to teach the beginner anything but words.[21]

W. H. Winch has spoken out clearly on this matter of deducing principles of child psychology from observing adults: "Some of the principles appealed to are true; some are false; but nearly all of them are tainted by what I have previously called the diminished-adult view of the child-mind. Our own psychological processes are put into the child, diminished in strength, but similar in form. . . . Repetition bores us; so we say it bores the young child. As a matter of fact, he loves it." Later he said: "I am well aware that middle-aged psychologizing attaches interest to its interests, not those of the child. Because it is interested in 'meanings' rather than 'words' it ascribes the same interest to the young child."[22]

When an adult reads, he usually does so to get the thought of what he is reading. This is a clear pointer for the reading specialist; the child should at the very outset get the thought of what he is reading. We have seen that this idea was set forth in Boston about 1870. It is now vigorously supported by reading experts. Anderson and Dearborn discuss it under the term "comprehension." The idea that reading is thought-getting is a truism centuries old. A reference to it is found in the preface of some Latin *Disticha* attributed to a pseudo-Cato of the third or fourth century A.D. The unidentifiable Cato tells his "dear son" to read these maxims or precepts and understand them "for to read and not understand is not to read at all" (*legere enim*

---

[21] *Philosophische Studien*, II (1885), 647–48.
[22] W. H. Winch, *Teaching Beginners to Read in England* (Bloomington, Ill., 1925), pp. 9, 50.

et non intellegere neclegere est).[23] The rigorous application of this old obvious fact to the child learning to read is the new element in the situation. Specialists feel sure that unless care is exercised with the beginner at this opening stage, unless he is assuredly familiar with the meaning of each and every word he reads, he is destined to be a "word-caller," a "parrot-reader," and to "bark at print."

This attempt to save the child comes too late in his vocabulary acquiring. Most of those who face their teacher for the first time have permanently tucked away in their heads a great many terms, the meanings of which they will never know and perhaps never particularly care to know. Consider the words in italics: Ride a *cockhorse;* A *Diller* a dollar; *Crosspatch draw the latch; Ladybird, ladybird,* fly away home; Thomas-a-Tattamus took two *T's,* To tie two *tups* to two tall trees.

Nearly all the reading adults do is done silently. Inevitably there arose soon after 1900 an enthusiasm for silent reading. Anderson and Dearborn examined this approach with their usual thoroughness. Huey had called the attention of educators to the idea in 1908, but much earlier Farnham had spoken disparagingly of oral reading. In 1922 Emma Watkins wrote *How to Teach Silent Reading to Beginners.* In her method the children did not utter a word while learning to read. The teacher held up cards telling them what to do. The most celebrated of the exponents of the system was James E. McDade, an official in the Chicago Public Schools about 1937, and to his work Anderson and Dearborn give considerable attention.[24]

The number and type of these "research studies" supporting the analytical method of teaching to read are sufficiently suggested by what has been given. The impact of such studies upon those already favorably disposed toward their findings has no doubt been substantial. But upon those less sympathetic, the effect has been slight to say the least. Stanley M. Elam, the editor of *Phi Delta Kappan,* wrote in the issue of June, 1965: "Much of this research is poorly

23 Emil Baehrens, *Poetae Latini Minores,* III (Leipzig, 1881), 214.
24 Anderson and Dearborn, *op. cit.,* pp. 152–53, 162, 173–74.

designed, its results inconclusive or contradictory. Sometimes it even appears that the conclusions are distorted by vested interests." Diack with his usual forthrightness says:

Perhaps I am giving the impression that research into reading during the past fifty years has been singularly unprofitable. This is an impression I am reluctant to give, but there is very little I can do about it, for in some years of reading on this subject I came across nothing in the way of research which I felt showed something that a mixture of keen observation and shrewd commonsense could not have found out—except perhaps the clever photography of Buswell and a few others which produced much more accurate records of eye-movements in reading than had existed before.[25]

Fraiberg regards these research studies as a barricade erected by proponents of the present method. She points out that "These findings, as well as the assumption on which reading research has been based, have been given a rough going over by a number of critics." She mentions scholars who have shown that much of this research "is of low quality, conducted by poorly trained people, and is little influenced by findings in other disciplines."[26]

[25] Diack, *op. cit.*, p. 179.
[26] Fraiberg, *op. cit.*, p. 59.

IN CONCLUSION

The fact is well established that children taught by a carefully worked out synthetic plan read much better and read sooner than those taught by an analytic method, or by any combination of approaches in which the analytic element predominates. The evidence for this statement is abundant and is constantly being augmented.

Those experimenting with synthetic reading systems in which children learn letters and sounds at the outset, even in kindergarten, are greatly encouraged by their success and are constantly expanding their efforts. The Bloomfield or Linguistic method is now embodied in attractive primers prepared by Barnhart and is being extensively tested with gratifying results.

The *Royal Road Readers* and the reading system of which they are a part are becoming increasingly well known in this country. The Phonovisual method already mentioned has succeeded so well that there is now in Washington, D.C., the Phonovisual Products, Inc. The second i.t.a. International Conference was held at Lehigh University in August, 1965, with over two hundred and fifty registrants from this country and abroad. Most of the leading publishers have reading systems, and those who don't wish they had. It appears that the winds of change are now blowing more strongly than ever in the field of elementary reading instruction.

Not long before his death, Dean William S. Gray and I, in one of our frequent "sidewalk seminars," were talking about the ever-present subject of reading. With reference to the numerous articles appearing in the press, I asked him if there had ever been a time when there was so much being said and written about reading. He answered that so far as he knew there never had been and that he regarded it as an excellent thing, his hope being that everybody would learn more, and that the children would profit.

The problem is certainly not a simple one. It appears that skilful educators have done all they possibly could with the present analytic method. And yet teachers utilizing all the improvements made in the current method are not able to get their children into reading as quickly as those using one or another of the synthetic systems. Many advocates of the present method feel strongly that in this instance the race should not be to the swift, that the paramount issue is not that of making fluent, capable readers, that is, "pronouncers," as they express it, in as short a time as possible. Dr. Anna D. Cordts in 1962 expressed the orthodox view:

It has long been known that when a child has been taught the sounds of the letters before he has learned to read for meaning, he has to unlearn the habit of attending to the sounds in order to be free to concentrate on what the sentence is telling him. When wrong habits of reading have become firmly fixed in the mind of a child it is exceedingly difficult to uproot them. It has been done, but rarely without a great deal of re-teaching over a long period of time.[1]

Nancy Larrick, as we have seen, was generous in her praise of the readiness with which the children in the Bethlehem i.t.a. project were reading and writing, but she did not endorse the program. Certainly Colonel Parker never gave anyone the impression that the word method which he so heartily endorsed and used was a quick way of getting a child to the reading stage. He said: "Two years at least should be spent with the average child in learning to

[1] See "Phonics in Reading: Where Do They Belong?" in *New Jersey Education Association Review*, September, 1962, pp. 28–30.

read First Reader reading, and the third year may be profitably spent in commanding Second Reader reading. There is immense economy in going very slowly."[2]

The originators of the word method felt that children should not be taught to read before they were eight or ten years old. For them, one of the attractive features of Parker's approach was that it did not make a fetish of reading. Released from the tyranny of reading, the child had time to study science, geography, history, chemistry, woodwork, cooking, and anything else he saw people doing in the world about him.

Styles come and go in education as in everything else. As long ago as 1925 Winch said that the only thing the matter with the ABC method was that it went out of style.[3] Those devoted to the present method are by no means averse to changes in the reading program so long as they do not change the fundamental principle that reading is best presented to the child as an analytical process, and that reading for meaning at the outset is insisted upon. They have no objection to the child's learning letters and sounds, but they feel these should come incidentally as the need arises. They insist that this kind of training should be deferred until the child has done a fair amount of reading for meaning with words he has memorized. Considering the silliness of the contents of children's primers, this intense devotion to the beginner's getting the meaning of what he reads is puzzling.

The beginner, with his reading readiness well established, is usually set to learning a sight vocabulary of perhaps fifty to one hundred words. In working on this first stage of his instruction, the child reads prepared texts limited to the words he has memorized. This step is followed by what Duker and Nally call "The Fledgling Reading Program." At this level the children acquire from three to four hundred additional sight words by memorizing them.

While acquiring his sight vocabulary, the child learns word-attack skills. He is drilled in tricks of recognition. If

2 Quoted in Lelia E. Partridge, *Notes of Talks on Teaching* (4th ed.; New York, 1883), pp. 65–66.

3 W. H. Winch, *Teaching Beginners to Read in England* (Bloomington, Ill., 1925), p. 59.

such words as "*can-car, train-three, can-ran, ran-run* or *play-played*" confuse him, "they suggest the need on the part of some children for help in noting the features which differentiate words, such as difference in configuration or general shape, in larger components and in letter composition or sequence. For example, the confusion between *can* and *car* must be cleared up by noting the difference in the last letter." With a battery of these word-attack skills, such as utilizing picture clues, guessing from context, structural analysis, and phonetic analysis, the child emerges from the "Fledgling" program to the "Novice Reading Program," which he reaches within two or three years after kindergarten. By the time he is in the fifth or sixth grade he will be ready for the "Apprentice Program."[4]

This charting of the child's route through the different stages of his reading program, as set forth by Duker and Nally with liberal use of the manual for teachers prepared by Arthur I. Gates for use with his own system, may not be typical of the more general practice. Just how reading is taught in the thousands of public schools varies widely; but in general, in all of them, memorizing perhaps three or four hundred words is an indispensable feature. And memorizing words is dull and taxing labor.

The view expressed early and often that a word is as easy to memorize as a letter does not state the case fairly. No doubt twenty-six words could be found which the child could memorize as readily as he could the alphabet. But this kind of achievement is not the question at issue. The problem is whether the child will find memorizing three or four hundred words as easy as memorizing the names of the twenty-six letters.

As has been pointed out, one of the first things noticed about the application of the word method in its unadulterated form was that children could not memorize enough words to do worthwhile reading. If the other form of the "new method" had been chosen, that in which instruction in letters and sounds followed at once the consideration of

4 Sam Duker and Thomas P. Nally, *The Truth About Your Child's Reading* (New York, 1956), p. 93.

the word, this resort to phonics as a helping device would not have been needed. Phonics re-entered the program as just another of the many attack skills. Apparently teachers today often receive little or no training in the subject, but regard it as merely an incidental aid to the analytical approach. With such phonetic competence as they have (often no greater than that of Horace Mann as noted in chapter 7), some teachers exhibit what Bloomfield referred to as "the crassest ignorance of elementary phonetics."[5] For example:

Dr. Flesch states that any alphabetical language is necessarily phonetic; that, in fact, the two words mean the same thing. He makes the further statement that research studies show that 87 per cent of the English language is phonetic. We would like to see such a study. Linguists themselves are unable to agree on what constitutes a phonetic word. For the English language, which does not lend itself to pronunciation by phonetic rules, such rules would have to be extended indefinitely to cover an infinite variety of exceptions. For example, the letter "a" carries almost 50 different sounds when used alone or in diagrams [sic] in the English language. Can you easily cite a logical rule for the pronunciation of get and gem?[6]

From what has been shown in this study, the usual method employed in the public schools for teaching a child to read involves a decided risk for the learner. It has been pointed out that during World War I, in a test made on one and a half million soldiers, approximately twenty-five per cent of them were found unable to do functional reading. The reading ability of these young men was undoubtedly typical. How many millions of those remaining at home— either below or above the age of soldiers—were unable to read well, we shall never know. As we have seen, approximately the same percentage of British servicemen during World War II were found to be similarly handicapped in reading. In 1929 Dr. William S. Gray and Ruth Munroe

[5] Leonard Bloomfield, *Language* (New York, 1933), p. 500.
[6] Duker and Nally, *op. cit.*, p. 144. The authors may have found the mistake which they repeated here in Irving H. Anderson and Walter F. Dearborn, *Psychology and Teaching of Reading* (New York, 1952), p. 209. Anderson and Dearborn misunderstood Ernest Horn in his article "The Child's Early Experience with the Letter A," *Journal of Educational Psychology*, XX (1929), 161–68. What Horn said was that in a list of words he presented "there were forty-seven different sound-letter associations for the letter *a* in words actually occurring in First, Second, and Third readers."

undertook an investigation into the reading habits of adults. They reported, among other things, that: "First, a surprisingly large number of adults have never been taught to read. In the second place, many adults who went to school as children have read so little since, that they are unable now to read even a simple newspaper account or a letter."[7]

How many of these non-readers there were in 1929 we do not know. The suspicion that there were millions of them is justified by what has just been said. In a book which appeared in 1951, Dr. Gray was cited as having "estimated that one-half of the adult population is 'functionally illiterate'—that is, unable to read with ordinary comprehension those books and magazines which have been designed for unselected lay audiences of today."[8]

A well-known magazine recently quoted Morton Botel, a national reading expert, as having said, "Up to 15 million children are so seriously retarded in reading that they cannot understand their textbooks."[9] In a recent issue of the *Saturday Review*, the Dean of the School of Law at the University of Pittsburgh told how difficult it was in graduate schools to bring students to a point at which they could read and write reasonably well.[10] Fraiberg, in June, 1965, quoted Jacques Barzun's comment on his highly selected graduate students at Columbia: "I find one in ten who needs coaching in the elements of literacy—spelling, pronunciation, sentence structure and diction. And these students cannot write because they cannot read."[11]

From a consideration of such estimates as these one must seriously question the reading competency of those who managed to escape being classified as functional illiterates. How many of them were just on the border line? The American Institute of Public Opinion has for twenty years or more been regularly surveying the reading habits of Ameri-

[7] William S. Gray and Ruth Monroe, *The Reading Interests and Habits of Adults* (New York. 1929), p. 263.

[8] John James De Boer, et al., *Teaching Secondary English* (New York, 1951), p. 161.

[9] *Parade*, April 5, 1964, p. 13.

[10] Thomas M. Cooley II, "A Law School Fights Graduate Illiteracy," *Saturday Review*, August 12, 1965, pp. 39–41.

[11] Selma Fraiberg, "The American Reading Problem," *Commentary*, June, 1965, p. 61.

cans and those in foreign lands. Summarizing what the Institute had found in a recent survey, the editor of *Science* wrote in the issue of April 27, 1956:

> The reading habits of our high-school and college graduates are likewise depressing: 57 percent of our high-school and 26 percent of our college graduates have not read a single book for the past year. A special study confined to college graduates showed that five out of six had not read a serious book outside their fields of special interest during the preceding several months. . . . Only 17 percent of all adults were reading a book at the time they were interviewed; the comparable figure in 1937 was 29 percent. The trend is apparently downward.[12]

Is it possible that this neglect of reading results in some measure from the lack of ease with which people now read? Is the present reading program, where great stress is placed on memorizing words and on the use of books with restricted vocabularies, making any contribution to such statistics as these?

Without question, the reading situation in this country today is bad. What is the fundamental reason for it? May Ayres Burgess explained that many of our soldiers in World War I had learned to read but had later forgotten the skill. Dr. Gray in 1929 thought that "many adults who went to school as children have read so little since" that they forgot how. It would be impossible to quote any higher authorities for this wholesale forgetting than the two just mentioned. I think their explanation of the situation was correct. Moreover, I strongly suspect, as they apparently did not, that the chief reason for this lamentable forgetting on the part of those who had earlier been able to read a little was the analytical method by which they had been taught. The following facts, well known to everybody, incline me to this view.

There was never a time in Western Europe when classical Greek was spoken. As one of the three classical languages, it was in former times widely studied, and proficiency in it was, and still is, generally accepted as a safe indication of a scholarly individual. In the days when the study of Greek was common in high schools and colleges, schoolboys

[12] *Science,* April 27, 1956, p. 703.

undertook the study of it pretty much as the modern child tries to read English according to the conventional method. Many five- and six-year-old children today know some, perhaps all, of the letters. They are not acquainted with the sounds for which the letters stand. Similarly, boys—and many girls as time went on—began the study of Greek with a knowledge of most of the letters of the Greek alphabet. They recognized them by their resemblance to letters in their own language. They did not know the sounds for which these letters stood, and they were, of course, destined never to know.

To be sure, when the student of Greek undertook his work, his teacher instructed him in pronunciation; but even so, the boy was forced by circumstances under which he labored to do his utmost to learn words largely by the way they looked on the printed page. Henry Bradley expressed the situation well: "Now observe that for us moderns a Greek or Latin word is primarily a succession of letters of the alphabet, not a succession of sounds. True, we do pronounce it, after a fashion, but still we feel that the essential thing is the written form, not the spoken one."[13]

To put the matter simply, the student of Greek was, according to the teachings of reading experts, in an advantageous position for learning to read that language. He had to do precisely what the specialists insist today's child should do when he tries to learn to read his own language; he had to go directly from the sight of the printed word to its meaning without the interposition of sound. According to this theory, a child is not particularly aided in learning to read by having been born into a world of speech sounds. True, from infancy he has depended upon these sounds to give him meaning and they have served him well. He has accumulated a vocabulary of thousands of words that he knows by their sounds only. But now that he is in school the experts insist he should no longer concentrate his attention on the sounds of words but on trying to memorize their physical appearance. He should note their over-all configuration, how much of them projects above or below

---

[13] *Collected Papers of Henry Bradley* (Oxford, 1928), p. 178.

the line, how many odd-shaped combinations of crooked marks such as *sh, th, ch, gh,* how many little monkey face *o*'s, and how many monkey tails, such as *y* has, he can find and use as structural clues by which to hold the words in his memory together with their meanings.

His teacher is at hand to help. She shepherds him closely. She knows that this is a critical time, that "pressure to teach children to recognize words by the way they sound, instead of the way they look is increasing. Beginners in reading are again being drilled on the names of the letters and their sounds. . . . It seems incredible that children in a public school of America would be subjected to such antiquated instruction after a half a century of research and experiment."[14]

The student of Greek certainly had the advantage here. The sounds of the letters and words with which he dealt had no meaning for him; he was not at all tempted to pronounce them as he grappled with almost every form he met, attempting to go directly from it to its meaning. He followed perfectly the prescription given by Duncan for the child trying to learn English, his own language: "There are two reasons for not making the approach to reading through sounds of letters. Letter-sounds have no meaning for children. . . . Secondly, such an approach is psychologically unsound, because all of us, bright adults and backward pupils alike, tend to see in whole words." The student of Greek did his work in silence, again following Duncan's prescription precisely: "My considered view, however, is that most reading from even the earliest stages should be silent."[15]

With the help of his teacher and grammar, the student of Greek provided himself with as many word-attack skills as he possibly could. The physical configuration of words, their structural analysis, prefixes, suffixes, roots, stems, endings, were elementary for him. Encouraged by his teacher he guessed from context on the slightest excuse. It

---

[14] Dr. Anna Cordts, "Phonics in Reading: Where Do They Belong?" *New Jersey Education Association Review,* September, 1962, pp. 28–30.

[15] John Duncan, O.B.E., *Backwardness in Reading Remedies and Prevention* (London, Toronto, Wellington, Sidney, 1953), pp. 29, 41.

is remarkable that reading specialists did not discover early that the study of Greek is all but perfectly adapted to the exemplification of their theories of how a child should be taught to read.

Dr. Huey, a modern, made Greek his favorite study through secondary school and college. Of course he did not study it in the usual way but began with the sentence method and treated "particular letters in reading" with "persistent inattention." This disregard of letters left him, at the end of his college course, "hesitant in naming or recognizing several capital letters of the Greek alphabet, perhaps incapable of recognizing one or two of them when seen in isolation."[16] Such a long period of enjoying Greek should have left him at least able to read with assurance the names of the fraternity houses on his campus.

The fact is, however, that no matter how attentively pupils studied Greek, in the end they had, in the vast majority of cases, such an insecure grasp of it that within a few years after graduation, what they had memorized slipped away from them. Nor was the situation improved when the study of modern languages was substituted for Greek and Latin. Certainly the teachers are now better prepared. They can usually speak the languages they teach, and they do their best to make their students familiar with sounds, but circumstances are much against them. From year's end to year's end most of those who today study Spanish, French, and German, never have any occasion for speaking the language they study. In the main, most of them study it by an analytic method for reading purposes only, trying to memorize whole words and to go directly from the word on the printed page to its meaning. Sounds play a minor role in what they do.

As their method of attack approximates that of their forefathers who studied the classical languages, so the rate of their forgetting parallels that of their predecessors. Within a few months or years after their last recitation, the most industrious of them find that the little ability they had acquired has vanished. They are unable to speak an intelligent

16 Edmund Burke Huey, *Psychology and Pedagogy of Reading* (New York, 1908), p. 103.

sentence or even to read the title of a scholarly article in the language. The lasting results secured by these students of modern languages are so meager, the forgetting follows so closely upon graduation, that Bloomfield, a modern language teacher himself, thought what was learned "scarcely good enough to counter a movement for abolishing the instruction."[17]

The experience of generations of students of Latin and Greek, and the efforts now being made by high school and college students to learn to read various modern languages by essentially analytic methods, where the student tries to go from the appearance of the word on the page to its meaning, shows the lack of wisdom in trying to teach a child to read his own language by analytic means, and suggests clearly why he so readily forgets what little he has learned, if his stay in school has been brief.

In 1908 Edward L. Thorndike of Teachers College of Columbia University said, "at least 25 out of 100 children of the white population of our country who enter school stay only long enough to learn to read simple English, write such words as they commonly use, and perform the four operations for integers without serious errors. A fifth of the children (white) entering city schools stay only to the fifth grade."[18] Such children were among the non-readers of the World War I soldiers.

The most remarkable thing about the present method of teaching to read is that such a large percentage of pupils, perhaps seventy-five per cent or more, escape classification as "crippled" or functional illiterates. What their actual competence and reading range is we do not know, but that so many of them read as well as they do is surprising. A partial explanation may be that some teachers of beginners have not, and are not, paying close attention to what those in places of authority are telling them. After all, teachers of first-graders have considerable freedom in the exercise of their duties.

One such teacher of my acquaintance, now retired, explained her success in teaching reading by saying that she

[17] Leonard Bloomfield, *Language* (New York, 1933), p. 504.
[18] Leonard P. Ayres, *Laggards in Our Schools* (New York, 1909), p. 9.

locked the door of her classroom, pulled down the window shades, and taught the children letters and sounds, and was pleased with the results of her bootlegging. Fraiberg mentions that often teachers condemned to work with the Dick-and-Jane type of primers expressed their opinions to her "in language that is rich in gastrointestinal metaphor." These rebels in the classrooms may well be a much larger body than anyone suspects.

For several years the indications have been becoming clearer that more and more children are getting better and earlier instruction in reading than was formerly the case. Some reading experts feel free to speak of the ABC's with approval. These old "idiot marks" may achieve respectability again if things continue to move in the present direction.

As long ago as 1962, Donald D. Durrell wrote:

> Psychological, psychiatric, neurological, and sociological explanations of reading failure appear to us to be unimportant and misleading. . . . The two major weaknesses of non-readers are the inability to identify separate sounds in spoken words and the lack of familiarity with printed letters. . . . The adult who tries to read Greek or Sanskrit without knowing the different letters can appreciate the task of the child unfamiliar with letters. If a child can tell the names of letters or identify letters named, his chances of reading are enhanced. If he can both name and write letters his chances are good indeed. . . . Probably one of the most valuable abilities that the home or kindergarten can contribute to success in beginning reading is the ability to name and to write letters. It is difficult to understand the reluctance in some quarters to teach letter names.[19]

Along with this approval of letter-learning at the beginning of formal schooling goes less resentment than was formerly felt by teachers and educators in general at the interest shown in reading "on the part of persons in related disciplines, such as sociologists, psychologists, psychiatrists, neurologists, linguists and those concerned with child development."[20]

---

[19] Donald D. Durrell, "Learning Factors in Beginning Reading," in *Teaching Young Children to Read*, ed. W. G. Cutts (Washington, 1964), pp. 71 ff.

[20] Helen M. Robinson, "A Look Ahead by the Research Director," in Cutts, *op. cit.*, p. 127.

The attitude of professionals and laymen alike appears now to be more favorable than it once was to the conclusion that no matter how a child is taught to read, he comes sooner or later to the strait gate and the narrow way: he has to learn letters and the sounds for which they stand. There is no evidence whatever that he will ultimately do this better from at first not doing it at all.

BIBLIOGRAPHY

Abercrombie, David. "What Is a 'Letter'?" *Lingua,* II (August, 1949–50), 54–63.

American Annals of Education and Instruction, I (1831) and II (1832). This was a continuation of the *American Journal of Education;* the paging is somewhat erratic in the first part of the first volume.

American Institute of Instruction, VIII (1838), 211–39; XIV (1844), 143–83. The fifty-three small volumes of this publication were devoted to the introductory discourses and lectures delivered before the American Institute of Instruction from 1830 to 1882.

Anderson, Irving H., and Dearborn, Walter F. *The Psychology and Teaching of Reading.* New York, 1952.

Anderson, Lewis F. *History of Common School Education.* New York, 1909.

Annual Report, Common Schools of Cincinnati. Cincinnati, 1857. This report, the 28th, was signed by Andrew W. Rickoff.

Austin, Mary C. *The Torch Lighters: Tomorrow's Teachers of Reading.* Cambridge, Mass., 1961.

Bache, Alexander Dallas. *Report on Education in Europe to the Trustees of Girard College for Orphans.* Philadelphia, 1839.

Bardeen, C. W. *The Orbis Pictus of John Amos Comenius.* Syracuse, N. Y., 1887. Bardeen explains that he used the 1728 edition of the translation of the *Orbis* made by Charles Hoole.

Baugh, Albert C. *A History of the English Language.* New York, 1935.

Bloomfield, Leonard. *Language.* New York, 1933.

Bloomfield, Leonard, and Barnhart, Clarence L. *Let's Read: A Linguistic Approach.* Detroit, 1961.

Board of Supervisors for the Public Schools of Boston. *Method of Teaching Reading in the Primary Schools.* An undated thirty page brochure embodying Colonel Parker's views on reading.

Bradley, Henry. *The Collected Papers of Henry Bradley.* With a Memoir by Robert Bridges. Oxford, 1928.

Brinsley, John. *Ludus Literarius.* London, 1612.

Burgess, May Ayres. *The Measurement of Silent Reading.* New York, 1921.

Carpenter, Rhys. "The Alphabet in Italy," *American Journal of Archaeology,* XLIX (2d series, 1945), 452–64.

Carter, James G. *Essays Upon Popular Education Containing a Particular Examination of the Schools of Massachusetts.* Boston, 1826. A sixty page booklet edited from articles previously published in the *Boston Patriot.*

Comenius, Johann Amos. *Joh. Amos Comenii orbis sensualium pictus . . . Written by the author in Latin and High Dutch . . . Tr. into English by Charles Hoole M.A. for the Use of Young Latin Scholars.* New York, 1810. This work by Comenius appeared in 1657 and was at once translated by Hoole who signed his "Translator's Preface": "From my School in Lothbury, London, Jan. 25, 1658." The New York printing was a reproduction of the 12th London edition.

Common School Journal (1838–48). This publication was founded by Horace Mann, who edited it until he left office in 1848. After his departure it soon expired.

Compayré, Gabriel. *History of Pedagogy.* Translated by W. H. Payne. 2d ed. Boston, 1907. The original French edition appeared in 1884.

Connecticut Common School Journal, I (1838); II (1839); III (1840); IV (1841).

Course of Study. University of Chicago, 1900——. This was the title (July, 1900–June, 1901) of what later became the *Elementary School Journal.*

Cremin, Lawrence A. *The Transformation of the School; Progressivism in American Education 1876–1957.* New York, 1961.

Curti, Merle. *The Social Ideas of American Educators.* Paterson, N. J., 1959. This is a new and revised edition of a work which was first published in 1935 by Charles Scribner's Sons. It is the tenth volume of the Report of the American Historical Association on the Social Studies in the Schools.

Cutts, W. G. (ed.). *Teaching Young Children to Read.* Proceedings of a Conference November 14–16, 1962, U. S. Department of Health, Education and Welfare, Office of Education. Washington, D. C.: Government Printing Office, 1964.

Daniels, J. C., and Diack, Hunter. *Progress in Reading.* Nottingham, [1956]. I have supplied the date from a statement on p. 122 of Hunter Diack, *In Spite of the Alphabet.*

Danielsson, Bror (ed.). *John Hart's Works on English Orthography and Pronunciation.* Stockholm, 1955.

De Pencier, Ida B. *The History of the Laboratory Schools, The University of Chicago, 1896–1957.* Chicago, 1960.

Dewey, John. *The School and Society.* Chicago, 1899.

——. "The University School," *University (of Chicago) Record,* I (1896), 417–22. I am indebted to Professor Robert L. McCaul, who supplied me with a mimeograph copy of this article.

Diack, Hunter. *In Spite of the Alphabet.* London, 1965.

Dictionary of American Biography. New York, 1928–36.

Dionysius of Halicarnassus. Edited by W. Rhys Roberts. New York, 1910.

Dobson, E. J. *English Pronunciation 1500–1700.* 2 vols. Oxford, 1957.

Documents Accompanying the Journal of the Senate and House of Representatives of the State of Michigan at the Regular Session of 1853. Lansing, 1853.

Downing, John. *To Bee or Not to Be: The New Augmented Roman Alphabet Explained and Illustrated.* London, Toronto, New York, 1962.

————. *Experiments With An Augmented Alphabet for Beginning Readers in British Schools.* London, n.d. This fifty-six page booklet was presented by the author as a paper at the 27th Educational Conference sponsored by the Educational Records Bureau in the City of New York, November 1 and 2, 1962.

Duker, Sam, and Nally, Thomas P. *The Truth About Your Child's Reading.* New York, 1956.

Farnham, George L. *The Sentence Method.* Syracuse, N. Y., 1887.

Fechner, Heinrich, *Grundriss der Geschichte der wichtigsten Leselehrarten.* Berlin, 1884.

Fénelon, François de Salignac de la Mothe-. *Adventures of Telemachus.* Translated from the French by Dr. [John] Hawkesworth. New York, 187?

Flesch, Rudolph. *Why Johnny Can't Read.* New York, 1955.

Freeman, Kenneth J. *Schools of Hellas.* 3d ed. London, 1932. The first edition was published in 1907.

Fries, Charles C. *Linguistics and Reading.* New York, 1962.

Gallaudet, Edward Miner. *Life of Thomas Hopkins Gallaudet.* New York, 1888.

Gedike, Friedrich. *Aristoteles und Basedow oder Fragmente über Erziehung und Schulwesen bei den Alten und Neuren.* Berlin and Leipzig, 1779.

————. *Einige Gedanken über die Ordnung und Folge der Gegenstände des jugendlichen Unterrichts.* Berlin, 1791.

Gelb, I. J. *A Study of Writing.* Chicago, 1952.

Giffin, William M. *School Days in the Fifties. With an Appendix Containing an Autobiographical Sketch of Francis Wayland Parker.* Chicago, 1906.

Gray, William S., and Monroe, Ruth. *The Reading Interests and Habits of Adults.* New York, 1929.

Gray, William S. *On Their Own in Reading.* Chicago, 1948.

————. *Summary of Investigations Relating to Reading.* Chicago, 1925.

Hall, G. Stanley. *Educational Problems.* 2 vols. New York, 1911.

Hanna, Jean S., and Paul R. "Spelling As A School Subject: A Brief History," *National Elementary Principal,* XXXVIII (May, 1959), 8–23.

Harrison, Maurice. *The Story of the Initial Teaching Alphabet.* New York, Toronto, London, 1964.

Haugen, Einar. "First Grammatical Treatise: The Earliest Germanic Phonology." This appeared as a supplement to *Language.* Language Monograph No. 25 (October–December, 1950).

Henderson, Ellen C. *You Can Teach a Child That Reading Can Be Fun.* New York, 1956.

Hendrickson, G. L. "Ancient Reading," *Classical Journal,* XXV (1929–30), 182–96.

Hill, Thomas. *The True Order of Studies.* New York, 1882.

Hodge, Frederick Webb. *Handbook of American Indians North of Mexico.* In Two Parts. Washington, D. C., Part I, 1907; Part II, 1910.

Hodges, Richard. *The English Primose.* Edited by Dr. Heinrich Kauter. Heidelberg, 1930. The first edition was published in London in 1644.

Hollis, Andrew Phillip. *The Contribution of the Oswego Normal School to Educational Progress in the United States.* Boston, 1898.

Hoole, Charles. *A New Discovery of the Old Art of Teaching School.* This edition has an introduction and notes by Thiselton Mark. Syracuse, N. Y., 1912. The work first appeared in 1660.

Huey, Edmund Burke. *The Psychology and Pedagogy of Reading.* New York, 1908.

Jacotot, J. J. *Enseignement universel . . . Langue maternelle.* 3d ed. Louvain, 1827. In this the author gives detailed instruction to one who would use his method.

Jagger, J. H. *The Sentence Method.* Glasgow, 1929.

Keagy, J. M. *An Essay on English Education Together With Some Observations on the Present Mode of Teaching the English Language.* Harrisburg, Pa., 1824. On the inside of the front cover there is an "Advertisement" explaining that this is an extract from a series of articles on education "written some years ago, and first published in the Morning Chronicle of Baltimore, in the Spring of 1819."

Kehr, Karl. *Die Praxis der Volksschule.* 10th Improved Edition. Gotha, 1895. The first edition was in 1880.

———. *Geschichte des Methodik des deutschen Volksschulunterrichts.* Gotha, 1889. This is Volume I of the 2d edition of a six volume work, 1888–91, made up of the work of various contributors. The first 121 pages of the first volume comprise a scholarly sketch by Kehr of the history of instruction in reading in the primary and elementary schools of Germany.

Kern, Artur and Edwin. *Lesen und lesenlernen.* Freiburg im Breisgau, 1937. This is the second edition of a work which appeared earlier as *Ist unsere Lesenmethode richtig?* On pages 107–32 there is a brief history of reading method.

Knight, Edgar W. (ed.). *Reports on European Education.* New York, 1930.

Koerner, James D. (ed.). *The Case for Basic Education.* Boston, 1959.

Lamport, Harold Boyne. "A History of the Teaching of Beginning Reading." Unpublished Ph.D. dissertation, School of Education, University of Chicago, 1935.

Leavitt, Robert Keith. *Noah's Ark: A Short History of the Original Webster Dictionaries.* Springfield, Mass., 1947.

Livengood, W. W. *Our Heritage.* Cincinnati, 1947. A brochure by the Editor-in-Chief and Vice President of the American Book Co.

Lynd, Albert. *Quackery in the Public Schools.* Boston, 1953.

Mann, Horace. *A Lecture on the Best Mode of Preparing and Using Spelling-Books.* Boston, 1841.

———. *Seventh Annual Report of the Board of Education Together with the Seventh Annual Report of the Secretary of the Board.* Boston, 1844.

———. *Reply to the "Remarks" of Thirty-one Schoolmasters.* Boston, 1844.

Mann, Mary Peabody. *Life of Horace Mann.* Centennial edition in facsimile. Washington, D. C., 1937.

March, Francis A. *The Spelling Reform.* Washington, D. C., 1893.

McCaul, Robert L. "Dewey and the University of Chicago," *School and Society,* LXXXIX (March 25, 1961), 152–57; (April 8, 1961), 179–83; (April 22, 1961), 202–6.

———. "Dewey's Chicago," *School Review,* Summer, 1959, pp. 258–80.

Milne, J. Grafton. "Relics of Graeco-Egyptian Schools," *Journal of Hellenic Studies,* XXVIII (1908), 121–32.

Monroe, Paul (ed.). *A Cyclopedia of Education.* 5 vols. New York, 1911–13.

Morley, Thomas. *A Plaine and Easie Introduction to Practicall Musicke.* With an introduction by Edmund H. Fellowes. (The Shakespeare Association Facsimiles No. 14.) London, 1937.

Mueller, Friedrich Max. *Lectures on the Science of Language.* Series 1, 2. London, 1861–64.

Murray, William, and Downs, L. W. *Children Learn to Read.* London, 1955.

Neef, J. *The Method of Instructing Children Rationally in the Arts of Writing and Reading.* Philadelphia, 1813.

Nilsson, Martin P. "Die Übernahme und Entwickelung des Alphabets durch die Griechen," *Historisk-filologiske Meddelelser,* I (1918), 6–36.

Oxford English Dictionary. 13 vols. Oxford, 1933.

Palmer, Thomas H. "On the Evils of the Present System of Primary Instruction," *American Institute of Instruction,* VIII (1838), 211–39.

Partridge, Lelia E. *Notes of Talks on Teaching, Given by Francis W. Parker, at the Martha's Vineyard Summer Institute, July 17 to August 19, 1882.* 4th ed. New York, 1885.

———. *The "Quincy Methods" Illustrated.* New York, 1885.

Pedersen, Holger. *Linguistic Science in the Nineteenth Century.* Authorized translation from the Danish by John Webster Spargo. Northwestern University, Cambridge, Mass., 1931.

Pei, Mario. *The Story of English.* New York, 1952.

Peirce, C. "On Reading," *American Institute of Instruction,* XIV (1844), 143–83. This lecture was delivered August 15, 1843. Peirce was the Principal of the Normal School at Lexington, Mass.

Plato. *The Republic.* Translated with Introduction and Notes by Francis Macdonald Cornford. Oxford, 1941.

Pochmann, Henry A. *German Culture in America.* Madison, Wis., 1957.

Quintilian (Marcus Fabius Quintilianus). *Quintilian's Institute of Oratory.* Literally translated with notes by the Rev. John Selby Watson. 2 vols. London, 1875.

Reeder, Rudolph Rex. *Historical Development of School Readers.* New York, 1900.

Remarks on the Seventh Annual Report of the Hon. Horace Mann. Boston, 1844.

Rice, J. M. *The Public-School System of the United States.* New York, 1893.

Sailing into Reading. Washington, D. C., 1960. The manuscript for this forty page brochure was originally prepared by Dr. Nila Banton Smith.

Sandys, Sir John Edwin. *A History of Classical Scholarship.* 3 vols. New York, 1958. First published in Cambridge, 1903–8.

Skeat, Walter W. *A Primer of English Etymology.* 6th ed., rev. Oxford, 1924.

Smith, Nila Banton. *American Reading Instruction.* New York, 1934. Dr. Smith is Director, The Reading Institute, New York University, New York City

Smith, Sir Thomas. *De recta & emendata Linguae Anglicae Scriptione.* Edited by Dr. Otto Deibel. Halle, 1913. This treatise appeared first in 1568.

Some Arguments for and Against Reformed English Spelling. A Report prepared for the Canadian Conference on Education. Kingston, Ont., 1962. Professor Dean of Queen's University, Kingston, was the chairman of the committee that drew up this report.

Sprengling, Martin. *The Alphabet: Its Rise and Development from the Sinai Inscriptions.* Chicago, 1931.

Stewart, Dugald. *The Collected Works of Dugald Stewart.* Edited by Sir William Hamilton. 11 vols. London, 1854–60.

Tauber, Abraham. *Spelling Reform in the United States.* Ann Arbor, Mich.: University Microfilms, 1958. This is a Columbia University thesis.

Taylor, J. Orville. *The District School.* New York, 1834.

Vogel, Theodor Moritz. *Leben und Verdienste Valentin Ickelsamers.* Leipzig, 1894.

Walcutt, Charles C. (ed.). *Tomorrow's Illiterates: The State of Reading Instruction Today.* Boston, 1961.

Walton, George A. *Report of Examinations of Schools in Norfolk County, Massachusetts.* Boston, 1880.

Warfel, Harry R. *Noah Webster, Schoolmaster to America.* New York, 1936.

Watson, E. H. *The Spelling Reform Question Discussed.* New York, 1880.

Wells, William Harvey. *In Memoriam.* Chicago, 1887. This was a small volume brought out by his friends after his death.

Williams, Ralph W. "Reading and Evolution," *Journal of Developmental Reading,* IV (Autumn, 1960), 3–11.

Wood, John. *Account of the Edinburgh Sessional School, and the Other Parochial Institutions for Education Established in that City in the year 1812.* Edinburgh, 1840. This work first appeared in 1828.

Wright, Thomas, and Halliwell, James Orchard. *Reliquiae Antiquae.* 2 vols. in 1. London, 1841–43.

Ziebarth, Dr. Erich. *Aus der Antiken Schule.* Bonn, 1913.

INDEX